Jaguar Boo  rica

D0379648

Series Editors

WILLIAM H. BEEZLEY, Neville G. Penrose Chair of Latin
American Studies, Texas Christian University
COLIN M. MACLACHLAN, Professor and Chair, Department
of History, Tulane University

Volumes Published

John E. Kicza, ed., *The Indian in Latin American History: Resistance,
Resilience, and Acculturation* (1993). Cloth ISBN 0-8420-2421-2
Paper ISBN 0-8420-2425-5

Susan E. Place, ed., *Tropical Rainforests: Latin American Nature and
Society in Transition* (1993). Cloth ISBN 0-8420-2423-9
Paper ISBN 0-8420-2427-1

Paul W. Drake, ed., *Money Doctors, Foreign Debts, and Economic
Reforms in Latin America from the 1890s to the Present* (1994).
Cloth ISBN 0-8420-2434-4   Paper ISBN 0-8420-2435-2

John A. Britton, ed., *Molding the Hearts and Minds: Education,
Communications, and Social Change in Latin America* (1994).
Cloth ISBN 0-8420-2489-1   Paper ISBN 0-8420-2490-5

Darién J. Davis, ed., *Slavery and Beyond: The African Impact on Latin
America and the Caribbean* (1995). Cloth ISBN 0-8420-2484-0
Paper ISBN 0-8420-2485-9

David J. Weber and Jane M. Rausch, eds., *Where Cultures Meet: Frontiers
in Latin American History* (1994). Cloth ISBN 0-8420-2477-8
Paper ISBN 0-8420-2478-6

Gertrude M. Yeager, ed., *Confronting Change, Challenging Tradition:
Women in Latin American History* (1994). Cloth ISBN 0-8420-2479-4
Paper ISBN 0-8420-2480-8

Linda Alexander Rodríguez, ed., *Rank and Privilege: The Military and
Society in Latin America* (1994). Cloth ISBN 0-8420-2432-8
Paper ISBN 0-8420-2433-6

Gilbert M. Joseph and Mark D. Szuchman, eds., *I Saw a City Invincible:
Urban Portraits of Latin America* (1996). Cloth ISBN 0-8420-2495-6
Paper ISBN 0-8420-2496-4

Roderic Ai Camp, ed., *Democracy in Latin America: Patterns and Cycles* (1996). Cloth ISBN 0-8420-2512-X   Paper ISBN 0-8420-2513-8

Oscar J. Martínez, ed., *U.S.-Mexico Borderlands: Historical and Contemporary Perspectives* (1996). Cloth ISBN 0-8420-2446-8 Paper ISBN 0-8420-2447-6

William O. Walker III, ed., *Drugs in the Western Hemisphere: An Odyssey of Cultures in Conflict* (1996). Cloth ISBN 0-8420-2422-0 Paper ISBN 0-8420-2426-3

Richard R. Cole, ed., *Communication in Latin America: Journalism, Mass Media, and Society* (1996). Cloth ISBN 0-8420-2558-8 Paper ISBN 0-8420-2559-6

U.S.-Mexico
Borderlands

U.S.-Mexico Borderlands

Historical and Contemporary Perspectives

Oscar J. Martínez
Editor

Jaguar Books on Latin America
Number 11

A Scholarly Resources Inc. Imprint
Wilmington, Delaware

Scholarly Resources Inc.
104 Greenhill Avenue
Wilmington, DE 19805-1897

Library of Congress Cataloging-in-Publication Data

U.S.-Mexico borderlands: historical and contemporary perspectives /
  Oscar J. Martínez, editor.
      p.   cm. — (Jaguar books on Latin America; no. 11)
  Includes bibliographical references (p.).
  Includes filmography (p.)
  ISBN 0-8420-2446-8 (cloth: alk. paper). — ISBN 0-8420-2447-6
(paper : alk. paper)
  1. Mexican-American Border Region—History. 2. Mexican-American
Border Region—History—Sources. I. Martínez, Oscar J. (Oscar Jáquez),
1943–. II. Series.
F786.M423 1995
972'.1—dc20   95-21781
                                                                    CIP

Acknowledgments

I would like to thank the many people who provided assistance and support for this project. My good friends and Jaguar series coeditors William H. Beezley and Colin M. MacLachlan eased the process significantly with timely encouragement and very helpful editorial suggestions. Without the availability of excellent materials on the borderlands published by other scholars, writers, and journalists, it would have been impossible to assemble this type of anthology. I was also fortunate to be able to choose from many fine primary documents, official and otherwise. Permission to reprint, given by numerous presses, journals, newspapers, authors, and others, is gratefully acknowledged. Finally, I thank Linda Pote Musumeci of Scholarly Resources for her contributions during the copyediting stage of the manuscript.

About the Editor

Oscar J. Martínez has spent most of his life in the U.S.-Mexico border-lands, taking part in and observing transboundary and cross-cultural interaction at close range. His family migrated from the interior of Mexico to Ciudad Juárez in the 1940s, moved to El Paso in the 1950s, and eventually settled permanently in Los Angeles. Before becoming professor of history at the University of Arizona in 1988, he taught and directed research programs at the University of Texas at El Paso for more than a decade. He has written or edited six other books and numerous articles and chapters of books on the history of the borderlands, including *Border People: Life and Society in the U.S.-Mexico Borderlands* (1994). Professor Martínez is also a former president of the Association of Borderlands Scholars.

Contents

Introduction, **xiii**

I The Making of the Boundary, **1**

Essays

1 RICHARD GRISWOLD DEL CASTILLO, The Treaty of Guadalupe Hidalgo, **2**

2 ANGELA MOYANO PAHISSA, The Mesilla Treaty, or Gadsden Purchase, **10**

Documents

3 Texas Declaration of Independence, **13**

4 Treaty of Velasco, **17**

5 Treaty of Guadalupe Hidalgo, **20**

6 Gadsden Treaty, **38**

II Border Strife, **45**

Essays

7 OSCAR J. MARTÍNEZ, Filibustering and Racism in the Borderlands, **46**

8 JOSEPH F. PARK, The Apaches in Mexican-American Relations, 1848–1861, **50**

Documents

9 COMISIÓN PESQUISADORA DE LA FRONTERA DEL NORTE, Report to the President, **58**

10 U.S. CONGRESS, SPECIAL HOUSE COMMITTEE, Texas Frontier Troubles, **66**

11 JUAN NEPOMUCENA CORTINA, Proclamation, **74**

12 CONGRESSIONAL INVESTIGATIVE BOARD, El Paso Troubles in Texas, **78**

III The Rise in Transborder Interaction, 85

Essay
13 MIGUEL TINKER SALAS, Sonora: The Making of a Border Society, 1880–1910, **86**

Documents
14 C. PERALES, Why the Border Needs the Free Zone, **98**

15 MATÍAS ROMERO, Why the Free Zone Should Not Exist, **101**

16 JOSÉ VASCONCELOS, A Mexican Schoolboy's Experiences in Eagle Pass, Texas, **103**

IV The Mexican Revolution, 107

Essays
17 MARDEE BELDING DE WETTER, Revolutionary El Paso, 1910–11, **108**

18 LINDA B. HALL AND DON M. COERVER, The Arizona-Sonora Border and the Mexican Revolution, **116**

Documents
19 SEÑORA FLORES DE ANDRADE, Conspiring against Porfirio Díaz, **134**

20 Plan de San Diego, **139**

21 J. T. CANALES, A Chicano Lawyer Blasts the Texas Rangers, **142**

V Boom and Bust, 149

Essays
22 OSCAR J. MARTÍNEZ, Prohibition and Depression in Ciudad Juárez-El Paso, **151**

23 THOMAS E. SHERIDAN, *La Crisis*, **162**

Document
24 SELDEN C. MENEFEE, Mexican Migratory Workers in South Texas: Crystal City, 1938, **170**

VI Interdependence: Blessings and Curses, 175

Essays
25 Lawrence A. Herzog, Border Commuter Workers and Transfrontier Metropolitan Structure along the U.S.-Mexico Border, **176**

26 Bill Lenderking, The U.S.-Mexican Border and NAFTA: Problem or Paradigm? **190**

Documents
27 Sandy Tolan, *La Frontera*: Land of Opportunity or Place of Broken Dreams? **203**

28 Michael Quintanilla and Peter Copeland, Mexican Maids: El Paso's Worst-kept Secret, **213**

29 Bob Duke, Border Ignored: Congressmen Fight Nationwide Indifference, **222**

VII A World Apart, 227

Essays
30 Tom Miller, The Borderblasters, **228**

31 Daniel D. Arreola and James R. Curtis, Tourist Landscapes, **236**

Documents
32 Peter Copeland, Border *Ambiente*, **244**

33 María Puente, So Close, Yet So Far: San Diego, Tijuana Bridging Gap, **249**

34 Oscar J. Martínez, "*La Frontera*," **256**

Suggested Readings, **259**
Suggested Films, **263**

Introduction

This book introduces readers to the unique world of the U.S.-Mexican borderlands, the region where the United States and Latin America have interacted with one another most intensely. Since the early nineteenth century, borderlanders have witnessed protracted conflict rooted in the vastly unequal power relationship between Mexico and the United States. But they have also experienced many positive influences arising from the economic, social, and cultural interdependence found in the area. Conflict and interdependence, two fundamental themes in the evolution of the borderlands, are the focus of this introduction as they are throughout the volume.[1]

Each section includes essays and documents that convey a general idea of salient problems and issues confronted by borderlanders during different stages in the evolution of the area. The reader will find original materials such as treaties, proclamations, official reports, manifestoes, advocacy statements, memoirs, and journalistic accounts. Both U.S. and Mexican authors are represented in the selections.

The Boundary and International Conflict[2]

International borders are likely to be the scene of conflict due to such basic factors as vague territorial limits, unclear title to natural resources, ethnic rivalries, and restrictions on the movement of goods and people across the political line. Where frontier conditions exist, lawlessness is also frequently a problem. In remote, sparsely populated areas the restraints that govern residents of settled regions are at best weak. Underfinanced local governments struggle ineffectively to exert their authority over wide expanses of territory. The international line itself represents a powerful escape valve for fugitives from the law. Bigots and racists also tend to take advantage of the prejudices that run strong in isolated communities. In short, at the outer edges of nations, oppressors and transgressors of all shades enjoy shields from punishment that are not available in the heartland. In the history of the U.S.-Mexican border, these and other problems have complicated relations between the two countries, making life difficult for the area's residents during periods of heightened animosity.

The Texas rebellion (1836) and the U.S.-Mexican War (1846–1848) exemplified the border-focused conflict in the first half of the nineteenth century. Disorder and bloodshed continued after the demarcation of the new political line following the signing of the Treaty of Guadalupe Hidalgo (1848) and the Gadsden Treaty (1853). In the post-1848 period one of the greatest sources of strife arose from recurring transboundary Indian raids. As depredations into its territory continued year after year, Mexico bitterly protested the seeming indifference of the United States to the problem. In turn, the United States filed its own complaints against Mexico.

Problems with slave hunters, smugglers, robbers, cattle thieves, and desperate characters of all shades who congregated in the borderlands further increased the tension between the two countries. The general lawlessness characteristic of many Americans living along the border led to defiance of Mexico's territorial integrity, including repeated filibustering expeditions into several northern states. Among the many foreigners who sought to establish empires or colonies on Mexican soil, none is better known than William Walker, whose invasion of Baja California and Sonora in 1853 was, however, short-lived. Yet, the U.S. frontier, especially in Texas, also endured depredations from criminal elements. These lawbreakers used the Mexican borderlands as their base of operations. Cattle rustling and smuggling particularly disturbed the Texans. Mexican retaliatory raids fomented by Anglo oppression, such as Juan N. Cortina's exploits in the Brownsville-Matamoros region in the 1850s, fanned racial hatred even more.

By the late 1870s relations between the United States and Mexico had become strained almost to the breaking point as each country accused the other of failing to suppress border lawlessness. With the advent of the railroads in the 1880s and the subsequent influx of more civilized settlers and influences, however, marauding and raiding activities declined. During the next three decades the frontier experienced relative peace and order.

The Mexican Revolution of 1910 introduced a new era of instability, with Mexican bandits and revolutionaries raising havoc in the Texas and New Mexico borderlands. For a time, residents in the U.S. border states lived in fear that extremists from the neighboring country, aided by militant Mexican Americans, would attempt to retake land lost by Mexico in the nineteenth century. The tensions of the decade occasioned several crossings by U.S. troops into Mexican territory, including the unsuccessful chase of Pancho Villa by General John J. Pershing in 1916. War between the two countries seemed likely at mid-decade, but the crisis abated as the violent phase of the revolution waned and as the United States turned its attention toward World War I. Thereafter, confrontation over borderlands violence ceased to be a major diplomatic issue between the two nations.

Interdependence in the Borderlands[3]

The regionalistic tendencies of the borderlands originated in the early history of New Spain's (colonial Mexico's) northern frontier. Beginning in the sixteenth century, Spaniards pushed northward from central Mexico and founded settlements in modern-day Tamaulipas, Nuevo León, Coahuila, Chihuahua, Sonora, Texas, New Mexico, Arizona, and California. Isolation and a harsh environment shaped a way of life in the north that was different from that found in the core of New Spain. A spirit of independence developed throughout El Norte (the North), and, eventually, political drift contributed to the separation of what is now the U.S. Southwest from Mexico. Mexicans living in Texas and California in particular felt neglected by the government in Mexico City, and their discontent played into the hands of Anglo-American expansionists who wanted the far northern Mexican frontier incorporated into the United States.

With the signing of the Treaty of Guadalupe Hidalgo, the Mexican north was split in two, with approximately one half of the territory remaining in Mexico and the other half going to the United States. Thereafter, each subregion belonged to a separate political system, but the economic ties that had existed before continued to grow, despite the presence of an international boundary.

Irrigated agriculture, ranching, and mining—industries that dated back to pre-Columbian times and the Spanish colonial era—received new impetus as migrants arrived in greater numbers. Cattle production soared in California, Texas, Chihuahua, and Sonora. Mining operations increased in New Mexico and along the Arizona-Sonora frontier. Commercial agriculture also expanded, although the full blossoming of this industry awaited the development of the modern irrigation systems that occurred in the early twentieth century with the construction of large dams and canals in New Mexico, Arizona, and California.

American investors soon discovered numerous business opportunities in the Mexican border region, especially in Chihuahua and Sonora. U.S. railroad companies, such as the Mexican Central Railroad, built important lines intended to link the mining and ranching areas of northern Mexico to processing centers and consumer markets in the United States. After 1876, U.S. entrepreneurs in Mexico were particularly favored in their activities by President Porfirio Díaz, who believed that Mexico's modernization depended on the country's ability to attract capital from abroad. In 1910, on the eve of Díaz's downfall, about one fourth of the

American capital invested in Mexico was concentrated in Coahuila, Nuevo León, Chihuahua, and Sonora.

The dependent status of the Mexican border region on the United States at the turn of the century is well illustrated by the presence of the *Zona Libre*, or Free Trade Zone, in the border cities. Free trade between Mexico and the United States had existed in certain communities after 1858, but President Díaz extended this privilege along the entire border in 1885, pleasing *fronterizos* (borderlanders) who had lobbied for official recognition of their unique needs. While it lasted, the *Zona Libre* stimulated significant commercial activity in the Mexican border communities, but it also created considerable resentment in the interior of the country, where it was seen as both a detriment to the growth of native industries and an unwarranted special favor to one part of the nation. The Mexican government finally eliminated the *Zona Libre* in 1905, justifying its action on the grounds that the country's railroad system now reached most of the border region.

By the 1920s the external orientation of the Mexican border region was even more accentuated as Prohibition in the United States drove Americans into Mexico in search of liquor and other vices not readily available north of the boundary. Tourism flourished all along the border but especially in Ciudad Juárez and Tijuana, where ordinary and famous *norteamericanos* found bars, casinos, cabarets, racetracks, and other establishments ready to satisfy their needs for recreation and entertainment. The Great Depression and the end of Prohibition in 1933 temporarily terminated the tourist boom along the border, but tourism resurfaced with renewed vigor during the World War II and Korean War years.

In recent decades the traditional interdependence between the two sides of the border has increased dramatically. The most important cause of this expanded integration has been U.S. demand for Mexican labor. During World War II the two nations initiated a guest worker arrangement known as the Bracero Program, allowing millions of Mexicans to work in U.S. agriculture under contract with employers. At the same time, millions of undocumented peasants crossed the border to satisfy the tremendous need for cheap labor that existed in both the rural and urban American economies. The pattern of large-scale Mexican immigration into the Southwest that began in the 1940s has continued into the present. Despite passage of major restrictionist legislation by the U.S. Congress in 1986, it remains questionable whether such laws can significantly alter undocumented migration while the underground labor system in the borderlands continues to be highly institutionalized and very profitable.

Another contemporary manifestation of transborder interdependence is the pronounced trade between the two countries. The economies of

U.S. border cities, such as Laredo and El Paso, are heavily dependent on Mexican consumers from directly across the border as well as from Mexico's interior. The special "rapid" train from Chihuahua City to Ciudad Juárez (a four-hour ride), inaugurated in the 1980s, is a dramatic example of the magnetism that El Paso has for Chihuahua City residents who like to buy American products. Apparently, the *rápido* was created especially for shoppers, who could arrive at the border by eleven in the morning, make their purchases in El Paso, and begin their return trip by six in the evening. The heavy dependence of American border cities on Mexican consumers has been demonstrated most dramatically by the drastic declines in business that followed recent devaluations of Mexican currency, particularly those in 1982 and 1994 when the greatest reductions in Mexican buying power took place.

Just as the American border cities depend on Mexican shoppers and tourists, so do the Mexican cities depend on Americans. The importance of the American trade to Mexico is illustrated by the establishment, in the 1960s, of Mexico's Programa Nacional Fronterizo (PRONAF), a government initiative that had as a central goal the physical improvement of Mexican border cities to make them more attractive to foreign visitors. In addition, the PRONAF sought to make more national goods available to the local clientele, thereby lessening the need for border Mexicans to shop on the American side.

The economic interdependence at the border is also evidenced by the Border Industrialization Program (BIP), a Mexican initiative consisting mostly of the *maquiladora* program, which involves foreign-owned assembly plants located in the Mexican borderlands, most of them directly on the border. Many factories have tandem operations on the American side, making the program binational in nature. The BIP began in 1965, a time of great unemployment along the border because the end of the Bracero Program left many former braceros stranded in border cities. The presence of abundant and inexpensive labor close to the United States encouraged countless American multinational companies as well as Japanese and other foreign firms to locate in Mexico. By the early 1990s about two thousand assembly plants employed more than five hundred thousand Mexican workers. The program grew so rapidly that it became the second most important generator of foreign exchange for Mexico, behind oil and ahead of tourism.

The greatest socioeconomic changes in the borderlands have taken place since World War II, when the U.S. government began to invest enormous amounts of capital throughout the Southwest in military installations, defense-related industries, and infrastructure projects such as highways. The infusion of these external funds stimulated the entire economy, helping to convert the U.S. border region into one of the most dynamic areas in the country. As an extension of the U.S. Southwest, northern Mexico benefited considerably from these trends, as well as from the national industrialization policies promoted from Mexico City during the same period. Not surprisingly, El Norte emerged as one of the most modern and prosperous regions within the Mexican republic.

In the last quarter of the twentieth century, both sides of the border sported a greatly expanded economy capable of sustaining substantially larger populations than had been possible previously. Traditional extractive and agricultural industries were pushed into the background and were replaced by manufacturing and high-tech industries that relied heavily on government spending. Trade and services became ever-growing sectors of the region's economy. Urban centers throughout the binational borderlands assumed a new look, evolving from isolated, underdeveloped towns into modern, vibrant metropolises. Some cities achieved national prominence within their respective countries. At the border, communities like Ciudad Juárez-El Paso and Tijuana-San Diego became highly integrated binational centers of great significance for both nation-states.

The economic expansion spurred impressive population growth as well. By 1990, 13.2 million people lived in the Mexican border states compared to 3.8 million four decades earlier; north of the boundary, the population of the U.S. border states more than doubled, rising from 19.7 million to 51.9 million. Thus, the combined population of the greater borderlands totaled 65.1 million by 1990. The number of people residing in the Mexican border *municipios* (municipalities) in 1990 was 3.8 million, and the population of the U.S. border counties was 5.1 million, for a combined total of 8.9 million.[4]

Conclusion

Conflict and interdependence are deeply embedded in the historical experience of border Mexicans, Mexican Americans, and Anglo-Americans. In the constant oscillation between friction and good neighborliness it is the latter that has prevailed over the long run. As we gaze toward the next century, increased cooperation and the forging of closer ties are likely to overshadow confrontation, but controversies will continue to receive the greatest attention in the media, thus distorting the reality of daily life at the border.

It is important to keep this broader vision in mind to better interpret the significance of contemporary border incidents, the building of walls and fences on the U.S. side, and the American tirades against Mexicans and other Latin American immigrants. Proposition 187, the harsh anti-immigrant referendum passed in California in 1994, has certainly created significant international and interethnic discord. Despite that, extant economic relations, legal border crossings, tourism, and the myriad other ties that still bind people from both sides will continue to grow and to thrive.

With the enactment of the North American Free Trade Agreement in 1994, borderlanders have entered a new era. The interdependence that now pervades the region will become even more intense in the future, leading to de facto integration in many sectors of society. Borderlanders will feel the effects of that increased interaction most acutely, but fewer and fewer people who reside in central areas of Mexico and the United States will be left untouched as the force of transnationalism radiates beyond the frontier.

Notes

1. Historical overviews of conflict and interdependence in the borderlands are provided in Raúl A. Fernández, *The United States-Mexico Border: A Politico-Economic Profile* (Notre Dame: University of Notre Dame Press, 1977); Oscar J. Martínez, *Border Boom Town: Ciudad Juárez since 1848* (Austin: University of Texas Press, 1978); idem, *Border People: Life and Society in the U.S.-Mexico Borderlands* (Tucson: University of Arizona Press, 1994); idem, *Troublesome Border* (Tucson: University of Arizona Press, 1988); Angela Moyano Pahissa, *México y Estados Unidos: Orígenes de una relación, 1819–1861* (México, D.F.: Secretería de Educación Pública, 1985); J. Fred Rippy, *The United States and Mexico* (New York: Knopf, 1926); and César Sepúlveda, *La frontera norte de México: Historia, conflictos, 1762–1975* (México, D.F.: Editorial Porrúa, 1976).

2. This section is based largely on Martínez, *Troublesome Border*. See also Rippy, *The United States and Mexico*.

3. This section draws heavily from Martínez, *Border People*, chap. 2.

4. *Censos generales de población* (México, D.F.: Dirección General de Estadística, 1950, 1990); U.S. Bureau of the Census, *Censuses of Population* (Washington, DC: U.S. Government Printing Office, 1950, 1990).

I The Making of the Boundary

The creation of the U.S.-Mexican boundary is best understood as a long historical process that began in the sixteenth century when England, Spain, and France competed for control of North America and that ended in the midnineteenth century when the United States absorbed large portions of the Mexican northern frontier through annexation, warfare, and purchase. Critical events in this process include the Texas rebellion (1836), which resulted in the detachment of Texas from Mexico, and the U.S.-Mexican War (1846–1848), which led to U.S. acquisition of California, Arizona, New Mexico, Nevada, Utah, and portions of Wyoming, Colorado, Kansas, and Oklahoma. The final transfer of territory occurred in 1854 when the United States purchased the Mesilla strip, consisting of present-day southwestern New Mexico and southern Arizona.

Mexico's devastating loss of territory is remembered by its people as one of the most critical junctures in the country's history. For generations afterward Mexicans remained deeply distrustful of the United States; Mexico had to be on its guard lest it lose more territory to its land-hungry neighbor. Politicians and diplomats proceeded with extreme caution when conducting negotiations with American officials. For the United States the lands acquired from Mexico truly expanded its possibilities of becoming a great and powerful nation. Americans now had a vast domain that extended from coast to coast, substantially boosting internal and external trade. The Mexican cession also yielded additional fertile lands and abundant gold, silver, copper, and other valuable resources. Thus, for both nations the making of the boundary proved to be a determining factor in their development.

Selections 1 and 2 provide significant background material on the two most important treaties pertaining to the boundary, the Treaty of Guadalupe Hidalgo and the Gadsden Treaty. Documents featured in Selections 3 through 6 include these two treaties plus the Texas Declaration of Independence and the Treaty of Velasco.

1 Richard Griswold del Castillo ◆
The Treaty of Guadalupe Hidalgo

*Ratification of the Treaty of Guadalupe Hidalgo (see Selection 5) trig-
gered considerable debate in both the United States and Mexico, as historian Richard Griswold del Castillo points out in this selection. In
Washington, the discussion centered on the amount of land to be acquired
from Mexico and whether slavery should be extended to these territories.
In Mexico City, the concerns expressed included the possible loss of more
land and the fate of Mexicans in the ceded areas. The legality of the treaty
was questioned in both countries, but its proponents prevailed.*

The final stage in the making of the Treaty of Guadalupe Hidalgo lasted
from the signing of the treaty on February 2, 1848, to the exchange
of ratifications on May 30, 1848. During this period both Mexican and
U.S. statesmen deliberated over the articles in the treaty. The U.S. Congress made several significant changes that the Mexican government accepted only after a protocol was drafted. In its final form the Treaty of
Guadalupe Hidalgo was still an imperfect document. Ambiguities and
errors in the treaty led to boundary disputes, a near renewal of warfare,
and the drafting of another treaty, in 1854, that ceded even more territory
to the United States.

U.S. Ratification

An immediate consequence of the signing of the treaty on February 2,
1848, was to initiate a debate in Washington, D.C., over the desirability
of ratification. President [James K.] Polk, after a long consultation with
his cabinet on Sunday and Monday, February 20 and 21, decided to accept the treaty and to ask Congress to ratify it. This was a decision based
primarily on his appraisal of the likelihood of continued congressional
support for the war. Polk's view was that Congress would probably reject
requests for further war appropriations and that this would lead to an even
less favorable treaty.[1] In his message to Congress he recommended not
only ratification but also the deletion of Article X, which dealt with
land grants, and a secret article relating to the extension of the period for
ratification.

From *The Treaty of Guadalupe Hidalgo: A Legacy of Conflict*, 43–53, 211–
12. © 1990 University of Oklahoma Press. Reprinted by permission of the University of Oklahoma Press.

Article X was an explicit statement protecting Mexican land grants, particularly those in Texas. Polk objected to the provision on the grounds that it would revive old land grants and throw into question the grants made by the Texas government since their declaration of independence in 1836. Further, Polk argued, "public lands within the limits of Texas belong to that state, and this government has no power to dispose of them, or to change the conditions of grants already made."[2]

Even with the president's endorsement, when the treaty came before the Senate, it was not assured of passage. Secretary of State Buchanan and Secretary of the Treasury Walker openly opposed it because it would not gain enough territory for the Republic. The opposition party, the Whigs, were against the treaty for the opposite reason: It would annex too much territory, which eventually would increase the slavocracy's power in Congress. Upon a motion by Sam Houston the Senate voted to conduct its deliberations in secret and as a result there are no exact records of the debate.[3]

One roadblock to a speedy passage of the treaty was the possibility that the Senate Foreign Relations Committee, which had to issue its report prior to the debate, might recommend rejection of the document on the basis that Nicholas Trist had been an unauthorized agent. Only Polk's personal intervention with the committee chair, Ambrose H. Sevier, resulted in a noncommittal rather than a negative report.

Finally, on February 28, the Senate met in executive session. For eleven days the various factions traded arguments. The Whigs, led by Daniel Webster, who feared a growth of the southern section and slavery, opposed the treaty. Some northern Democrats rejected the treaty because they were morally against the war. Some opposed it because they were political rivals of the president. Others like Sam Houston and Jefferson Davis did not want the treaty because it did not annex more of the Mexican territories; Houston favored retaining the territory as far south as the state of Vera Cruz while Davis wanted to annex most of the northern Mexican states.

The treaty remained largely intact because of each faction's opposition to the proposals of the others. Motions to modify, to either expand or retract, the boundary were defeated. The Senate defeated an attempt to insert the language of the Wilmot Proviso, restricting slavery in the new territories. Article X was stricken as recommended by the president; language in Article IX was changed by substituting language from the Louisiana and Florida treaties; Article XI was changed to allow the United States to sell arms and ammunition to Indians in its territories; and the secret article lengthening the time allowed for ratification was omitted. The Senate made a few other minor changes that did not affect the substance of the treaty. During the debate, President Polk exerted his influence on a number of senators by personal visits and pledges of support. Just before the final vote, a powerful opponent of the treaty, former President John Quincy Adams, died. This removed a major rallying point for the opposition, and the mourning period that followed delayed the Senate debate long enough for the senators to assess the mood of public opinion, which was strongly in favor of the treaty and an end to the war.

On March 10, 1848, the Senate voted to ratify the modified version by a vote of 38 to 14, four more than the required two-thirds majority. The vote followed sectional rather than party lines, with the majority of northerners opposing.[4]

Mexican Ratification

It now remained for Mexico to ratify the treaty. Buchanan attempted to gain Mexican acceptance by writing a letter of explanation to the Mexican minister of foreign relations, Luis de la Rosa. Buchanan argued that changes in Article IX dealing with the rights of citizenship were primarily the result of the Senate's wish not to violate precedents established in treaties negotiated with France and Spain. Article IX in its original form forcefully maintained the civil and property rights of the former Mexican citizens. . . .

Buchanan maintained that the Senate amendment of the original was justified because in Florida and Louisiana, "no complaint has ever been made by the original or other inhabitants that their civil or religious rights have not been amply protected."[5] In this he chose to ignore the litigious territorial history of Louisiana where there had been numerous public complaints and lawsuits by the native French against the American administration of New Orleans in the early years.[6] Buchanan's overestimation of the benefits of protection afforded ethnic minorities under the Constitution extended to his rationale for the deletion of Article X from the treaty. . . .

This article struck to the heart of a question that would be the basis for hundreds of lawsuits and many instances of injustice against the former Mexican landholders. The treaty makers knew well that most of the Mexican citizens occupying land grants in the ceded territories did not have perfect title to their lands and that the majority were in the process of fulfilling the requirements of Mexican law. Frequent changes in political administrations, the notorious slowness of the Mexican bureaucracy, and many individual circumstances had made it difficult for Mexican landholders to obtain clear title in an expedient way. Article X would have allowed them to complete the process under an American administration.

The article specifically recognized the unique condition of the Mexican land-grant claimants in Texas, most of whom had been dispossessed of their lands by Anglo Texans following Texas independence. The article would allow them to resurrect their claims and fulfill the conditions of Mexican law.[7]

In his letter to the Mexican minister, Buchanan said that Article X was so outrageous that if it were a part of the treaty "it would be a mere nullity" and that "the Judges of our courts would be compelled to disregard it." He went on in prolix fashion: "It is to our glory that no human power exists in this country which can deprive the individual of his property without his consent and transfer it to another. If the grantees of lands in Texas, under the Mexican government, possess valid titles, they can maintain their claims before our courts of justice."[8] The language of Article X applied to New Mexico and California as well. For the next five decades the territorial, state, and supreme courts would be occupied with sorting out "perfect" and "imperfect" land grants and dispossessing those who occupied the land in 1848. The absence of specific treaty protections for the holder of unperfected grants threw them on the mercy of the American courts. In 1848 Buchanan had an unbridled optimism about the ability of the judicial system to dispense justice; subsequent decisions, however, created a heritage of ill will between Mexican settlers and Anglo immigrants.

Realizing that these amendments and deletions might prevent the Mexican Congress from ratifying the treaty, President Polk sent with the modified document two commissioners to explain the changes and to accept the Mexican ratification on the spot. Senator Ambrose Sevier, chair of the Senate Foreign Relations Committee, and Nathan Clifford, the attorney general, arrived in Mexico in mid-April, and on May 3, 1848, the Mexican Congress convened to debate the modified version of the treaty.

In the period following the signing of the treaty, a vocal opposition formed. Before the congressional debates, the opponents of the treaty, led by Manuel Crescencio Rejón, published their arguments against ratification and stimulated debate over whether to continue the war. Rejón, a liberal from Yucatán, had helped draft the 1824 constitution and had served as minister of relations under Herrera and Santa Anna. Rejón believed that Mexico could win a protracted guerrilla war. Other liberals, such as Melchor Ocampo and Benito Juárez, shared this view and opposed the Treaty of Guadalupe Hidalgo.

Regón's opposition was published in an 1848 broadside entitled "Observations on the Treaty of Guadalupe Hidalgo."[9] His argument against the treaty was contained in fifteen closely reasoned juridical sections of this treatise. Rejón believed that the treaty would mean the inevitable economic subordination of Mexico by the United States. He predicted that the new boundary, by bringing American commerce closer to the heartland of Mexico, would lead [to] the Americanization of Mexico. He said, "We will never be able to compete in our own markets with the North American imports. . . . The treaty is our sentence of death."[10] Rejón criticized those who thought that the Mexican citizens in the ceded territories would be protected. He believed that American racism would prevent their being treated justly: "The North Americans hate us, their orators deprecate us even in speeches in which they recognize the justice of our cause, and they consider us unable to form a single nation or society with them." For Rejón the treaty would only delay "the absolute loss of our political existence as a republic."[11]

The juridical arguments Rejón advanced were that the treaty violated Mexican laws because it had been drafted clandestinely without input from Congress or the states. There had been no open discussion of the treaty prior to the debates over ratification. The treaty had not been published, and the signing of the treaty violated the constitution. In a word, Rejón argued that the government had exceeded its authority in agreeing to alienate its national territory. The Mexican government also had violated international law and precedent.[12] Although the government had argued that the territory being ceded was worthless, Rejón placed a high value on the lands, especially California. In his argument he called California "our priceless flower" and "our inestimable jewel."[13] By coincidence gold had been discovered a few weeks before Rejón wrote these words, but neither he nor the rest of the world would learn of it until the midsummer of 1848.[14]

In response to Rejón's arguments, Bernardo Couto, one of the original commissioners, published the commissioners' arguments in favor of the treaty. The recurring theme in the writings of treaty advocates was that, by ending the war, the treaty had saved Mexico from possible obliteration as a nation. If the war had continued, they argued, all of Mexico probably would have been annexed by the United States. The negotiators wrote: "The treaty not only prevents any increase of our losses by a continuation of the war, but recovers the greater part of that which was subjected to the arms of the conquerors; it may be more properly called a treaty of recovery rather than one of alienation."[15]

Regarding the territory and people being lost, the commissioners adopted a stoic attitude: "It can hardly be said that we lose any power, since that which we cede is almost all uninhabited and uncultivated. . . . We lose in our rich hopes for the future, but if we know how to cultivate and defend the territory that the treaty preserves or has rescued for us, we shall find it sufficient to console us for our past misfortunes."[16]

Couto naïvely argued that the rights of the former Mexican citizens would be protected because, in American law, "every treaty has a superiority and preference under civil legislation." The proponents asserted that the treaty provisions for citizenship and property rights in Articles VIII and IX would be sufficient to protect the former Mexican citizens. They were wrong: American local, state, and national courts later ruled that the provisions of the treaty could be superseded by local laws.[17]

Manuel de la Peña y Peña also published his arguments in favor of the treaty. He emphasized the extraordinary concern he and his fellow commissioners had felt for their abandoned Mexican populations. "If it had been possible," he wrote, "I would have enlarged the territorial cession with the condition of freeing the Mexican population living there." To resume the war, he continued would endanger their safety and condition; terrible sacrifices were necessary to end the war.[18]

On May 7, 1847, the Mexican Congress opened its debates on the treaty. At that time Peña y Peña, another commissioner, was acting president. His support for ratification was important, especially because he addressed freshman deputies and senators whose future political life might depend on their alliance with the president.

In considering the treaty, the Congress heard a report from Minister of War Anaya outlining the military situation. They then listened to a detailed report from Luis de la Rosa, minister of the treasury, outlining financial justifications for a treaty. Finally, the Chamber heard a report from the commissioners explaining the provisions of the treaty.[19]

The military situation was not good. Besides the American occupation, factions opposing the treaty had made sporadic attempts at rebellion against the federal government. In Aguascalientes, General Paredes y Arrillaga pronounced against the government and captured Guanajuato for a few months until the city was recaptured by federal troops.[20] In early May 1848 the governments of Coahuila and Tamaulipas declared that they would not recognize the Treaty of Guadalupe if it were ratified.[21] Benito Juárez, then governor of Oaxaca, formally announced that his state would oppose the treaty and keep fighting.[22] In addition protests against the treaty came from the state governments of Chihuahua, Zacatecas, Jalisco, and Mexico. As if this were not sufficient, several potentially dangerous Indian rebellions called for immediate action; in San Luis Potosí the Xichu Indians razed missions and buildings throughout a hundred-square-mile area.

Opposition to the treaty was strongest in the Chamber of Deputies. José María Cuevas, brother of the Luis Cuevas who had signed the treaty, spoke eloquently in opposition, moving the delegates to a standing ovation and lengthy demonstration.[23] The published arguments of Senators

Mariano Otero and Manuel Crescencio Rejón against the treaty were influential. Oral arguments in favor of ratification came from the minister of foreign relations, Luis de la Rosa; the minister of war, Pedro Anaya; and the president of the Chamber, Francisco Elorriaga.²⁴ Finally, on May 19, the deputies met and voted 51 to 35 for ratification. Then the Senate took up the debate. There was less intense opposition in this body, the principal leader being Mariano Otero. After three days of discussion, the modified treaty passed by a vote of 33 to 4.²⁵

In ratifying the Treaty of Guadalupe Hidalgo, the majority of the Mexican Congress chose the lesser of two evils. Not to ratify the document would have meant continued American military occupation, a prolonged financial disaster for the Mexican government, and the probable loss of additional territory. In accepting the treaty, the politicians admitted that the loss of territory was inevitable and that a treaty would liberate Mexico from foreign domination while preventing further erosion of national territory. Most of the delegates probably accepted Peña y Peña's characterization: It was a treaty of recovery rather than of cession.²⁶

Notes

1. David Pletcher, *The Diplomacy of Annexation: Texas, Oregon, and the Mexican War* (Columbia: University of Missouri Press, 1973), p. 558.
2. Senate Executive Documents No. 52, 30th Congress, 1st session, 4–5.
3. Ibid., 9.
4. Robert Selph Henry, *The Story of the Mexican War* (New York: Frederick Unger, 1950), pp. 386–388. The most complete documentary collection regarding the treaty and its ratification is assembled in David Hunter Miller, *Treaties and Other International Acts of the United States of America*, vol. 5, *Mexico, 1848* (Washington, DC: Government Printing Office, 1937), pp. 207–428. The best account of the Senate's ratification debates is Ralph A. Rowley, "Precedents and Influences Affecting the Treaty of Guadalupe-Hidalgo" (Master's thesis, University of New Mexico, 1970), pp. 78–96.
5. Miller, 5:255.
6. See François Xavier Martin, *The History of Louisiana From the Earliest Periods* (New Orleans: James A. Gresham, 1882), pp. 322–323.
7. Conditions required by the federal government usually included five actions: (1) presentation of a petition describing the parcel along with a map (*diseño*) to the local government official; (2) examination of the land to ascertain its availability and the filing of a report (*informe*); (3) the issuance of a formal grant by the local government (*expediente*); (4) approval of the grant by the territorial or state Assembly or Deputation; and (5) approval by the central government. See William W. Robinson, *Land in California* (Berkeley: University of California Press, 1948).
8. Miller, 5:255.
9. Later these broadsides were published as *Pensamiento Político* (México, D.F.: UNAM, 1968). See "Observations on the Treaty of Guadalupe Hidalgo," in that work, pp. 93–145.

10. Ibid., pp. 119–20.

11. Ibid., pp. 122, 123.

12. Ibid., pp. 127–33.

13. Ibid., pp. 127, 133.

14. The news of the discovery of gold in Alta California did not reach Mexico City until after the ratification of the treaty. Although gold was discovered on January 24, 1848, John Marshall and John Sutter tried to keep the discovery secret. It was not until the middle of May that news reached San Francisco. See J. S. Holliday, *The World Rushed In: The California Gold Rush Experience* (New York: Simon & Schuster, 1981).

15. *Siglo XIX*, June 2, 1848, 3:2.

16. Ibid., June 7, 1848, 3:4.

17. Ibid., June 10, 1848, 3:3.

18. Ibid., June 2, 1848, 1:5.

19. José María Roa Bárcena, *Recuerdos de la invasión norteamericana (1846–1848)*, vol. 3 (1883; Reprint, México, D.F.: Editorial Porrua, 1947), 3:323.

20. Francisco de Paula de Arrangoiz, *Mexico desde 1808 hasta 1867* (1872; Reprint, México, D.F.: Editorial Porrua, 1969), p. 401.

21. *Siglo XIX*, May 19, 1848, 3:6.

22. *Algunos documentos sobre el tratado de Guadalupe y la situación de México durante la invasión Americana* (México, D.F.: Editorial Porrua, 1970), p. 380.

23. Roa Bárcena, p. 304.

24. *Algunos documentos*, pp. 51–65, 168–92.

25. Dennis E. Berge, "Mexican Response to United States Expansionism, 1841–1848" (Ph.D. diss., Berkeley, 1965), pp. 304–306.

26. *Siglo XIX*, June 2, 1848, 3:2.

2 Angela Moyano Pahissa ◆
The Mesilla Treaty, or Gadsden Purchase

The Gadsden Treaty (Selection 6), known in Mexico as El Tratado de La Mesilla, aroused indignation among Mexicans because it resulted in the loss of additional territories to the United States. As Angela Moyano Pahissa indicates, Washington took advantage of political instability south of the border to accomplish its objectives. Moyano Pahissa, a Mexican historian, is particularly critical of the bullying tactics of the expansionist U.S. negotiator James Gadsden.

The problem over the Mesilla Valley emerged directly from the discussions concerning the border. According to the Treaty of Guadalupe Hidalgo, the commissioners charged with delimiting the border had to finish their work within a year of ratification. They began much later than that, and the Mexican delegation quickly accused the North American delegation of being more interested in other matters.

By the end of the 1840s interest had arisen in the United States for the building of a railroad line to the Pacific. During the conquest of New Mexico (in 1846), Lieutenant William Emory had investigated which area would yield the best route. According to his studies, the appropriate site was a depression in the Gila River Valley southwest of El Paso. That detail was not communicated to Nicholas Trist [U.S. negotiator of the Treaty of Guadalupe Hidalgo], and the border was fixed north of the place identified by Emory. As the two countries continued wrangling [in the early 1850s], the land in question, known as La Mesilla, was occupied by a group of New Mexicans who did not want to live in U.S. territory and decided to found a town south of New Mexico.

Meanwhile, geographers and land surveyors engaged in polemics. The border commissioners determined that the Disturnell Map, which was used by the negotiators of the Treaty of Guadalupe Hidalgo, contained errors. Immediately both sides tried to obtain more territory for their respective countries. Finally a settlement was negotiated, but A. B. Gray, one of the members of the U.S. commission, was not present during the talks, and upon his return he refused to accept the accord, thus bringing about a renewal of the controversy. The Mexican commissioners com-

From *México y Estados Unidos: Origenes de una relación, 1819–1861* (México, D.F.: Secretaría de Educación Pública, 1985), 242–43, 248, 251–54, trans. Oscar J. Martínez. Reprinted by permission of the author.

plained that their U.S. counterparts lacked interest in reaching agreement on the location of the boundary, being more interested in the proposed railroad line. . . .

On July 15, 1853, the U.S. secretary of state, an expansionist, issued diplomatic instructions to James Gadsden. His [Gadsden's] principal objective was to settle the Mesilla controversy, although he was also ordered to seek the abrogation of Article XI of the Treaty of Guadalupe Hidalgo, pertaining to cross-border Indian incursions, and to obtain concessions in the Isthmus of Tehuantepec. . . .

From the start, Gadsden invoked the principle of natural borders, stating that valleys and rivers united people while mountains and deserts divided them. Thus, he pressed Mexico for territorial concessions extending to the Sierra Madre mountains. . . . From the documents that detail the negotiations, Gadsden emerges as a rude and pushy man whose job it was to buy, in whatever way possible, what his masters craved.

At the time, Mexico faced much political instability because of the conflict between conservatives and liberals. The newspaper *El Siglo XIX* published an article in which it revealed a proposal by the conservatives to seek an alliance with Spain and the reestablishment of the monarchy. In their view that was the only way to obtain protection from the territorial ambitions of the United States, which had first desired Texas, then California, now La Mesilla, and tomorrow Tehuantepec. The national economy was in a disastrous situation. Desperate for funds, President Antonio López de Santa Anna even imposed taxes based on the number of windows in a house and on dogs, whose owners would pay one peso every month for each animal. . . .

It was in the midst of such a catastrophic confusion, when political movements were coming and going, that the United States issued instructions to its functionaries for the purchase of La Mesilla. The expansionist administration of Franklin Pierce formulated five options for the purchase of territory from Mexico. . . . The first plan, encompassing 124 million square miles, included the Baja California peninsula, half of Tamaulipas, almost all of Nuevo León and Coahuila, and fractions of Durango, Chihuahua, and Sonora. The price would be 50 million pesos. The second proposal, comprising 50,000 square miles of territory, would include a stretch of land south of the boundary that would detach portions of all the border states, plus the area that links Sonora and Baja California; the United States would pay 35 million pesos. The third proposal consisted of 68,000 square miles, all in Baja California, with a price tag of 30 million pesos. The fourth plan excluded Baja California and offered 20 million pesos. The fifth plan, with a price tag of 15 million pesos, limited itself to the territory thought necessary for the proposed railroad. . . .

Gadsden, upon learning about the overtures of the conservatives to European nations, threatened warfare that would lead to U.S. annexation of northern Mexico, including Baja California. . . . It is therefore understandable why Santa Anna would accept the last offer. . . . Santa Anna's behavior during the war with the United States [1846–1848] seemed traitorous, or at least highly suspicious. On this occasion, however, he did all he could to cede as little territory as possible. . . .

Concerning the article [VIII] that dealt with the Isthmus of Tehuantepec, this was an error that would sour the relations between the two nations for many years. Mexico authorized the construction of a railway and a road across the isthmus. The U.S. government was anxious to establish a foothold in the commerce between east and west, and it placed its hopes in Tehuantepec. The Mesilla Treaty . . . granted U.S. citizens transit rights without passport requirements. Furthermore, it guaranteed that there would be no interference in the flow of goods and people, that transit fees would not be charged, that the United States would have the right to transport mail, that Mexico would open a seaport at the terminal point of the railway, and that an arrangement would be worked out for the transit of U.S. troops and munitions. The last provision was the most dangerous part of the treaty because it gave the United States the right to protect the route.

The treaty encountered much opposition in the United States. The acquired territory was insignificant and arid. Mexico was saved by North American internal politics. The United States found itself in the midst of a great political conflict provoked by the incorporation of Kansas and Nebraska into the Union. Once again the country was caught up in a violent controversy over slavery. . . . President Pierce . . . threatened the Senate with shouldering the responsibility for a possible war with Mexico if it rejected the treaty and asked for additional territories. The Congress accepted the treaty, with a payment of 10 million pesos [for the ceded land].

In Mexico, the discussions over the treaty had been conducted in secret. The treaty became known after ratification in July 1854. The argument was made that the semiarid lands that had been sold had no value. Besides, Mexico was not prepared for a second war with the United States in case that country wanted to take the Mesilla Valley by force.

3 Texas Declaration of Independence

The roots of the Texas rebellion of 1836 lay in American westward expansionism and in the inability of Mexico, a poor, unstable country in the earliest stages of nation-building, to stop that surge. In the early 1820s, Mexico allowed thousands of Anglo-Americans to settle in Texas in an effort to populate a distant and weakly protected frontier province. Within a decade, an estimated thirty thousand Anglos vastly outnumbered the thirty-five hundred local Mexicans. Anglo unhappiness with Mexico's administration of Texas surfaced in different forms, including demands for more political representation, religious freedom, unobstructed trade, and recognition of slavery. When President Antonio López de Santa Anna imposed a centralist government on the province in 1834, Texans clamored for a return to the federalist constitution of 1824. Chronic discontent led to disregard for laws, localized uprisings, talk of sedition, and, eventually, full-scale insurgency.

On March 2, 1836, following a series of skirmishes and battles between Texan rebels and Mexican troops, fifty-nine delegates from the insurgent forces, including three Mexicans, gathered at Washington-on-the-Brazos and declared the independence of Texas from Mexico. With the aid of sympathetic Americans in the adjacent United States, the Texans succeeded in their effort to establish an independent republic. Annexation to the United States followed in 1845.

When a government has ceased to protect the lives, liberty, and property of the people, from whom its legitimate powers are derived, and for the advancement of whose happiness it was instituted, and, so far from being a guarantee for the enjoyment of those inestimable and inalienable rights, becomes an instrument in the hands of evil rulers for their oppression: When the Federal Republican Constitution of their country, which they have sworn to support, no longer has a substantial existence, and the whole nature of their government has been forcibly changed, without their consent, from a restricted federative republic, composed of sovereign states, to a consolidated, central, military despotism in which every interest is disregarded but that of the army and the priesthood—both the eternal enemies of civil liberty, the ever-ready minions of power, and the usual instruments of tyrants. When, long after the spirit of the constitution has departed, moderation is, at length, so far lost by those in power that even the semblance of freedom is removed, and the forms

From Eugene C. Barker, ed., *Texas History* (Dallas: Turner Company, 1929), 242–45.

themselves, of the constitution discontinued; and so far from their petitions and remonstrances being regarded the agents who bear them are thrown into dungeons; and mercenary armies sent forth to force a new government upon them at the point of the bayonet: When in consequence of such acts of malfeasance and abdication, on the part of the government, anarchy prevails, and civil society is dissolved into its original elements—In such a crisis, the first law of nature, the right of self-preservation—the inherent and inalienable right of the people to appeal to first principles and take their political affairs into their own hands in extreme cases—enjoins it as a right towards themselves and a sacred obligation to their posterity to abolish such government and create another, in its stead, calculated to rescue them from impending dangers, and to secure their future welfare and happiness.

Nations, as well as individuals, are amenable for their acts to the public opinion of mankind. A statement of a part of our grievances is, therefore, submitted to an impartial world, in justification of the hazardous but avoidable step now taken of severing our political connection with the Mexican people, and assuming an independent attitude among the nations of the earth.

The Mexican government, by its colonization laws, invited and induced the Anglo-American population of Texas to colonize its wilderness under the pledged faith of a written constitution that they should continue to enjoy that constitutional liberty and republican government to which they had been habituated in the land of their birth, the United States of America. In this expectation they have been cruelly disappointed, inasmuch as the Mexican nation has acquiesced in the late changes made in the government by General Antonio López de Santa Anna, who, having overturned the constitution of his country, now offers us the cruel alternative either to abandon our homes, acquired by so many privations, or submit to the most intolerable of all tyranny, the combined despotism of the sword and the priesthood.

It has sacrificed our welfare to the state of Coahuila, by which our interests have been continually depressed through a jealous and partial course of legislation carried on at a far distant seat of government, by a hostile majority, in an unknown tongue; and this too, notwithstanding we have petitioned in the humblest terms, for the establishment of a separate state government, and have, in accordance with the provisions of the national constitution, presented to the general Congress a republican constitution which was, without just cause, contemptuously rejected.

It incarcerated in a dungeon, for a long time, one of our citizens, for no other cause but a zealous endeavor to procure the acceptance of our constitution and the establishment of a state government.

It has failed and refused to secure on a firm basis, the right of trial by jury, that palladium of civil liberty, and only safe guarantee for the life, liberty, and property of the citizen.

It has failed to establish any public system of education, although possessed of almost boundless resources (the public domain) and, although it is an axiom, in political science, that unless a people are educated and enlightened it is idle to expect the continuance of civil liberty, or the capacity for self-government.

It has suffered the military commandants stationed among us to exercise arbitrary acts of oppression and tyranny; thus trampling upon the most sacred rights of the citizen and rendering the military superior to the civil power.

It has dissolved by force of arms, the State Congress of Coahuila and Texas, and obliged our representatives to fly for their lives from the seat of government; thus depriving us of the fundamental political right of representation.

It has demanded the surrender of a number of our citizens, and ordered military detachments to seize and carry them into the interior for trial; in contempt of the civil authorities, and in defiance of the laws and the constitution.

It has made piratical attacks upon our commerce, by commissioning foreign desperadoes, and authorizing them to seize our vessels, and convey the property of our citizens to far distant ports for confiscation.

It denies us the right of worshipping the Almighty according to the dictates of our own conscience; by the support of a national religion calculated to promote the temporal interests of its human functionaries rather than the glory of the true and living God.

It has demanded us to deliver up our arms, which are essential to our defense, the rightful property of freemen, and formidable only to tyrannical governments.

It has invaded our country, both by sea and by land, with intent to lay waste our territory and drive us from our homes; and has now a large mercenary army advancing to carry on against us a war of extermination.

It has, through its emissaries, incited the merciless savage, with the tomahawk and scalping knife, to massacre the inhabitants of our defenseless frontiers.

It has been, during the whole time of our connection with it, the contemptible sport and victim of successive military revolutions; and has continually exhibited every characteristic of a weak, corrupt, and tyrannical government.

These, and other grievances, were patiently borne by the people of Texas until they reached that point at which forbearance ceases to be a virtue. We then took up arms in defence of the national constitution. We appealed to our Mexican brethren for assistance. Our appeal has been made in vain. Though months have elapsed, no sympathetic response has yet been heard from the Interior. We are, therefore, forced to the melancholy conclusion that the Mexican people have acquiesced in the destruction of their liberty, and the substitution therefor of a military government—that they are unfit to be free and incapable of self-government.

The necessity of self-preservation, therefore, now decrees our eternal political separation.

We, therefore, the delegates, with plenary powers, of the people of Texas, in solemn convention assembled, appealing to a candid world for the necessities of our condition, do hereby resolve and declare that our political connection with the Mexican nation has forever ended; and that the people of Texas do now constitute a free sovereign and independent republic, and are fully invested with all the rights and attributes which properly belong to independent nations; and, conscious of the rectitude of our intentions, we fearlessly and confidently commit the issue to the decision of the Supreme Arbiter of the destinies of nations.

4 Treaty of Velasco

As the Texas rebellion raged, a decisive battle took place on April 21, 1836, in San Jacinto, a site near present-day Houston. The Texans forced General Antonio López de Santa Anna, who was captured after the battle, to declare an armistice; to order Mexican troops to evacuate Texas; and to commit himself, upon his return to Mexico City, to work toward official recognition of Texas independence. The agreement, which was signed in Velasco, became known as the Treaty of Velasco. Because Santa Anna signed this document under duress, the Mexican congress repudiated it, but Texas persisted in claiming it to be valid.

Santa Anna requested that the treaty consist of a public and a private agreement, and his captors acceded. What is most significant in the secret portion of the accord for understanding the eventual location of the boundary between Texas and Mexico is Santa Anna's implicit acceptance of the Rio Grande as the dividing line. Despite Mexico's rejection of the treaty and the abundant evidence that the historical boundary of Texas was actually the Nueces River, Washington followed the Texan interpretation when the annexation of Texas ensued in 1845, further complicating U.S. relations with Mexico.

PUBLIC AGREEMENT

Articles of Agreement entered into between His Excellency David G. Burnet, President of the Republic of Texas, of the one part, and His Excellency General Antonio López de Santa Anna, President-General-in-Chief of the Mexican Army, of the other part:

Article 1. General Antonio López de Santa Anna agrees that he will not take up arms, nor will he exercise his influence to cause them to be taken up, against the people of Texas, during the present war of independence.

Article 2. All hostilities between the Mexican and Texan troops will cease immediately, both on land and water.

Article 3. The Mexican troops will evacuate the territory of Texas, passing to the other side of the Rio Grande del Norte.

Article 4. The Mexican army, in its retreat, shall not take the property of any person without his consent and just indemnification, using only such articles as may be necessary for its subsistence, in cases where the owners may not be present, and remitting to the commander of the

From the El Paso Public Library, Special Collections, Southwest Room, El Paso, Texas.

army of Texas, or to the commissioners to be appointed for the adjustment of such matters, an account of the property consumed, the place where taken, and the name of the owner, if it can be ascertained.

Article 5. That all private property, including horses, cattle, negro slaves, or indentured persons of whatever denomination, that may have been captured by any portion of the Mexican army, or may have taken refuge in the said army, since the commencement of the late invasion, shall be restored to the commander of the Texan army, or to such other persons as may be appointed by the government of Texas to receive them.

Article 6. The troops of both armies will refrain from coming into contact with each other; and, to this end, the commander of the army of Texas will be careful not to approach within a shorter distance of the Mexican army than five leagues.

Article 7. The Mexican army shall not make any other delay on its march than that which is necessary to take up their hospitals, baggage, &c., and to cross the rivers. Any delay, not necessary to these purposes, to be considered an infraction of this agreement.

Article 8. By express, to be immediately despatched, this agreement shall be sent to General Filisola, and to General T. J. Rusk, commander of the Texan army, in order that they may be apprized of its stipulations; and, to this end, they will exchange engagements to comply with the same.

Article 9. That all Texan prisoners now in possession of the Mexican army, or its authorities, be forthwith released, and furnished with free passports to return to their homes; in consideration of which a corresponding number of Mexican prisoners, rank and file, now in possession of the government of Texas, shall be immediately released. The remainder of the Mexican prisoners, that continue in possession of the government of Texas, to be treated with due humanity; any extraordinary comforts that may be furnished them to be at the charge of the government of Mexico.

Article 10. General Antonio López de Santa Anna will be sent to Vera Cruz, as soon as it shall be deemed proper.

The contracting parties sign this instrument for the above-mentioned purposes, by duplicate, at the port of Velasco, this the 14th day of May 1836.

DAVID G. BURNET,
ANT°. LÓPEZ DE SANTA ANNA.

SECRET AGREEMENT

Antonio López de Santa Anna, General-in-Chief of the Army of Operations, and President of the Republic of Mexico, before the Government established in Texas, solemnly pledges himself to fulfill the Stipulations contained in the following Articles, so far as concerns himself:

Article 1. He will not take up arms, nor cause them to be taken up, against the people of Texas, during the present war for independence.

Article 2. He will give his orders that, in the shortest time, the Mexican troops may leave the territory of Texas.

Article 3. He will so prepare matters in the cabinet of Mexico, that the mission that may be sent thither by the government of Texas may be well received, and that by means of negotiations all differences may be settled, and the independence that has been declared by the convention may be acknowledged.

Article 4. A treaty of commerce, amity, and limits, will be established between Mexico and Texas, the territory of the latter not to extend beyond the Rio Bravo del Norte.

Article 5. The present return of General Santa Anna to Vera Cruz being indispensable for the purpose of effecting his solemn engagements, the government of Texas will provide for his immediate embarkation for said port.

Article 6. This instrument, being obligatory on one part as well as on the other, will be signed in duplicate, remaining folded and sealed until the negotiations shall have been concluded, when it will be restored to his excellency General Santa Anna; no use of it to be made before that time, unless there should be an infraction by either of the contracting parties.

Port of Velasco, May the 14th, 1836.

ANT°. LÓPEZ DE SANTA ANNA,
DAVID G. BURNET.

James Collingsworth, *Secretary of State.*
Bailey Hardeman, *Secretary of the Treasury.*
P. H. Grayson, *Attorney-General.*

5 Treaty of Guadalupe Hidalgo

The Treaty of Guadalupe Hïdalgo (see Selection 1) ended the U.S.-Mexican War, which lasted from April 1846 to February 1848. Hostilities commenced after the U.S. annexation of Texas in 1845 and the subsequent failed attempts to de-escalate tensions over pending disagreements, mutual threats, and bungled diplomacy. A shooting incident in a disputed zone on the Texas-Tamaulipas frontier led to a declaration of war in Washington. The hostilities culminated with the invasion of Mexico City and the signing of a treaty in the nearby town of Guadalupe.

The following parts of the Treaty of Guadalupe Hidalgo are especially significant: Article V, which defines the new border between the two nations; Articles VIII and IX, which detail the citizenship, property, and religious rights accorded the Mexicans who were incorporated into the United States; and Article XI, which obligates the United States to stop Indian incursions into Mexico.

T*reaty signed at Guadalupe Hidalgo February 2, 1848*

Senate advice and consent to ratification, with amendments, March 10, 1848[1]

Ratified by the President of the United States, with amendments, March 16, 1848[1]

Ratified by Mexico May 30, 1848

Ratifications exchanged at Querétaro May 30, 1848

Entered into force May 30, 1848

Proclaimed by the President of the United States July 4, 1848

Articles V, VI, and VII amended and article XI abrogated by treaty of December 30, 1853[2]

Article XXI continued in effect by convention of March 24, 1908[3]

Articles II–IV, XII–XV, and XVII–XX terminated upon fulfillment of terms

9 Stat. 922; Treaty Series 207[4]

In the name of Almighty God:

The United States of America, and the United Mexican States, animated by a sincere desire to put an end to the calamities of the war which

From Charles I. Bevans, ed., *Treaties and Other International Agreements of the United States of America, 1776–1949*, 13 vols. (Washington, DC: U.S. Department of State, 1972), 9:791–806.

unhappily exists between the two Republicans, and to establish upon a solid basis relations of peace and friendship, which shall confer reciprocal benefits upon the citizens of both, and assure the concord, harmony and mutual confidence, wherein the two Peoples should live, as good Neighbours, have for that purpose appointed their respective Plenipotentiaries: that is to say, the President of the United States has appointed Nicholas P. Trist, a citizen of the United States, and the President of the Mexican Republic has appointed Don Luis Gonzaga Cuevas, Don Bernardo Couto, and Don Miguel Atristain, citizens of the said Republic; who, after a reciprocal communication of their respective full powers, have, under the protection of Almighty God, the author of Peace, arranged, agreed upon, and signed the following

TREATY OF PEACE, FRIENDSHIP, LIMITS AND SETTLEMENT BETWEEN THE UNITED STATES OF AMERICA AND THE MEXICAN REPUBLIC

ARTICLE I

There shall be firm and universal peace between the United States of America and the Mexican Republic, and between their respective Countries, territories, cities, towns and people, without exception of places or persons.

ARTICLE II

Immediately upon the signature of this Treaty, a convention shall be entered into between a Commissioner and Commissioners appointed by the General in Chief of the forces of the United States, and such as may be appointed by the Mexican Government, to the end that a provisional suspension of hostilities shall take place, and that, in the places occupied by the said forces, constitutional order may be reestablished, as regards the political, administrative and judicial branches, so far as this shall be permitted by the circumstances of military occupation.[5]

ARTICLE III

Immediately upon the ratification of the present treaty by the Government of the United States, orders shall be transmitted to the Commanders of their land and naval forces, requiring the latter, (provided this Treaty shall then have been ratified by the Government of the Mexican Republic and the ratifications exchanged)[6] immediately to desist from blockading any Mexican ports; and requiring the former (under the same condition) to commence, at the earliest moment practicable, withdrawing all troops of the United States then in the interior of the Mexican Republic, to points, that shall be selected by common agreement, at a distance from the sea-ports, not exceeding thirty leagues; and such evacuation of the interior of the Republic shall be completed with the least possible delay: the Mexican Government hereby binding itself to afford every facility in it's [sic] power for rendering the same convenient to the troops, on their march and in their new positions, and for promoting a good understanding between them and the inhabitants. In like manner, orders shall be dispatched to the persons in charge of the custom houses at all ports occupied by the forces of the United States, requiring them (under the same condition) immediately to deliver possession of the same to the persons authorized by the Mexican Government to receive it, together with all bonds and evidences of debt for duties on importations and on exportations, not yet fallen due. Moreover, a faithful and exact account shall be made out, showing the entire amount of all duties on imports and on exports, collected at such Custom Houses, or elsewhere in Mexico, by authority of the United States, from and after the day of ratification of this Treaty by the Government of the Mexican Republic; and also an account of the cost of collection; and such entire amount, deducting only the cost of collection, shall be delivered to the Mexican Government, at the City of Mexico, within three months after the exchange of ratifications.

The evacuation of the Capital of the Mexican Republic by the Troops of the United States, in virtue of the above stipulation, shall be completed in one month after the orders there stipulated for shall have been received by the commander of said troops, or sooner if possible.

Article IV

Immediately after the exchange of ratifications of the present treaty, all castles, forts, territories, places and possessions, which have been taken or occupied by the forces of the United States during the present war, within the limits of the Mexican Republic, as about to be established by the following Article, shall be definitively restored to the said Republic, together with all the artillery, arms, apparatus of war, munitions, and other public property, which were in the said castles and forts when captured, and which shall remain there at the time when this treaty shall be duly ratified by the Government of the Mexican Republic. To this end, immediately upon the signature of this treaty, orders shall be despatched to the American officers commanding such castles and forts, securing against the removal or destruction of any such artillery, arms, apparatus of war, munitions, or other public property. The city of Mexico, within the inner line of intrenchments surrounding the said city, is comprehended in the above stipulations, as regards the restoration of artillery, apparatus of war, &c.

The final evacuation of the territory of the Mexican Republic, by the forces of the United States, shall be completed in three months from the said exchange of ratifications, or sooner, if possible: the Mexican Government hereby engaging, as in the foregoing Article, to use all means in it's power for facilitating such evacuation, and rendering it convenient to the troops, and for promoting a good understanding between them and the inhabitants.

If, however, the ratification of this treaty by both parties should not take place in time to allow the embarkation of the troops of the United States to be completed before the commencement of the sickly season, at the Mexican ports on the Gulf of Mexico; in such case a friendly arrangement shall be entered into between the General in Chief of the said troops and the Mexican Government, whereby healthy and otherwise suitable places at a distance from the ports not exceeding thirty leagues shall be designated for the residence of such troops as may not yet have embarked, until the return of the healthy season. And the space of time here referred to, as comprehending the sickly season, shall be understood to extend from the first day of May to the first day of November.

All prisoners of war taken on either side, on land or on sea, shall be restored as soon as practicable after the exchange of ratifications of this treaty. It is also agreed that if any Mexicans should now be held as captives by any savage tribe within the limits of the United States, as about to be established by the following Article, the Government of the said United States will exact the release of such captives, and cause them to be restored to their country.

ARTICLE V[7]

The Boundary line between the two Republics shall commence in the Gulf of Mexico, three leagues from land, opposite the mouth of the Rio Grande, otherwise called Rio Bravo del Norte, or opposite the mouth of it's deepest branch, if it should have more than one branch emptying directly into the sea; from thence, up the middle of that river, following the deepest channel, where it has more than one to the point where it strikes the Southern boundary of New Mexico; thence, westwardly along the whole Southern Boundary of New Mexico (which runs north of the town called *Paso*) to it's western termination; thence, northward, along the western line of New Mexico, until it intersects the first branch of the river Gila; (or if it should not intersect any branch of that river, then, to the point on the said line nearest to such branch, and thence in a direct line to the same;) thence down the middle of the said branch and of the said river, until it empties into the Rio Colorado; thence, across the Rio Colorado, following the division line between Upper and Lower California, to the Pacific Ocean.

The southern and western limits of New Mexico, mentioned in this Article, are those laid down in the Map, entitled *"Map of the United Mexican States, as organized and defined by various acts of the Congress of said Republic, and constructed according to the best authorities. Revised edition. Published at New York in 1847 by J. Disturnell"*: Of which Map a Copy is added to this Treaty,[8] bearing the signatures and seals of the Undersigned Plenipotentiaries. And, in order to preclude all difficulty in tracing upon the ground the limit separating Upper from Lower California, it is agreed that the said limit shall consist of a straight line, drawn from the middle of the Rio Gila, where it unites with the Colorado, to a point on the Coast of the Pacific Ocean, distant one marine league due south of the southernmost point of the Port of San Diego, according to the plan of said port, made in the year 1782, by Don Juan Pantoja, second sailing-Master of the Spanish fleet, and published at Madrid in the year 1802, in the Atlas to the voyage of the schooners *Sutil* and *Mexicana*: of which plan a Copy is hereunto added,[9] signed and sealed by the respective Plenipotentiaries.

In order to designate the Boundary line with due precision, upon authoritative maps, and to establish upon the ground landmarks which shall show the limits of both Republics, as described in the present Article, the two Governments shall each appoint a Commissioner and a Surveyor, who, before the expiration of one year from the date of the exchange of ratifications of this treaty, shall meet at the Port of San Diego, and proceed to run and mark the said Boundary in it's whole course to the mouth of the Rio Bravo del Norte. They shall keep journals and make out plans of their operations; and the result, agreed upon by them, shall be deemed a part of this treaty, and shall have the same force as if it were inserted therein. The two Governments will amicably agree regarding what may be necessary to these persons, and also as to their respective escorts, should such be necessary.

The Boundary line established by this Article shall be religiously respected by each of the two Republics, and no change shall ever be made therein, except by the express and free consent of both nations, lawfully given by the General Government of each, in conformity with it's own constitution.

ARTICLE VI[10]

The vessels and citizens of the United States shall, in all time, have a free and uninterrupted passage by the Gulf of California, and by the river

Colorado below it's confluence with the Gila, to and from their possessions situated north of the Boundary line defined in the preceding Article: it being understood that this passage is to be by navigating the Gulf of California and the river Colorado, and not by land, without the express consent of the Mexican Government.

If, by the examinations which may be made, it should be ascertained to be practicable and advantageous to construct a road, canal, or railway, which should, in whole or in part, run upon the river Gila, or upon it's right or it's left bank, within the space of one marine league from either margin of the river, the Governments of both Republics will form an agreement regarding it's construction, in order that it may serve equally for the use and advantage of both countries.

ARTICLE VII

The river Gila, and the part of the Rio Bravo del Norte lying below the southern boundary of New Mexico, being, agreeably to the fifth Article, divided in the middle between the two Republics, the navigation of the Gila and of the Bravo below said boundary shall be free and common to the vessels and citizens of both countries; and neither shall, without the consent of the other, construct any work that may impede or interrupt, in whole or in part, the exercise of this right: not even for the purpose of favoring new methods of navigation. Nor shall any tax or contribution, under any denomination or title, be levied upon vessels or persons navigating the same, or upon merchandise or effects transported thereon, except in the case of landing upon one of their shores. If, for the purpose of making the said rivers navigable, or for maintaining them in such state, it should be necessary or advantageous to establish any tax or contribution, this shall not be done without the consent of both Governments.

The stipulations contained in the present Article shall not impair the territorial rights of either Republic, within it's established limits.

ARTICLE VIII

Mexicans now established in territories previously belonging to Mexico, and which remain for the future within the limits of the United States, as defined by the present Treaty, shall be free to continue where they now reside, or to remove at any time to the Mexican Republic, retaining the property which they possess in the said territories, or disposing thereof and removing the proceeds wherever they please; without their being subjected, on this account, to any contribution, tax or charge whatever.

Those who shall prefer to remain in the said territories, may either retain the title and rights of Mexican citizens, or acquire those of citizens of the United States. But, they shall be under the obligation to make their election within one year from the date of the exchange of ratifications of this treaty: and those who shall remain in the said territories, after the expiration of that year, without having declared their intention to retain the character of Mexicans, shall be considered to have elected to become citizens of the United States.

In the said territories, property of every kind, now belonging to Mexicans not established there, shall be inviolably respected. The present owners, the heirs of these, and all Mexicans who may hereafter acquire said property by contract, shall enjoy with respect to it, guaranties equally ample as if the same belonged to citizens of the United States.

ARTICLE IX[11]

The Mexicans who, in the territories aforesaid, shall not preserve the character of citizens of the Mexican Republic, conformably with what is stipulated in the preceding article, shall be incorporated into the Union of the United States and be admitted, at the proper time (to be judged of by the Congress of the United States) to the enjoyment of all the rights of citizens of the United States according to the principles of the Constitution; and in the mean time shall be maintained and protected in the free enjoyment of their liberty and property, and secured in the free exercise of their religion without restriction.

ARTICLE X[12]

ARTICLE XI[13]

Considering that a great part of the territories which, by the present treaty, are to be comprehended for the future within the limits of the United States, is now occupied by savage tribes, who will hereafter be under the exclusive control of the Government of the United States, and whose incursions within the territory of Mexico would be prejudicial in the extreme; it is solemnly agreed that all such incursions shall be forcibly restrained by the Government of the United States, whensoever this may be necessary; and that when they cannot be prevented, they shall be punished by the said Government, and satisfaction for the same shall be exacted: all in the same way, and with equal diligence and energy, as if the same incursions were meditated or committed within it's own territory against it's own citizens.

It shall not be lawful, under any pretext whatever, for any inhabitant of the United States, to purchase or acquire any Mexican or any foreigner residing in Mexico, who may have been captured by Indians inhabiting the territory of either of the two Republics; nor to purchase or acquire horses, mules, cattle or property of any kind, stolen within Mexican territory by such Indians.[14]

And, in the event of any person or persons, captured within Mexican territory by Indians, being carried into the territory of the United States, the Government of the latter engages and binds itself, in the most solemn manner, so soon as it shall know of such captives being within it's territory, and shall be able so to do, through the faithful exercise of it's influence and power, to rescue them, and return them to their country, or deliver them to the agent or representative of the Mexican Government. The Mexican Authorities will, as far as practicable, give to the Government of the United States notice of such captures; and it's agent shall pay the expenses incurred in the maintenance and transmission of the rescued captives; who, in the mean time, shall be treated with the utmost hospitality by the American Authorities at the place where they may be. But if the Government of the United States, before receiving such notice from Mexico, should obtain intelligence through any other channel, of the existence of Mexican captives within it's territory, it will proceed forthwith to effect their release and delivery to the Mexican agent, as above stipulated.

For the purpose of giving to these stipulations the fullest possible efficacy, thereby affording the security and redress demanded by their true spirit and intent, the Government of the United States will now and hereafter pass, without unnecessary delay, and always vigilantly enforce, such laws as the nature of the subject may require. And finally, the sacredness of this obligation shall never be lost sight of by the said Government, when providing for the removal of the Indians from any portion of the said territories, or for it's being settled by citizens of the United States; but on the contrary, special care shall then be taken not to place it's Indian occupants under the necessity of seeking new homes, by committing those invasions which the United States have solemnly obliged themselves to restrain.

ARTICLE XII

In consideration of the extension acquired by the boundaries of the United States, as defined in the fifth Article of the present treaty, the Government of the United States engages to pay to that of the Mexican Republic the sum of fifteen Millions of Dollars.[15]

Immediately after this Treaty shall have been duly ratified by the Government of the Mexican Republic, the sum of three Millions of Dollars shall be paid to the said Government by that of the United States at the city of Mexico, in the gold or silver coin of Mexico. The remaining twelve Millions of Dollars shall be paid at the same place, and in the same coin, in annual instalments of three Millions of Dollars each, together with interest on the same at the rate of six per centum per annum. This interest shall begin to run upon the whole sum of twelve millions, from the day of the ratification of the present treaty by the Mexican Government, and the first of the instalments shall be paid at the expiration of one year from the same day. Together with each annual instalment, as it falls due, the whole interest accruing on such instalment from the beginning shall also be paid.[16]

ARTICLE XIII

The United States engage moreover, to assume and pay to the claimants all the amounts now due them, and those hereafter to become due, by reason of the claims already liquidated and decided against the Mexican Republic, under the conventions between the two Republics, severally concluded on the eleventh day of April eighteen hundred and thirty-nine,[17] and on the thirtieth day of January eighteen hundred and forty three:[18] so that the Mexican Republic shall be absolutely exempt for the future, from all expense whatever on account of the said claims.

ARTICLE XIV

The United States do furthermore discharge the Mexican Republic from all claims of citizens of the United States, not heretofore decided against the Mexican Government, which may have arisen previously to the date of the signature of this treaty: which discharge shall be final and perpetual, whether the said claims be rejected or be allowed by the Board of Commissioners provided for in the following Article, and whatever shall be the total amount of those allowed.

ARTICLE XV

The United States, exonerating Mexico from all demands on account of the claims of their citizens mentioned in the preceding Article, and considering them entirely and forever cancelled, whatever their amount may be, undertake to make satisfaction for the same, to an amount not exceeding three and one quarter millions of dollars. To ascertain the validity and amount of those claims, a Board of Commissioners shall be established by the Government of the United States, whose awards shall be final and conclusive: provided that in deciding upon the validity of each claim, the board shall be guided and governed by the principles and rules of decision described by the first and fifth Articles of the unratified convention, concluded at the city of Mexico on the twentieth day of November one thousand eight hundred and forty-three; and in no case shall an award be made in favor of any claim not embraced by these principles and rules.

If, in the opinion of the said Board of Commissioners, or of the claimants, any books, records or documents in the possession or power of the Government of the Mexican Republic, shall be deemed necessary to the just decision of any claim, the Commissioners or the claimants, through them, shall, within such period as Congress may designate, make an application in writing for the same, addressed to the Mexican Minister for Foreign Affairs, to be transmitted by the Secretary of State of the United States; and the Mexican Government engages, at the earliest possible moment after the receipt of such demand, to cause any of the books, records or documents, so specified, which shall be in their possession or power, (or authenticated copies or extracts of the same) to be transmitted to the said Secretary of State, who shall immediately deliver them over to the said Board of Commissioners: *Provided* That no such application shall be made, by, or at the instance of, any claimant, until the facts which it is expected to prove by such books, records or documents, shall have been stated under oath or affirmation.

Article XVI

Each of the contracting parties reserves to itself the entire right to fortify whatever point within it's territory, it may judge proper so to fortify, for it's security.

Article XVII

The Treaty of Amity, Commerce and Navigation, concluded at the city of Mexico on the fifth day of April A.D. 1831,[19] between the United States of America and the United Mexican States, except the additional Article, and except so far as the stipulations of the said treaty may be incompatible with any stipulation contained in the present treaty, is hereby revived for the period of eight years from the day of the exchange of ratifications of this treaty, with the same force and virtue as if incorporated therein; it being understood that each of the contracting parties reserves to itself the right, at any time after the said period of eight years shall have expired, to terminate the same by giving one year's notice of such intention to the other party.

Article XVIII

All supplies whatever for troops of the United States in Mexico, arriving at ports in the occupation of such troops, previous to the final evacuation thereof, although subsequently to the restoration of the Custom

Houses at such ports, shall be entirely exempt from duties and charges of any kind: the Government of the United States hereby engaging and pledging it's faith to establish and vigilantly to enforce, all possible guards for securing the revenue of Mexico, by preventing the importation, under cover of this stipulation, of any articles, other than such, both in kind and in quantity, as shall really be wanted for the use and consumption of the forces of the United States during the time they may remain in Mexico. To this end, it shall be the duty of all officers and agents of the United States to denounce to the Mexican Authorities at the respective ports, any attempts at a fraudulent abuse of this stipulation, which they may know of or may have reason to suspect, and to give to such authorities all the aid in their power with regard thereto: and every such attempt, when duly proved and established by sentence of a competent tribunal, shall be punished by the confiscation of the property so attempted to be fraudulently introduced.

ARTICLE XIX

With respect to all merchandise, effects and property whatsoever, imported into ports of Mexico, whilst in the occupation of the forces of the United States, whether by citizens of either republic, or by citizens or subjects of any neutral nation, the following rules shall be observed:

I. All such merchandise, effects and property, if imported previously to the restoration of the Custom Houses to the Mexican Authorities, as stipulated for in the third Article of this treaty, shall be exempt from confiscation, although the importation of the same be prohibited by the Mexican tariff.

II. The same perfect exemption shall be enjoyed by all such merchandise, effects and property, imported subsequently to the restoration of the Custom Houses, and previously to the sixty days fixed in the following Article for the coming into force of the Mexican tariff at such ports respectively: the said merchandise, effects and property being, however, at the time of their importation, subject to the payment of duties as provided for in the said following Article.

III. All merchandise, effects and property, described in the two rules foregoing, shall, during their continuance at the place of importation, and upon their leaving such place for the interior, be exempt from all duty, tax or impost of every kind, under whatsoever title or denomination. Nor shall they be there subjected to any charge whatsoever upon the sale thereof.

IV. All merchandise, effects and property, described in the first and second rules, which shall have been removed to any place in the interior, whilst such place was in the occupation of the forces of the United States, shall, during their continuance therein, be exempt from all tax upon the sale or consumption thereof, and from every kind of impost or contribution, under whatsoever title or denomination.

V. But if any merchandise, effects or property, described in the first and second rules, shall be removed to any place not occupied at the time by the forces of the United States, they shall, upon their introduction into such place, or upon their sale or consumption there, be subject to the same duties which, under the Mexican laws, they would be required to pay in such cases, if they had been imported in time of peace through the Maritime Custom Houses, and had there paid the duties, conformably with the Mexican tariff.

VI. The owners of all merchandise, effects or property, described in the first and second rules, and existing in any port of Mexico, shall have the right to reship the same, exempt from all tax, impost or contribution whatever.

With the respect to the metals, or other property, exported from any Mexican port, whilst in the occupation of the forces of the United States, and previously to the restoration of the Custom House at such port, no person shall be required by the Mexican Authorities, whether General or State, to pay any tax, duty or contribution upon any such exportation, or in any manner to account for the same to the said Authorities.

Article XX

Through consideration for the interests of commerce generally, it is agreed, that if less than sixty days should elapse between the date of the signature of this treaty and the restoration of the Custom Houses, conformably with the stipulation in the third Article, in such case, all merchandise, effects and property whatsoever, arriving at the Mexican ports after the restoration of the said Custom Houses, and previously to the expiration of sixty days after the day of the signature of this treaty, shall be admitted to entry; and no other duties shall be levied thereon than the duties established by the tariff found in force at such Custom Houses at the time of the restoration of the same. And to all such merchandise, effects and property, the rules established by the preceding Article shall apply.

Article XXI

If unhappily any disagreement should hereafter arise between the Governments of the two Republics, whether with respect to the interpretation of any stipulation in this treaty, or with respect to any other particular concerning the political or commercial relations of the two Nations, the said Governments, in the name of those Nations, do promise to each other, that they will endeavour, in the most sincere and earnest manner, to settle the differences so arising, and to preserve the state of peace and friendship, in which the two countries are now placing themselves: using, for this end, mutual representations and pacific negotiations. And if, by these means, they should not be enabled to come to an agreement, a resort shall not, on this account, be had to reprisals, aggression or hostility of any kind, by the one Republic against the other, until the Government of that which deems itself aggrieved, shall have maturely considered, in the spirit of peace and good neighbourship, whether it would not be better that such difference should be settled by the arbitration of Commissioners appointed on each side, or by that of a friendly nation. And should such course be proposed by either party, it shall be acceded to by the other, unless deemed by it altogether incompatible with the nature of the difference, or the circumstances of the case.

ARTICLE XXII

If (which is not to be expected, and which God forbid!) war should unhappily break out between the two Republics, they do now, with a view to such calamity, solemnly pledge themselves to each other and to the world, to observe the following rules: absolutely, where the nature of the subject permits, and as closely as possible in all cases where such absolute observance shall be impossible.

I. The merchants of either Republic, then residing in the other, shall be allowed to remain twelve months (for those dwelling in the interior) and six months (for those dwelling at the sea-ports) to collect their debts and settle their affairs; during which periods they shall enjoy the same protection, and be on the same footing, in all respects, as the citizens or subjects of the most friendly nations; and, at the expiration thereof, or at any time before, they shall have full liberty to depart, carrying off all their effects, without molestation or hinderance: conforming therein to the same laws, which the citizens or subjects of the most friendly nations are required to conform to. Upon the entrance of the armies of either nation into the territories of the other, women and children, ecclesiastics, scholars of every faculty, cultivators of the earth, merchants, artisans, manufacturers, and fishermen, unarmed and inhabiting unfortified towns, villages or places, and in general all persons whose occupations are for the common subsistence and benefit of mankind, shall be allowed to continue their respective employments, unmolested in their persons. Nor shall their houses or goods be burnt, or otherwise destroyed; nor their cattle taken, nor their fields wasted, by the armed force, into whose power, by the events of war, they may happen to fall; but if the necessity arise to take anything from them for the use of such armed force, the same shall be paid for at an equitable price. All churches, hospitals, schools, colleges, libraries, and other establishments for charitable and beneficent purposes, shall be respected, and all persons connected with the same protected in the discharge of their duties and the pursuit of their vocations.

II. In order that the fate of prisoners of war may be alleviated, all such practices as those of sending them into distant, inclement or unwholesome districts, or crowding them into close and noxious places, shall be studiously avoided. They shall not be confined in dungeons, prison-ships, or prisons; nor be put in irons, or bound, or otherwise restrained in the use of their limbs. The officers shall enjoy liberty on their paroles, within convenient districts, and have comfortable quarters; and the common soldier shall be disposed in cantonments, open and extensive enough for air and exercise, and lodged in barracks as roomy and good as are provided by the party in whose power they are for it's own troops. But, if any officer shall break his parole by leaving the district so assigned him, or any other prisoner shall escape from the limits of his cantonment, after they shall have been designated to him, such individual, officer or other prisoner, shall forfeit so much of the benefit of this article as provides for his liberty on parole or in cantonment. And if any officer so breaking his parole, or any common soldier so escaping from the limits assigned him, shall afterwards be found in arms, previously to his being regularly exchanged, the person so offending shall be dealt with according to the established laws of war. The officers shall be daily furnished by the party in whose power they are, with as many rations, and of the same articles as are allowed either in kind or by commutation, to officers of equal rank in it's own army; and all others shall be daily furnished with such ration as is allowed to a common soldier in it's own service: the value of all which supplies shall, at the close of the war, or at periods to be agreed upon between the respective commanders, be paid by the other party on a mutual adjustment of accounts for the subsistence of prisoners; and such accounts shall not be mingled with or set off against any others, nor the balance due on them be withheld, as a compensation or reprisal for any cause whatever, real or pretended. Each party shall be allowed to keep a commissary of prisoners, appointed by itself, with every cantonment of prisoners, in possession of the other: which commissary shall see the prisoners as often as he pleases; shall be allowed to receive, exempt from all duties or taxes, and to distribute whatever comforts may be sent to them by their friends; and shall be free to transmit his reports in open letters to the party by whom he is employed.

And it is declared that neither the pretence that war dissolves all treaties, nor any other whatever shall be considered as annulling or suspending the solemn covenant contained in this article. On the contrary, the state of war is precisely that for which it is provided; and during which it's stipulations are to be as sacredly observed as the most acknowledged obligations under the law of nature or nations.

ARTICLE XXIII

This treaty shall be ratified by the President of the United States of America, by and with the advice and consent of the Senate thereof; and by the President of the Mexican Republic, with the previous approbation of it's General Congress: and the ratifications shall be exchanged in the City of Washington, or at the seat of government of Mexico,[20] in four months from the date of the signature hereof, or sooner if practicable.

In faith whereof, we, the respective Plenipotentiaries, have signed this Treaty of Peace, Friendship, Limits and Settlement, and have hereunto affixed our seals respectively. Done in Quintuplicate, at the City of Guadalupe Hidalgo, on the second day of February in the year of Our Lord one thousand eight hundred and forty eight.

N. P. TRIST	[SEAL]
LUIS G. CUEVAS	[SEAL]
BERNARDO COUTO	[SEAL]
MIG. ATRISTAIN	[SEAL]

Notes

1. For United States amendments to arts. III, IX–XII, and XXIII, see footnotes to those articles. An additional and secret article was stricken out pursuant to the Senate resolution. It reads as follows:

ADDITIONAL AND SECRET ARTICLE

Of the Treaty of Peace, Friendship, Limits and Settlement between the United States of America and the Mexican Republic, signed this day by their respective Plenipotentiaries.

In view of the possibility that the exchange of the ratifications of this treaty may, by the circumstances in which the Mexican Republic is placed, be delayed longer than the term of four months fixed by it's twenty-third Article for the exchange of ratifications of the same; it is hereby agreed that such delay shall not, in any manner, affect the force and validity of this Treaty, unless it should exceed the term of eight months, counted from the date of the signature thereof.

This Article is to have the same force and virtue as if inserted in the treaty to which it is an Addition.

In faith whereof, we, the respective Plenipotentiaries have signed this Additional and Secret Article, and have hereunto affixed our seals respectively. Done in Quintuplicate at the City of Guadalupe Hidalgo on the second day of February, in the year of Our Lord one thousand eight hundred and forty-eight.

N. P. Trist [seal]
Luis G. Cuevas [seal]
Bernardo Couto [seal]
Mig. Atristain [seal]

The text printed here is the amended text as proclaimed by the President.

2. TS 208, *post*, p. 812.

3. TS 500, *post*, p. 927.

4. For a detailed study of this treaty, see 5 Miller 207.

5. For text of military convention signed Feb. 29, 1848, see *post*, p. 807.

6. The phrase "and the ratifications exchanged" was added by the United States amendments.

7. For an amendment to art. V, see treaty of Dec. 30, 1853 (TS 208), *post*, p. 812.

8. For a reproduction of the Disturnell map, see 5 Miller (inside back cover).

9. For a reproduction of the plan of the Port of San Diego, see 5 Miller (opposite p. 236).

10. For amendments to arts. VI and VII, see treaty of Dec. 30, 1853 (TS 208), *post*, p. 814.

11. The United States amendment of art. IX substituted a new text. The text of art. IX as signed reads as follows:

The Mexicans who, in the territories aforesaid, shall not preserve the character of citizens of the Mexican Republic, conformably with what is stipulated in the preceding Article, shall be incorporated into the Union of the United States, and admitted as soon as possible, according to the principles of the Federal Constitution, to the enjoyment of all the rights of citizens of the United States. In the mean time, they shall be maintained and protected in the enjoyment of their liberty, their property, and the civil rights now vested in them according to the Mexican laws. With respect to political rights, their condition shall be on an equality with that of the inhabitants of Louisiana and the Floridas, when these provinces, by transfer from the French Republic and the Crown of Spain, became territories of the United States.

The same most ample guaranty shall be enjoyed by all ecclesiastics and religious corporations or communities, as well in the discharge of the offices of their ministry, as in the enjoyment of their property of every kind, whether individual or corporate. This guaranty shall embrace all temples, houses and edifices dedicated to the Roman Catholic worship; as well as property destined to it's support, or to that of schools, hospitals and other foundations for charitable or beneficent purposes. No property of this nature shall be considered as having become the property of the American Government, or as subject to be, by it, disposed of or diverted to other uses.

Finally, the relations and communications between the Catholics living in the territories aforesaid, and their respective ecclesiastical authorities, shall be open, free and exempt from all hindrance whatever, even although such authorities should reside within the limits of the Mexican Republic, as defined by this treaty;

and this freedom shall continue, so long as a new demarcation of ecclesiastical districts shall not have been made, conformably with the laws of the Roman Catholic Church.

12. Art. X, stricken out by the United States amendments, reads as follows:

All grants of land made by the Mexican Government or by the competent authorities, in territories previously appertaining to Mexico, and remaining for the future within the limits of the United States, shall be respected as valid, to the same extent that the same grants would be valid, if the said territories had remained within the limits of Mexico. But the grantees of lands in Texas, put in possession thereof, who, by reason of the circumstances of the country since the beginning of the troubles between Texas and the Mexican Government, may have been prevented from fulfilling all the conditions of their grants, shall be under the obligation to fulfill the said conditions within the periods limited in the same respectively; such periods to be now counted from the date of the exchange of ratifications of this treaty: in default of which the said grants shall not be obligatory upon the State of Texas, in virtue of the stipulations contained in this Article.

The foregoing stipulation in regard to grantees of land in Texas, is extended to all grantees of land in the territories aforesaid, elsewhere than in Texas, put in possession under such grants; and, in default of the fulfilment of the conditions of any such grant, within the new period, which, as is above stipulated, begins with the day of the exchange of ratifications of this treaty, the same shall be null and void.

The Mexican Government declares that no grant whatever of lands in Texas has been made since the second day of March one thousand eight hundred and thirty six; and that no grant whatever of lands in any of the territories aforesaid has been made since the thirteenth day of May one thousand eight hundred and forty-six.

13. Abrogated by treaty of Dec. 30, 1853 (TS 208), *post*, p. 814.

14. The United States amendments called for deletion, at the end of this paragraph, of the phrase "nor to provide such Indians with fire-arms or ammunition by sale or otherwise."

15. The following words were deleted at this place in accordance with the United States amendments:

. . . , in the one or the other of the two modes below specified. The Mexican Government shall, at the time of ratifying this treaty, declare which of these two modes of payment it prefers; and the mode so elected by it shall be conformed to by that of the United States.

First mode of payment: Immediately after this treaty shall have been duly ratified by the Government of the Mexican Republic, the sum of three Millions of Dollars shall be paid to the said Government by that of the United States at the city of Mexico, in the gold or silver coin of Mexico. For the remaining twelve millions of dollars, the United States shall create a stock, bearing an interest of six per centum per annum, commencing on the day of the ratification of this Treaty by the Government of the Mexican Republic, and payable annually at the city of Washington: the principal of said stock to be redeemable there, at the pleasure of the Government of the United States, at any time after two years from the exchange of ratifications of this treaty; six months public notice of the intention to redeem the same being previously given. Certificates of such stock, in proper form, for such sums as shall be specified by the Mexican Government, and transferable by the said Government, shall be delivered to the same by that of the United States.

16. The following concluding sentence was deleted from this paragraph in accordance with the United States amendments: "Certificates in proper form, for the said instalments respectively, in such sums as shall be desired by the Mexican Government, and transferable by it, shall be delivered to the said Government by that of the United States."

17. TS 205, *ante*, p. 783.

18. TS 206, *ante*, p. 788.

19. TS 203, *ante*, p. 764.

20. The phrase "or at the seat of government of Mexico" was added by the United States amendments.

6 Gadsden Treaty

Signed in 1853 and ratified in 1854, the Gadsden Treaty (see Selection 2) altered the existing U.S.-Mexican boundary by transferring additional lands from Mexico to the United States in exchange for $10 million. The ceded 29,640 square miles, which had formed parts of the Mexican states of Chihuahua and Sonora, were incorporated into the New Mexico Territory, including Arizona. The area included prime agricultural and ranching lands, rich silver and copper mines, and convenient flat terrain for the construction of a U.S. railroad line to the Pacific.

Agreement over several important issues that had caused controversy after 1848 are reflected in the treaty. First, the two nations solved a thorny dispute that had arisen over the exact location of the dividing line from the El Paso area to the Gila River (Article 1st). Second, the United States used its considerably stronger bargaining power to free itself from the obligation incurred in 1848 to restrain Indians residing on the U.S. side from launching raids into Mexico (Article 2nd). Third, the United States acquired remarkable transit rights in the Isthmus of Tehuantepec, the narrowest mass of land between the Gulf of Mexico and the Pacific Ocean (Article 8th); a treaty signed in 1937 terminated this imperialist clause.

T*reaty signed at México December 30, 1853*
Senate advice and consent to ratification, with amendments,
    April 25, 1854[1]
Ratified by Mexico May 31, 1854
Ratified by the President of the United States, with amendments,
    June 29, 1854[1]
Ratifications exchanged at Washington June 30, 1854
Entered into force June 30, 1854
Proclaimed by the President of the United States June 30, 1854
Article 8 terminated December 21, 1937, by treaty of April 13,
    1937[2]

10 Stat. 1031; Treaty Series 208

In the Name of Almighty God:

The Republic of Mexico and the United States of America desiring to remove every cause of disagreement, which might interfere in any man-

From Charles I. Bevans, ed. *Treaties and Other International Agreements of the United States of America, 1776–1949,* 13 vols. (Washington, DC: U.S. Department of State, 1972), 9:812–16.

ner with the better friendship and intercourse between the two Countries; and especially, in respect to the true limits which should be established, when notwithstanding what was covenanted in the Treaty of Guadalupe Hidalgo in the Year 1848,[3] opposite interpretations have been urged, which might give occasion to questions of serious moment: to avoid these, and to strengthen and more firmly maintain the peace, which happily prevails between the two Republics, the President of the United States has for this purpose, appointed James Gadsden Envoy Extraordinary and Minister Plenipotentiary of the same near the Mexican Government, and the President of Mexico has appointed as Plenipotentiary "ad hoc" His Excellency Don Manuel Diez de Bonilla Cavalier Grand Cross of the National and Distinguished Order of Guadalupe, and Secretary of State and of the Office of Foreign Relations, and Don José Salazar Ylarregui and General Mariano Monterde as Scientific Commissioners invested with Full powers for this Negotiation who having communicated their respective Full Powers, and finding them in due and proper form, have agreed upon the Articles following.

Article 1st

The Mexican Republic agrees to designate the following as her true limits with the United States for the future; Retaining the same dividing line between the two California's, as already defined and established according to the 5th Article of the Treaty of Guadalupe Hidalgo, the limits between the Two Republics shall be as follows: Beginning in the Gulf of Mexico, three leagues from land, opposite the mouth of the Rio Grande as provided in the fifth article of the treaty of Guadalupe Hidalgo, thence as defined in the said article, up the middle of that river to the point where the parallel of 31°47' north latitude crosses the same, thence due west one hundred miles, thence south to the parallel of 31°20' north latitude, thence along the said parallel of 31°20' to the 111th meridian of longitude west of Greenwich, thence in a straight line to a point on the Colorado river twenty english miles below the junction of the Gila and Colorado rivers, thence up the middle of the said river Colorado until it intersects the present line between the United States and Mexico.

For the performance of this portion of the Treaty each of the two Governments shall nominate one Commissioner to the end that, by common consent, the two thus nominated having met in the City of Paso del Norte, three months after the exchange of the ratifications of this Treaty may proceed to survey and mark out upon the land the dividing line stipulated by this article, where it shall not have already been surveyed and established by the Mixed Commission according to the Treaty of Guadalupe keeping a Journal and making proper plans of their operations. For this purpose if they should Judge it is necessary, the contracting Parties shall be at liberty each to unite to its respective Commissioner Scientific or other assistants, such as Astronomers and Surveyors whose concurrence shall not be considered necessary for the settlement and ratification of a true line of division between the two Republics; that line shall be alone established upon which the Commissioners may fix, their consent in this particular being considered decisive and an integral part of this Treaty, without necessity of ulterior ratification or approval, and without room for interpretation of any kind by either of the Parties contracting.

The dividing line thus established shall in all time be faithfully respected by the two Governments without any variation therein, unless of the express and free consent of the two, given in conformity to the principles of the Law of Nations, and in accordance with the Constitution of each country respectively.

In consequence, the stipulation in the 5th Article of the Treaty of Guadalupe upon the Boundary line therein described is no longer of any force, wherein it may conflict with that here established, the said line being considered annulled and abolished wherever it may not coincide with the present, and in the same manner remaining in full force where in accordance with the same.

ARTICLE 2ND

The government of Mexico hereby releases the United States from all liability on account of the obligations contained in the eleventh article of the treaty of Guadalupe Hidalgo, and the said article and the thirty third article of the treaty of amity, commerce and navigation between the United States of America and the United Mexican States concluded at Mexico, on the fifth day of April, 1831,[4] are hereby abrogated.

ARTICLE 3RD

In consideration of the foregoing stipulations, the government of the United State agrees to pay to the government of Mexico, in the city of New York, the sum of ten millions of dollars, of which seven millions shall be paid immediately upon the exchange of the ratifications of this treaty, and the remaining three millions as soon as the boundary line shall be surveyed, marked, and established.

ARTICLE 4TH

The Provisions of the 6th and 7th Articles of the Treaty of Guadalupe Hidalgo having been rendered nugatory for the most part by the Cession of Territory granted in the First Article of this Treaty, the said Articles are hereby abrogated and annulled and the provisions as herein expressed substituted therefor—The Vessels and Citizens of the United States shall in all Time have free and uninterrupted passage through the Gulf of California to and from their possessions situated North of the Boundary line of the Two Countries. It being understood that this passage is to be by navigating the Gulf of California and the river Colorado, and not by land, without the express consent of the Mexican Government, and precisely the same provisions, stipulations and restrictions in all respects are hereby agreed upon and adopted and shall be scrupulously observed and enforced by the Two Contracting Governments in reference to the Rio Colorado, so far and for such distance as the middle of that River is made their common Boundary Line, by the First Article of this Treaty.

The several Provisions, Stipulations and restrictions contained in the 7th Article of the Treaty of Guadalupe Hidalgo, shall remain in force only so far as regards the Rio Bravo del Norte below the initial of the said Boundary provided in the First Article of this Treaty That is to say below the intersection of the 31°47'30" parallel of Latitude with the Boundary Line established by the late Treaty dividing said river from its mouth upwards according to the 5th Article of the Treaty of Guadalupe.

Article 5th

All the provisions of the Eighth and Ninth, Sixteenth and Seventeenth Articles of the Treaty of Guadalupe Hidalgo shall apply to the Territory ceded by the Mexican Republic in the First Article of the present Treaty and to all the rights of the persons and property both civil and ecclesiastical within the same, as fully and as effectually as if the said Articles were herein again recited and set forth.

Article 6th

No Grants of Land within the Territory ceded by the First Article of This Treaty bearing date subsequent to the day Twenty fifth of September—when the Minister and Subscriber to this Treaty on the part of the United States proposed to the Government of Mexico to terminate the question of Boundary, will be considered valid or be recognized by the United States, or will any Grants made previously be respected or be considered as obligatory which have not been located and duly recorded in the Archives of Mexico.

Article 7th

Should there at any future period (which God forbid) occur any disagreement between the two Nations which might lead to a rupture of their relations and reciprocal peace, they bind themselves in like manner to procure by every possible method the adjustment of every difference, and should they still in this manner not succeed, never will they proceed to a declaration of War, without having previously paid attention to what has been set forth in Article 21 of the Treaty of Guadalupe for similar cases; which Article as well as the 22nd is here re-affirmed.

ARTICLE 8TH[5]

The Mexican government having on the 5th of February 1853 authorized the early construction of a plank and railroad across the Isthmus of Tehuantepec, and to secure the stable benefits of said transit way to the persons and merchandise of the citizens of Mexico and the United States, it is stipulated that neither government will interpose any obstacle to the transit of persons and merchandise of both nations; and at no time shall higher charges be made on the transit of persons and property of citizens of the United States than may be made on the persons and property of other foreign nations, nor shall any interest in said transit way, nor in the proceeds thereof, be transferred to any foreign government.

The United States by its Agents shall have the right to transport across the Isthmus, in closed bags, the mails of the United States not intended for distribution along the line of communication; also the effects of the United States government and its citizens, which may be intended for transit, and not for distribution on the Isthmus, free of custom-house or other charges by the Mexican government. Neither passports nor letters of security will be required of persons crossing the Isthmus and not remaining in the country.

When the construction of the railroad shall be completed, the Mexican government agrees to open a port of entry in addition to the port of Vera Cruz, at or near the terminus of said road on the Gulf of Mexico.

The two governments will enter into arrangements for the prompt transit of troops and munitions of the United States, which that government may have occasion to send from one part of its territory to another, lying on opposite sides of the continent.

The Mexican government having agreed to protect with its whole power the prosecution, preservation and security of the work, the United States may extend its protection as it shall judge wise to it when it may feel sanctioned and warranted by the public or international law.

ARTICLE 9TH

This Treaty shall be ratified, and the respective ratifications shall be exchanged at the City of Washington, within the exact period of six months from the date of its signature or sooner if possible.

In the testimony whereof, We the Plenipotentiaries of the contracting parties have hereunto affixed our hands and seals at Mexico the—Thirtieth (30th)—day of December in the Year of Our Lord one thousand eight hundred and fifty three, in the thirty third year of the Independence of the Mexican Republic, and the seventy eighth of that of the United States.

JAMES GADSDEN   [SEAL]
MANUEL DIEZ DE BONILLA   [SEAL]
JOSÉ SALAZAR YLARREGUI   [SEAL]
J. MARIANO MONTERDE   [SEAL]

Notes

1. As a result of the United States amendments, the terms of the treaty were radically altered: arts. 1 and 2 were rewritten; arts. 3 and 4 were rewritten and combined as art. 3; art. 8 was deleted; and there were several minor corrections of the text. For a detailed study of this treaty, and texts of the articles as signed, see 6 Miller 293.

The text printed here is the amended text as proclaimed by the President.

2. TS 932, *post*, p. 1023.

3. Treaty signed Feb. 2, 1848 (TS 207, *ante*, p. 791).

4. TS 203, *ante*, p. 764.

5. Art. 8 terminated by treaty of Apr. 13, 1937 (TS 932, *post*, p. 1023).

II Border Strife

The delimitation of the U.S.-Mexican border in the 1840s and 1850s concluded major territorial conflicts between the United States and Mexico, but other forms of border friction remained constant for much of the latter part of the nineteenth century. Indian raiding loomed large in the bilateral agenda into the 1880s, when the two neighbors initiated a series of accords that permitted "hot pursuit" of raiders into each other's territory. Filibustering, or unlawful invasions by adventurers and privateers, flourished in the 1850s, with Mexico the customary victim. Banditry, especially cattle rustling, triggered many confrontations. Ethnic discord along the Texas-Mexican frontier also spawned numerous incidents, with Chicanos bearing the brunt of the violence. In short, the border continued to take center stage in the tense relationship between the two neighbors. By the 1870s a new U.S.-Mexican war seemed inevitable, but diplomacy averted such a catastrophe.

The essays included in this section address three border controversies that followed the signing of the Treaty of Guadalupe Hidalgo: filibustering and ethnic tensions (Selection 7) and the difficulties encountered by the Apaches, Mexicans, and Anglo-Americans in Sonora-Arizona in their attempts to coexist in the border region (Selection 8). Selections 9 and 10 are documents that present the radically contrasting official Mexican and U.S. interpretations of instability along the border. Selection 11 is a proclamation issued by one of the most controversial figures of the 1850s and 1860s, Juan Nepomucena Cortina. Selection 12, the final item in this section, is an official U.S. report on the so-called Salt War in San Elizario, Texas.

7 Oscar J. Martínez ◆
Filibustering and Racism in the Borderlands

After the U.S.-Mexican War, power-hungry Anglo-Americans, Frenchmen, and others cast their eyes on the resource-rich and thinly populated northern tier of Mexican states. Numerous cross-border invasions ensued. North of the boundary, racial polarization marred the relationship between Mexicans and Anglo-Americans. These problems exacerbated an already dangerous climate in the borderlands.

Filibustering

In the literature and popular lore that circulated outside of Mexico during the late 1840s and early 1850s, northern Mexico was portrayed in colorful, exotic, and economically attractive terms. Many foreigners were led to believe that great opportunities to get rich existed just beyond the new border; they also thought that local Mexicans would be won over easily to the idea of alignment with outsiders because the Mexicans would thereby be "liberated" from domestic political tyrants and protected from the disorder that prevailed on the frontier. Although foreigners exaggerated the state of affairs in the border region, there is considerable truth to the perception that *norteños* lived in a precarious environment. Banditry, smuggling, and Indian depredations had kept the residents of Tamaulipas, Nuevo León, Coahuila, Chihuahua, and Sonora in turmoil for many years.

The Mexican government found it exceedingly difficult to provide the northern frontier with added protection because it was hampered by incessant internal strife and lack of revenues. Nevertheless, between 1848 and 1852 national leaders offered various proposals for the establishment of military-civilian colonies throughout northern Mexico. But despite official endorsement of several schemes, the effort did not get very far. Only a few colonies were established, and within a short period most of these disintegrated. Their failure is explained by poor planning, lack of resources, delays, and understandable hesitation on the part of colonists to move to the boundary area. With its defenses weakened and its population thinned by outmigration, northern Mexico became an attractive target for adventurers who thought little of violating any nation's territorial integrity.

There were many plots to invade portions of northern Mexico, with a number of these materializing into serious incursions. The following is a summary of major expeditions during the 1850s, the "Golden Age" of filibustering:[1]

1849–1855 Mexican rebel José María Carvajal led an on-again, off-again movement to establish a "Republic of Sierra Madre" in northeastern Mexico and South Texas. U.S. business interests and American volunteers were heavily involved in attacks on Mexican border towns. Opposition to Mexico's tariff laws constituted a primary motive for the insurrection.

1851–1852 Charles de Pindray led over 150 Frenchmen in a colonization effort in Sonora, which initially had the permission of Mexican officials. Suspicious of Pindray's motives, however, the government subsequently withheld support, which led to the disintegration of the colony.

1852–1854 Intending to carry out a French mining and colonization scheme in Sonora, Gaston Raousset de Boulbon arrived by sea with 150 followers, taking over Hermosillo, where his plan to "liberate" Sonora failed. He was tried and shot in 1854 following his last unsuccessful attempt to conquer Guaymas.

1853–1854 "King" of the filibusters William Walker and his followers invaded Baja California and Sonora, proclaiming them "Republics." Walker's invasion, which lasted eight months, was repelled by Mexican soldiers and volunteers. Walker and others were arrested and tried by U.S. authorities, but sympathetic juries acquitted them.

1857 Encouraged by expressions of support from a rebel faction in conflict-ridden Sonora, Henry A. Crabb led his "Arizona Colonizing Company" into that Mexican state, only to encounter strong opposition when the rival groups came to terms. Crabb's band was virtually exterminated.

American officials took measures to prevent filibustering, but these proved insufficient and ineffective, allowing the activity to flourish. Mexicans believed that Washington's indifference was rooted in tacit approval of the incursions, given the prospect that any territory taken from Mexico might eventually be annexed to the United States. Historian J. Fred Rippy concludes, however, that American officials made sincere efforts to deal with the problem but that they faced certain constraints in enforcing the law. First, the language in the U.S. neutrality statute was imprecise; second, the law provided for apprehending suspects after commission of the crime, not before, thus making it difficult to arrest individuals only thought to be planning incursions; and third, the filibusters had the sympathy and support of the public. Federal prosecutors found convictions difficult to come by in those areas where juries sided with the filibusters.[2]

In retrospect, filibustering failed for a variety of reasons, but firm opposition to the foreign invaders on the part of the Mexican people explains the collapse of most of the invasions. Although separatist tendencies existed for generations along Mexico's northern frontier, the intervention of foreigners in such movements was hardly seen in a positive light by the local population, especially after the experience in Texas in the 1830s and the massive loss of territory in 1848. Filibustering and pseudofilibustering added considerably to the legacy of distrust between Mexicans and Americans. Suspicions surfaced with regularity in Mexico City that Washington encouraged private attempts to detach more Mexican lands. As long as the dark cloud of possible foreign conquest of Mexico hovered in the background, it was difficult to sustain amiable and productive international relations.

Discrimination against Mexicans

Racial discrimination in the U.S. borderlands constituted one of the most vexing problems throughout the latter part of the nineteenth century.[3] Anglo-American intolerance toward Mexicans, which surfaced acutely during the Texas rebellion and the War of 1846–1848, intensified when waves of migrants from the southern United States settled in Texas, New Mexico, Arizona, and California following the signing of the Treaty of Guadalupe Hidalgo. Mexican Americans became a subordinated minority and were compelled to endure ethnic tensions that often disintegrated into violent encounters. At the personal level, Mexican Americans were subjected to continuous harassment, miscarriages of justice, land invasions, swindles, thefts, rapes, murders, and lynchings. Exposure to persecution and violence on an even larger scale transpired as well, as the following examples indicate:

> **Early 1850s** About two thousand native New Mexicans left their homes and crossed the border into Mexico when Anglos encroached upon their lands.
>
> **1857** Anglo cartmen attacked Mexican competitors in South Texas, killing seventy-five. This incident is known as "The Cart War."
>
> **1859–1860** Juan "Cheno" Cortina and sixty followers engaged Anglo lawmen in a series of skirmishes motivated by racial tensions. Over twenty people died in the raids (see Selection 11).

Early 1870s Cross-border Indian raiding and bandit depredations created an extremely unstable climate, leading to widespread
persecution of suspected offenders. Many innocent people died.

The mistreatment of Mexicans and Mexican Americans in the United
States was a continuing concern for the Mexican government, which reminded American authorities of their obligation under Articles VIII and
IX of the Treaty of Guadalupe Hidalgo to safeguard the rights of these
people. But the U.S. government, which cared little for the welfare of
minority groups, was in any case too distant from the problem. State and
local authorities, who were in a better position to intervene, were generally not sympathetic to the plight of people of Mexican descent, thus leaving these people vulnerable to exploiters and oppressors. Racism and
discrimination marred the legacy of the U.S. borderlands, continuing well
into the twentieth century.

Notes

1. J. Fred Rippy, *The United States and Mexico* (New York: Knopf, 1926);
Luis G. Zorrilla, *Historia de las relaciónes entre México y los Estados Unidos de
América, 1800–1958*, 2 vols. (México, D.F.: Editorial Porúa, 1977).

2. For example, twelve participants in the José María Carvajal incursions were
acquitted in Texas, and William Walker was declared innocent in California. Those
found guilty were seldom punished. Rippy, *United States and Mexico*, 96, 102,
171–72.

3. Discrimination against Mexicans and Mexican Americans in the nineteenth
century is well documented in Rodolfo Acuña, *Occupied America: A History of
Chicanos*, 3d ed. (New York: Harper and Row, 1988); and Carey McWilliams,
North from Mexico (New York: Greenwood Press, 1968).

8   Joseph F. Park ◆ The Apaches in
Mexican-American Relations, 1848–1861

Indian-white hostilities prevailed throughout the borderlands during the nineteenth century, but the problem was especially acute along the Sonora-Arizona frontier. The Apaches raided Mexican and Anglo-American settlements on both sides of the border in response to encroachment on their ancestral lands and to other resentments that the tribe held against outsiders. In this essay, Joseph F. Park discusses aspects of a troubled relationship among three ethnic groups and between two nations. He completed this study as a graduate student at the University of Arizona.

M uch of the enmity that existed between Arizona and Sonora in the decade following the Gadsden Purchase in 1853 arose from the failure of the United States to comply fully with Article XI of the Treaty of Guadalupe Hidalgo in 1848, which pledged prevention of Apache raiding across the border. . . .

After the Mexican War, Apache depredations increased. During 1849, Sonora suffered a series of terrible raids. In less than two weeks—January 10 to 23—eighty-six persons lost their lives at Santa Cruz, Bacoachi, Bavispe, and other frontier villages. After authorities tried unsuccessfully to negotiate a peace with the Apaches during the spring of 1850, a mass emigration of settlers from this region occurred. In January 1851, Ignacio Pesqueira, then a young captain in the national guard of Sonora, led a company of one hundred men to intercept a raiding party reported to be passing east of Arizpe with 1,300 head of cattle. At Pozo Hediondo, Pesqueira clashed with two hundred and fifty Pinals under Mangas Coloradas. At nightfall Pesqueira withdrew the remnants of his exhausted company, leaving twenty-six dead on the field. Infuriated by Chihuahua's responsibility for the defeat at Pozo Hediondo, Commander General José Mariá Carrasco issued a proclamation on February 10 warning Sonorans that anyone found dealing with the Apaches under any pretext would be judged a traitor and shot. On March 6, he invaded Chihuahua and near Janos killed twenty Apaches. His soldiers then collected the cattle and some sixty prisoners and distributed them among Sonoran haciendas and ranches. When Colonel Medina, presidio commander at Janos, reported this incident to the federal authorities, they approved of Carrasco's actions.

From *Arizona and the West* 3, no. 2 (Summer 1961): 129, 135–45, notes omitted. Reprinted by permission of Joseph Wilder.

The hostilities between Sonora and Chihuahua over the Apache inroads soon involved the Anglo-Americans who were settling in the Mexican Cession in increasing numbers. Their arrival in this region added nothing new to the contest, but broadened its scope. The Pinals and Chiricahuas had enjoyed refuge and an outlet for plunder in Chihuahua, but now found greater opportunities north of the new international line. This intensified the bitterness and suspicion Sonorans already felt toward Arizona.

Respecting the Apache problem, the United States introduced no new policy. Both settlers and government officials, ignoring Spanish precedents, stumbled along the same path of trial and error, precipitated the same series of mistakes, and arrived at basically the same method of Apache control. The United States early began negotiating formal treaties with Apache leaders—the most significant being that concluded by Colonel E. V. Sumner with Mangas Coloradas and other chiefs at Santa Fe, in 1852. Because previous treaties had not referred to Article XI of the Guadalupe Treaty, except to stipulate that the Indians should deliver up Mexican prisoners, it is doubtful that the government regarded these early pacts as anything more than official gestures toward compliance with that article. But treaty-making by the United States as an effective means of Apache control was doomed at the start, not only by a total ignorance of Apache life but also by bad faith in fulfilling promises of food and presents.

The principal defect in the Santa Fe treaty, and others of this type, was that it was structured along the "sovereign nations concept," which had been employed with some success in relations with eastern tribes. Governor Bustamante of Sonora earlier had rejected this method of dealing with the Apaches, believing that these tribes neither had formal political organization nor had chieftains who were empowered to negotiate treaties that would bind more than a handful of warriors. The informality of Apache government and the custom of raiding were shaped by environmental factors. Local groups often engaged in simple agriculture, but never developed the practice on a scale conducive to the formation of large, sedentary social units with complex forms of government. Instead, the Apaches relied principally on hunting and gathering, the band remaining the largest social unit; for foraging purposes, it was usually divided into small groups. Because the environment failed to support their needs, they raided Pima and Papago villages, as well as Mexican ranchos and pueblos. Thus, economic factors—particularly a shortage of food—frequently rendered inoperative those treaties designed to prevent raiding. On investigating an unexplained raid in 1850 on Doña Ana, New Mexico, Captain A. W. Bowman reported that the Apaches had suffered a shortage of game and had explained to him, "We must steal from somebody; and if you will not permit us to rob the Mexicans, we must steal from you, or fight you."

The raiding pattern served more than purely economic ends; it was a part of the Apache way of life. On minor forays, youths were trained and conditioned for prolonged sorties deep into Mexico. And many Apache ceremonies—the victory feast, distribution of plunder, social status—were rooted in the raiding complex. During the 1850s hatred of the white warped the raiding pattern into a form of retributive warfare against Mexico. The fierce Apache attacks now drove the Mexicans from the frontiers of *Apachería* and south to Magdalena, thus turning back an advance of two centuries and creating enmities that motivated acts of violence far in excess of those caused by conflict during a raid. In 1859, during a discussion with a station agent at Apache Pass, the Coyotero chief, Francisco, asked if the Apaches would still be permitted to steal from Sonora if the United States took the state from Mexico. The agent said that he thought not, and the old chief replied that "as long as he lived and had a warrior to follow him, he would fight Sonora, and he did not care if the Americans did try to stop it, he would fight till he was killed."

After the Santa Fe treaty in 1852, Congress turned to the dialectics of the slavery question, leaving western settlers to their own devices in dealing with the Apaches. Arizonans now found themselves in much the same plight as the isolated Mexican villagers below the border. Consequently, they entered upon the precarious course previously taken by settlers in western Chihuahua: seeking protection through private treaties with local Apache bands. The United States had failed at treaty-making on a tribal level, but Arizona miners and ranchers made bargains with local groups which proved generally successful, particularly when Indian needs could be met by raiding elsewhere.

In Arizona, Dr. Michael Steck, an Indian agent, negotiated the principal local treaties with the Apaches. En route to Arizona, Charles D. Poston, heading the initial Sonora Exploring and Mining Company expedition to Tubac, arranged through Dr. Steck for a meeting with several Apache chiefs at the Santa Rita del Cobre mines in 1856. Poston relates that "the chiefs said they wanted to be friends with the Americans, and would not molest us if we did not interfere with 'trade with Mexico.' On this basis we made a treaty and the Apaches kept it." During this period, there was much concern with the protection of the Overland Road because of its importance not only to westward immigration but as a means of booming Arizona's nascent mining industry. Dr. Steck, who favored a pacific policy with the Indians, in December, 1858, met with the Chiricahuas near Apache Pass and obtained their promise not to molest traffic on the Overland Road. On March 20, 1859, at Cañon del Oro, near Tucson, he made a similar agreement with three hundred Pinal warriors who reportedly represented 3,000 Indians.

The War Department, meanwhile, did little to protect southern Arizona, and in accordance with the Gadsden Treaty did nothing to stop raids across the border. Positive steps were taken, however, when the army established Fort Buchanan on the Sonoita River in 1856, and in June, 1857, in New Mexico skirmished near Mount Graham with a party of Mogollon Apaches who were said to have been involved in the killing of a Navajo agent at Zuñi. From southern Arizona, Sylvester Mowry sent Secretary of War John B. Floyd a plan to hem in the Apaches above the Gila River with a string of forts similar to the presidial line established by Spain. Floyd approved the plan, but Congress took no action; and after February, 1858, the few garrisons in southern Arizona were even reduced.

For several years, the system of local treaties and occasional military actions insured peace. Mining and exploratory work went ahead, and with some mines reporting a profit there were predictions that Tubac would become Arizona's largest city. To the east, however, the Apache Pass area was a beehive of excitement, for here raiding parties of the Chiricahuas and other tribes rendezvoused in full view of curious station agents and settlers. Here Cochise prepared his expeditions, and his warriors boasted of their projected raids into Mexico, even naming the villages they planned to sack. At Fort Buchanan, all was quiet, except for the incidental interest stirred by the sight of Indian parties passing the fort on their way down the Sonoita toward the Mexican border. Captain R. S. Ewell, the commanding officer, discharged his duties adequately, considering the fact that circumstances often required him to assume the role of both military and civil administrator in a land possessing neither law or government. But Ewell and a Colonel Douglas, as part owners of the nearby Patagonia Mine, were absorbed in its exploitation. On August 10, 1858, Ewell wrote to his niece, Elizabeth Ewell, of Maryland, concerning the operation of the mine:

> ... there are five openings here. The Chaplaincy is vacant and no questions asked of the applicant, pay $1,200 with house and fuel, and provisions at eastern prices. We want a scientific manager for the mine, good wages with a chance for outside speculation. . . . If I can clear by the mine $10,000, I shall take my line of march for the States and settle down. It sometimes gives me the chills for fear that it may turn out a failure—more from the wise "I thought so" of friends than the loss of money.

But Ewell's command of Fort Buchanan and his regard for the Apaches were reminiscent of Governor Vildósola's policies at the presidio of Pitic in the mideighteenth century. The conditions and morale of the troops were appalling. The post hardly justified its designation, being a collection of scattered adobe buildings, through which Apaches prowled at night; the men were required to carry arms, drawn and cocked, as a precaution when traveling between their quarters after dark. For some time the garrison consisted of infantry; then, two companies of dragoons arrived, mounted on worn-out mules and horses and armed with eight different types of guns, but only one type of ammunition. The troops neither exerted themselves to recover stolen stock nor were they inclined to pursue and punish the Indians for stealing. The Apaches soon learned that there was little to fear from Fort Buchanan. In view of conditions at the fort, it is understood why the owners of the Patagonia Mine, located in the same valley twelve miles to the south, soon followed the example of others in paying for protection by provisioning the Apache parties that stopped there for that purpose.

The weakness of this type of alliance soon became apparent. A majority of the settlers felt that the Apaches must first be defeated before pacific measures could be employed effectively. Others referred to the manifold advantages of forcing Sonora to pay in lives and property for Arizona's protection. "The Apache Indian is preparing Sonora for the rule of a higher civilization than the Mexican," Sylvester Mowry exclaimed in a speech before the Geographical Society in New York on February 3, 1859. "It is every day retreating farther south, leaving to us (when the time is ripe for our own possession) the territory without the population." On the other hand, some were dubious as to the outcome of such tactics. The editor of the Tucson W*eekly Arizonian* warned:

> We make treaties with the Indians to protect ourselves, and at the same time allow them to plunder our neighbors across the line, which they do to an extent almost beyond belief. The whole State of Sonora is ravaged by marauding bands of Apaches, who find safe retreat, and often a market for their booty, in Arizona Territory. It is, in fact, nothing more or less than legalized piracy upon a weak and defenseless State, encouraged and abetted by the United States government; and mark the consequences: The Mexicans retaliate upon us, and steal back their plundered stock, or its equivalent, whenever the opportunity offers.

Herman Ehrenberg, a local mine operator, pointed to other factors. Speaking of the Pinal treaty, he said:

> The consequences of this treaty must be the creation of bitter feeling all along the frontier [of the] State of Sonora. It must foster thieving in our country, unpunished by the authorities in Sonora, because we do not punish the Indian assassin and robber for his crimes in Sonora, and by his crossing the line, virtually protect and harbor him. . . . No quiet,

industrious Mexican will venture himself and family in our midst under the circumstances, to live or work; and if any hands at all come up, they will be the outcasts, the lazy, the desperadoes, in fact the worse than good for nothings. How can mining prosper under such circumstances. . . ?

The security promised by local treaties depended perilously upon the behavior of the individuals involved and upon their thorough acceptance of the status quo in a given area. Such security was difficult to maintain in view of the rapid influx of "outsiders." A display of bravado, a drunken act, or a foolhardy decision on the part of some greenhorn could forfeit many lives. On July 31, 1859, a tense situation developed at the Patagonia Mine when a workman named Freeman brandished a rifle at a party of Apaches approaching under a white flag. They dropped back, but one Indian waited, then fired a pistol at the mining crew without effect. Although cautioned by his fellow workers, Freeman returned the shot instantly. The Apaches retired, but as Freeman and others ascended a nearby ridge to watch them, another shot was heard and Freeman fell dead. To the relief of the Tubac community, this encounter passed without further effects.

Employed initially to protect regional interests the local treaty policy collapsed, ironically, through the avarice of a self-minded few. In [Raphael] Pumpelly's opinion, this was caused by abuses already notorious in the sordid history of Indian treaties:

Indian agents appointed to represent the Government, and distribute presents among the Indians, carry on with them a profitable but shameful trade, bartering not only arms and spirits, but the very presents of the Government, against horses and mules, which they know well the Apache must first steal from Mexicans and Americans. It was out of these thefts, made to fulfill the dishonest contracts entered into with Government officials, that the majority of the Indian troubles arose in Arizona.

The attempted arrest of Cochise by Lieutenant Bascom of Fort Buchanan on February 4, 1861, for kidnapping a boy belonging to one John Ward has been generally accepted as the incident which sparked the full-scale Apache wars in Arizona. At this time, seven Southern states had seceded and it was rumored that Fort Buchanan would be abandoned. Ward, whom Poston described as a drunk with a government hay contract, was one of several settlers financially interested in keeping the post activated—though hardly by moves that would provoke a war with the Apaches. At Bascom's request Cochise came to the fort, but became alarmed by the officer's conduct and with a knife slashed his way through the side of the meeting tent and escaped. Several of the Indians who failed to escape were among the first victims in a round of senseless retaliations which spread across southern Arizona and doomed a thousand lives above and below the border during the next decade.

During the spring the Apaches, forcing the troops to remain in garrison, confined their marauding largely to the Apache Pass area, but in early summer they entered the Santa Cruz Valley. One evening at dusk near Tubac they rode up to the Santa Rita Mining Company and killed H. C. Grosvenor, the field superintendent, and two Mexican workers. In June Tubac's alliance with the Apaches ended. One day, a group of excited Sonoran ranchers rode into town and requested aid in intercepting a herd of stock being driven by an Apache band northward over the Baboquivari plain toward a crossing on the Santa Cruz River near the Canoa Ranch. The Mexicans offered Poston and other officials of the Santa Rita Mines half the herd in return for their assistance, but the mine owner refused to furnish aid. Later, Poston justified his stand:

> The Apaches had not up to this time given any trouble; but on the contrary, passed within sight of our herds, going hundreds of miles into Mexico on their forays rather than break their treaty with the Americans. They could have easily carried off our stock by killing the few *vaqueros* kept with them on the ranch, but refrained from doing so from motives well understood on the frontiers.

The Sonorans rode on to the Canoa Ranch, headquarters of the Sopori Land and Cattle Company, where they made the same appeal to a Captain Tarbox, who with a group of men had arrived recently from Maine to set up a lumber camp in the Santa Rita Mountains. The men from Maine accepted the offer. Together, they ambushed the Indians and divided the herd. But on the next full moon, the Apaches attacked the Canoa Ranch, killing the entire lumber crew—including Richard Jones, superintendent of the Sopori Land and Cattle Company—and drove off two hundred and eighty head of stock. This raid broke the company financially.

With the spread of hostilities, Arizonans shared for the first time the plight suffered by Sonorans for generations. Lives were lost and property of every kind was left abandoned as the population deserted the Tubac region, some settlers taking refuge at Tucson or in fortified ranches. Others pulled out of southern Arizona entirely. "Never was desolation so sudden, so complete," wrote Sylvester Mowry, who had resigned his commission in the army to devote his full time to the operation of the Patagonia Mine. With its fortified hacienda and smelting works, the Patagonia was the only mine that remained in operation throughout this period.

However, out of the winds of chaos came some good. Faced with a common enemy, Arizonans and Sonorans took their first self-conscious steps toward cooperation, not only in meeting the Apache problem but also in resolving other problems which had disrupted sound relations between the two peoples.

9 Comisión Pesquisadora de la Frontera del Norte ◆ Report to the President

*In response to strong criticism from the U.S. government regarding bor-
der incidents, the Mexican government created a commission to look into
the causes of frontier violence. The commission's 1873 report refutes official American allegations, placing much of the blame for the chaos on
U.S. aggression. The excerpt here is a narration of numerous sovereignty
violations of Mexican territory by U.S. citizens.*

The Mexican frontier has been the constant victim of invasions organized in or departing from the United States. . . . The invasions to
which a political character have been ascribed were, in part, acts of plun-
dering; and some of these were accompanied by circumstances which were
really disgraceful.

At the beginning of September, 1851, José María Carbajal, subsequently a general of the republic, seconded by a great number of the inhabitants on the Mexican frontier, made a revolutionary proclamation at
the "Loba," Mexico, in which he set forth, as a political measure, the
expulsion of the army from the frontier, and, as a commercial measure,
the reduction of duties and the removal of prohibitions.

These ideas were extraordinarily popular in that part of the country.
The old army had behaved in an oppressive manner towards the towns on
the frontier, and this had rendered it exceedingly distasteful to them. The
commercial restrictions had reduced the towns on the line of the Bravo to
a state of misery, and the people were daily seen leaving with their means
for the United States.

General Carbajal, after having proclaimed these principles, established
himself at Rio Grande city, in Texas, where he commenced gathering together and organizing his elements for the purpose of crossing into Mexico
and combating there the existing authorities. The Mexicans who accompanied him knew nothing of his plans; they commenced understanding
them about the middle of September, 1851, when the force which had
been gathered together at Rio Grande City crossed from Texas into Mexico.

From *Reports of the Committee of Investigation Sent in 1873 by the Mexican Government to the Frontier of Texas* (New York: Baker and Goodwin, 1875),
184, 187–96. (Translation of original report entitled *Informe de la Comisión
Pesquisadora de la Frontera del Norte al Ejecutivo de la Unión.* México, D.F.,
1874.)

Among this force there were some thirty Americans, which greatly displeased the inhabitants of the frontier who had joined Carbajal; but all this was settled by his promise that they should be the only ones who he would receive in aid of the enterprise.

The result of the first action was unfavorable to the government; the town of Camargo was attacked, taken, and its garrison capitulated. A few days afterwards they advanced on Matamoros. From the day after their arrival in front of the town, parties of Americans, to the number of three or four hundred men, who publicly crossed the river at the Parades Garita and other points, commenced joining Carbajal's forces.

This produced a disagreeable impression upon those who participated in Carbajal's views. The people of Matamoros, among whom the plan of the "Loba" had been popular, decided to oppose the movement, seeing in it not a revolution, but an invasion. They considered that the governing spirit was filibustering, and that nothing but evil could result to the frontier by giving the question such a direction. The subsequent occurrence justified these fears. The Americans who crossed into Texas consisted of some companies of Texan volunteers (Rangers), who had been serving on the banks of the Bravo, and had just been discharged. General Carbajal enlisted them for six months. In his proclamation of the 25th of September, 1851, he explained the reasons which had decided him to take this step. The commander of these companies, and the second in command of the whole of the expedition, was Captain John S. Ford, whose conduct during the whole course of his life has ever been absolutely hostile to Mexico.

The movement counted upon the support of Charles Stillman, a merchant of wealth residing at Brownsville, who furnished it with considerable resources. The Americans residing in that city also supported it; several of them crossed in the afternoon, participated in the fighting, which took place during the night, and returned to Brownsville on the morning of the following day to attend to their business. Night and day they were crossing from that city into Mexico, by the public fords, both ammunition and provisions. Some houses were intentionally burned, and the conbustibles were obtained from the house of Charles Stillman. The siege lasted nine days, during which all these horrors were committed. About the end of October, the assailants were repulsed and compelled to retire. Everything showed that the movement had been perverted. From a political point of view, the prevailing spirit in the occurrences which had taken place, was a hostility on the part of the Texas frontier against that of Mexico. In its fiscal character, the movement degenerated into smuggling operations, in which the people of Brownsville were interested. For the inhabitants of the Texas side, it was a means of prosecuting the attempts began in 1848, and leading to the ruin of our towns on the Bravo, for the purpose of aiding the progress of their own. This latter, and the prejudices which had been created between both frontiers, explained the popularity of that movement on the Texas side, and the animosity displayed by the inhabitants of Matamoros in resisting the attack. The result of this was, that General Carbajal, after his retreat, was little by little abandoned by the Mexicans who had accompanied him. He took refuge with his force in Texas, and established his camp at the "Sal," in Hidalgo county.

Monterey—Lerado [sic] was menaced, during several months, by a party of the same adventurers under the command of James Willreison and E. Alt Evans, who crossed several times during the first half of 1852, and carried arms in the name of General Carbajal. Complaint was made to the commander at Fort McIntosh, and he replied that the acts in question were those of pillage, against which he could do nothing as a military officer. These adventurers were at Lerado, in Texas; they were supported there, and crossed to this side with impunity to commit these outrages.

In September of 1861 [sic: November 1851], General Carbajal with his forces crossed a second time; they went to Cerralvo, and were there defeated. In February of 1852, he made a third attempt near Camargo, was again defeated, and thereupon took refuge with his followers in Texas.

In these cases the enlistment, the gathering of the people, the camping, all was done publicly. The authorities of Starr county, which was the base for the organization, took a most active part. N. P. Norton, the district judge of the county, headed the last expedition of this kind in March, 1853. At this time no political principles were invoked; it was purely and simply acts of vandalism and robbery.

On the twenty-fifth of March, 1853, N. P. Norton crossed from the Texas side into Mexico, at Reynosa Biejo. He was accompanied by forty Americans and ten Texan Mexicans. He reached Reynosa on the 26th, where he arrested the alcalde and Francisco Garcia Treviño, whom he threatened to shoot if within two hours they did not deliver ($30,000) thirty thousand dollars. The former he shut up and kept a prisoner; his force disseminated itself through the town, plundered various houses, stole all the horses, mules, and arms which they could find. The people were only able to get together two thousand dollars, which were delivered to Norton. He abandoned Reynosa at five o'clock on the afternoon of the 26th, pursued by a force which had left Camargo; a slight skirmish took place, and in the night Norton crossed the river at the Capote ford. The only purpose of his expedition was robbery, and this was done by the first authority of the county. He and two of his accomplices were indicted at Brownsville for a violation of the United States neutrality laws; in June of 1855, that is two years after the indictment, a "*nolle prosequi*" was entered in the case.

Another class of aggressions comprises the cases in which open hostility was manifested against the Mexican nation. The first of these was the invasion of Piedras Negras, in 1855.

This expedition was organized at San Antonio, Texas; several men of means took part in the enterprise, and two hundred men who had served in the Rangers, constituted the force. The pretext was the pursuit of the tribe of Lipan Indians of whom the Texans complained, accusing them of being the authors of much of the injury suffered by them. It is probable, nevertheless, that one of the incentives was the capture of fugitive slaves, a great number of which had taken refuge on the frontier of Coahuila; the negotiations previously initiated with several persons at San Antonio makes this to be suspected. If successful, they would not stop there; a more extended field of operations would present itself to the adventurers, even the occupation of the country. Under the pretext then of the Lipans, there were necessarily concealed more extensive plans.

On the 25th of August, 1855, some Americans, residing at San Antonio, Texas, addressed Colonel Lanberg, who was in command of the frontier at Coahuila, inquiring from him upon what conditions he would deliver up the Negroes who had taken refuge in Mexico, how many could be recovered, how much would have to be paid for each delivered on the banks of the river, and the mode of payment. The finale of the letter contains a covert threat; it says: "Our future measures and proceedings will wholly depend upon the report made by you; in the mean time we are preparing to act promptly."

Colonel Lanberg gave a favorable reply, and suggested the idea of an arrangement by which the runaway negroes should be exchanged for the Mexican "peones" who had taken refuge in Texas; he also supported the project with the government of Nuevo León. The Commission, in passing, are compelled to condemn this attempt on the part of a government officer to make an exchange of human flesh, and this, at the same time, shows the necessity that Mexico should be represented on the frontier by men of high tone, and who, by their character, will command respect and consideration.

The government of Nuevo León, on the 11th of September, replied that, in fact, it was convinced of the injuries suffered by both frontiers, but that, in matters of this nature, it could not enter into arrangements with private individuals; that the proper party to initiate these was the governor of Texas, with whom it was ready to come to an arrangement, by making a provisional agreement, until the government in Mexico should be organized. The communication concluded in the following terms: "If,

notwithstanding the foregoing, the people of 'Bejar,' who have addressed
you (Colonel Lanberg), decide to invade our frontier with a view of recovering their runaway negroes and stolen horses, in this case you will be
compelled to repel force with force."

The communication of the government of Nuevo León requiring an
impossible condition, was a refusal, and it was fully understood by both
sides that an aggression was to follow. All these antecedents give reason
to believe that the question of the Lipans was but a pretext.

The expedition arrived at the bank of the river on the first of October,
1855; this same day twelve Americans opposite Piedras Negras seized
two skiffs, and carried them to the place on the river where the filibusters
were encamped, a league from Fort Duncan. The party crossed the river
without being molested, notwithstanding the publicity which had been
given to the expedition. On the 3d of October they were defeated by the
Mexican troops, at the place called the "Maroma"; after their defeat they
retreated, and arrived at Piedras Negras, which town they pillaged and
burned. The Mexican forces, which had been detained awaiting ammunition, arrived near Piedras Negras on the 6th, and there stopped, without
attacking the filibusters, because the commander of Fort Duncan had made
demonstrations to protect them. These demonstrations consisted in placing four pieces of cannon pointing upon Piedras Negras, while the invaders quietly crossed without molestation, carrying with them what they
had stolen from the place, and in full view of the civil authorities of Texas
and of the military authorities of the United States. After reaching the
other side, the filibusters made a breastwork of bags of flour, corn, and
sugar, which they had stolen at Piedras Negras, and from thence fired
upon the town, without the military authority at Fort Duncan interposing
any obstacle. The people at Piedras Negras informed the Mexican officer
commanding that during the continuance of the invaders in the town, two
companies from Fort Duncan crossed over every night to protect the filibusters, and retired again on the morning of the following day. Complaint
was made to the commander of the said fort concerning these hostile proceedings, and his reply is far from being satisfactory. The defeat of the
filibusters created a feeling of great indignation at San Antonio, Texas,
because a very different result had been expected. A meeting was held, at
which it was resolved to invite the people of Texas to join in a campaign
against the Mexican Indians, to request the government to furnish arms,
and that it should take the necessary measures for the purpose in view.
C. Jones, J. H. Callaghan, S. A. Willcox, T. Sutherland, Asa Mitchell, and
J. A. Maverick published the call, and appointed the 15th of November
for the meeting of the volunteers at the confluence of the Santa Clara and

Cibolo rivers. A committee was appointed to receive contributions, and the officers of the expedition were appointed.

Under the pretext of the Lipan Indians, a more extensive filibustering expedition was organized than the previous one had been. Capitalists took part in it, and in reality the question assumed that character which the difficulties between the frontiers have always assumed, when the greater influence is exercised by the Texans on the bank of the Rio Bravo. It was a war of invasion openly proclaimed, and the most remarkable feature was the publicity given to those acts, and the aid demanded from the government of Texas. If there existed but this fact, it would be sufficient to decide as to what is the cause of all the questions on the frontier, and what is the prevailing opinion among the inhabitants of Texas in the vicinity of the Rio Bravo. A short time after this call was made, the circumstances attending the defeat of the filibusters began to be known, and it was understood that the undertaking presented more difficulties than had at first been anticipated. The capitalists withdrew their names, while the attitude assumed by the government of the United States was sufficient to put an end to further attempts.

[Juan Nepomucena] Cortina's revolt in 1859, and his taking refuge in Mexico in 1860, were also made the pretext of invasion by the volunteers in the service of Texas. They were headed by John S. Ford, captain of one of the companies, and who had been in command of the filibusters, and the second in command of the expedition which attacked Matamoros.

The trouble began to be felt in January of 1860. At the end of this month, a party of Americans appeared in front of the Soledad ranche [*sic*] and fired upon families residing there, and, almost at the same time, eight of them were seen on our side in the direction of the same ranche. On the fourth of February, the Bolsa ranche was attacked and burned, and the occupants killed. An explanation of these disgraceful occurrences has been attempted in a supposititious attack on the steamer *Ranchero* by Cortina, a supposition which was sufficient for Mifflin Kennedy, the owner of that steamer, to swear that he suffered great losses.

General Scott, in his report to the war department at Washington, on the 19th of May, 1860, states that there was no such attack, and his statement is perfectly true. Cortina arrived at this ranche from up the river, remained there several days, and was about leaving the place because he was suspicious of it; during the night the *Ranchero* arrived with a force on board, and anchored in front of the Bolsa. The people on board fired several shots at the ranche which were replied to. The force then landed, concealing its movements, and surrounded the ranche. After sharp firing, Cortina retreated to a place in the neighborhood, where he remained until the following day, when American cavalry crossed over. So, far from the *Ranchero* having been attacked, she served as the means of an aggression against our frontier, an aggression which had been previously organized, and in the execution of which the steamer approached the Bolsa, and those who were on board of her opened hostilities against the Mexican lines.

There occurred then what took place on all the following invasions, an unoffending man was accidentally killed, another, Cleto Garcia, was arrested and hung by the volunteers as one of Cortina's friends, although he was a peaceable and inoffensive man; after the murdering, robbing, and burning the ranche, the volunteers stole horses, killed cattle, and then crossed the river at the Santa Maria ford.

Cortina's revolt was a critical period for the Mexican population on the left bank. All who were suspected of sympathizing with him were murdered without pity, their families compelled to fly, and their property stolen. The conduct initiated by the volunteers at the Bolsa was followed up on the occasion of the second invasion.

The military authorities at Matamoros received notice that Cortina was at the "Mesa" ranche, and sent a force in pursuit of him. They notified Major Heintzelman, of the U.S. Army, to be on the alert on the left bank, and the major communicated the notice to the troops who were at Brownsville and Edinburg. The Mexican forces arrived at the Mesa without having heard anything of Cortina, and departed again leaving a picket force of twenty-six men there. Ford, the captain of the volunteers, crossed at Rosario on the night of the 16th of March, and attacked the picket which had been left at the Mesa; some of the soldiers were killed, others dispersed, and the rest made prisoners. Captain Ford then discovered that they were Mexican forces, and explained by saying that it had been an error, as his scouts had informed him that Cortina was at the "Mesa." A youth at the ranche was wounded, several houses were pillaged, the money destined for the payment of the force stolen, but few articles were ever restored.

The disrespect towards our soil had inordinately increased with these people. The volunteers, instead of returning to Texas, went several leagues inward, and made incursions upon our frontier. They visited several ranches, made prisoners of the people, and pursued those who fled to the woods. They searched for Cortina's friends to hang them, and at the "Magueyes ranche" killed Elijio Tagle, stole horses, and several days after returned to Texas.

Ever seeking the friends of Cortina, or rather making use of this as a pretext, Captain Ford again crossed into Mexico at Reynosa Vieja, on the 4th of April, 1860, and shut the people up in some sheds, to prevent them from giving notice to the authorities at San Antonio de Reynosa, but these had had timely notice that an invasion was on foot, and soon learned what was going on, and that the Texan volunteers, to the number of sixty men, were within two leagues. The people were armed and ready; Ford penetrated the town to the principal square, and when he arrived there, the people showed themselves on the roofs of the houses, and at the heads of the streets, and gave Ford to understand that he was surrounded, and that they would not permit the slightest disorder. Ford stated that he had crossed upon the authority of General Guadalupe Garcia, and produced an order signed by him, authorizing him, Ford, to cross to the Bolsa ranche, and arrest Cortina, whom he was informed was there; he also demanded the delivery to him of such friends of Cortina as were at Reynosa. They answered him that their town was not the Bolsa, and that they had no friends of Cortina there. Ford found himself compelled to abandon the town and depart by the public ford, because they would not permit him to cross elsewhere, being suspicious of his intentions towards the ranches.

10   U.S. Congress, Special House Committee ◆
Texas Frontier Troubles

*This report reflects views of the border generally held by Americans in
and out of the government. Mexico is held responsible for much of the
region's lawlessness because it allegedly tolerated the activities of raiders and bandits, allowing them to take refuge on the Mexican side. Raids
by Juan Nepomucena Cortina in 1859 and 1860 (see Selection 11) receive special attention in the report. The authors, members of a House
Committee appointed to investigate depredations in South Texas, recommend sending more U.S. troops to the border and giving them authority
to cross into Mexico whenever necessary to capture marauders.*

This country is mostly prairie, about three hundred miles from the coast
to its upper line and an average width of one hundred and fifty miles,
covered with the most nutritious grasses, and is looked upon as among
the best pasture-land of all the fine pastures of Western Texas. Before the
revolutionary war of Texas, it contained vast herds of cattle, horses, and
sheep, the owners living partly on the lands and partly in the Mexican
towns west of the river. In 1835, just before the war, according to the
assessment-rolls of the towns on the Rio Grande, there were over three
millions of head of stock on these plains.[1] The war followed. During its
progress, and after its close, nearly all the inhabitants left, either withdrawing to the south of the river by order of the Mexican generals or
keeping close upon the river-bank, to be ready to cross. The stock was
abandoned and destroyed. None of the people remained to reside there,
as they were disarmed by Mexico and treated as enemies by Texas.[2] The
Indians commenced their devastating forays upon the defenseless country. On the early American maps that portion of Texas was marked as a
"desert," inhabited only by "large droves of wild horses and cattle." It is
far from being a desert, but the wild horses and cattle were there, the
remnants of former wealth. For years this country was the hunting ground
of "mustang-hunters," Americans, Mexicans, and Indians alike.

After the Mexican war the Government of the United States established military posts along the frontier, and the State of Texas kept several companies of "rangers" in the field, thus affording protection from
Indian incursions. The legislature of the State, in the year 1852, also passed
liberal laws confirming the titles of the old Mexican owners to their lands.

From 44th Cong., 1st sess., Report no. 343, February 29, 1876, pp. ii–vi,
xii–xiii, xvi–xvii.

The assertion made by a committee of investigation sent by the government of Mexico, that the Mexicans were deprived of their lands by legislation,[3] is directly contrary to the facts and without foundation. The legislation of the State has been of the most liberal character, and the decisions of the courts uniformly in favor of the old titles.

In consequence of this liberal legislation the Mexican residents returned about the year 1853, and re-established their stock-ranches, and in 1856, and since, Americans settled throughout the country, purchasing lands from the old owners, or acquiring the unlocated public domain under the laws of Texas. They were remarkably prosperous until the raids assumed a formidable character. From reports given to the committee it may be seen that, although agriculture is still in its infancy there, and the country still held and used alone by the herdsmen, the wealth was rapidly increasing.

In the report of the commission sent there in 1872, to investigate the raids, it is stated that, in the year 1870, the assessment-rolls in the counties of Cameron, Hidalgo, Starr, Webb, La Salle, Encinal, Duval, Zapata, and Nueces (the returns of two other counties, Live Oak and McMullen, not having been included) showed 299,193 cattle, and 73,593 horses; and now, even after the enormous losses by the raids, the following estimates give an idea of the exportations of that district:

The firm of Coleman, Mathis & Fulton, of Rockford, having contracted to ship cattle by Morgan's steamboat-line, supply, per annum, 50,000 steers, at the rate of $18 per head, or	$900,000
The packing and rendering establishments at Fulton consume 50,000 head of steers, worth $15 per head	750,000
The number of cattle driven north to the Kansas market is estimated at 75,000 at $12 per head	900,000
The export of wool from Corpus Christi was last year 6,000,000 pounds, at an average price of 22 cents	1,320,000

The number of mutton-sheep is not estimated.

All the figures given mean gold values.

History of the Raids

The history of the present raids can be said to have commenced with the Cortina war in 1859 and 1860. We will quote enough of the official account of Major Heintzelman, U.S.A., dated March 1, 1860, and contained in the Executive Documents of the first session of the Thirty-sixth Congress, Doc. No. 84, submitted to the House of Representatives by the

Secretary of War under a resolution of the House to give an outline of that war:

> Juan Nepomuceno Cortina, the leader of the banditti who have for the last five months been in arms on the Lower Rio Grande, murdering, robbing, and burning, is a ranchero, at one time claiming to be an American and at another a Mexican citizen. At the time General Taylor arrived on the banks of the Rio Grande he was a soldier in General Arista's army. He has for years been noted as a lawless, desperate man.
>
> Ten years ago he was indicted for murder, and the sheriff attempted to arrest him, which made him for a long period keep out of the way, until the witnesses were gone. In 1854 he again began to be seen about; but no effort was made to arrest him until in the spring of 1859 when he was indicted for horse-stealing, and he has since been a fugitive from justice. When he came to town he was always well armed or had some of his friends around him, making it dangerous to interfere with him. . . .
>
> On the 13th of July last he was in Brownsville with some of his ranchero friends, when a man who was formerly a servant of his was arrested by the city marshal for abusing a coffee-house keeper. Cortina attempted to rescue the man. He fired twice on the Marshal, the second shot wounding him in the shoulder. He mounted his horse, took the prisoner up behind him, and with his friends around him rode off, defying the authorities to arrest him. He escaped to Matamoras [*sic*] and there was treated with consideration and lauded as the defender of Mexican rights. . . .
>
> Before daylight on the morning of the 28th of September, Cortina entered the city of Brownsville with a body of mounted men, variously estimated at from forty to eighty, leaving two small parties of foot outside, one near the cemetery, the other near the suburbs of Framireño. The citizens were awakened by firing and cries of "Viva Cheno Cortina!" "Mueran los Gringos!"—Death to Americans! "Viva Mexico!" The city was already in his possession, with sentinels at the corners of the principal streets, and armed men riding about. He avowed his determination to kill the Americans; but assured Mexicans and foreigners that they should not be molested. Thus was a city of two thousand to three thousand inhabitants occupied by a band of armed banditti—a thing till now unheard of in these United States.
>
> He made his headquarters in the deserted garrison of Fort Brown, and sent mounted men through the streets hunting up their enemies. He broke open the jail, liberated the prisoners, knocked off their irons, and had them join him. He killed the jailor, Johnson, a constable named George Morris, young Neale, in his bed; and two Mexicans were after Glavecke, the wounded city marshal, and others.

We will not go further into the details of the war thus inaugurated. Cortina went to the Mexican side, and "he and his men stayed about Matamoros publicly, unmolested by the authorities."

Cortina established himself subsequently on the American side of the river above Brownsville, where he collected men and arms. He repulsed an attack made on his position by a number of Americans, assisted by national guards from Matamoros, with some artillery, on the 24th of October. The governor of Texas sent out forces against Cortina. Several fights took place in the chaparral, in which Cortina maintained his position. Major Heintzelman says:

> Cortina was now a great man. He had defeated the "Gringos," and his position was impregnable. He had the Mexican flag flying in his camp, and numbers were flocking to his standard. When he visited Matamoras, he was received as the champion of his race—as the man who would right the wrongs of the Mexicans and drive back the hated Americans to the Nueces.

Major Heintzelman arrived, in command of United States troops, on the night of the 5th of December at Brownsville. He took command, and, with a mixed force of United States troops, Texas rangers, and volunteers, dislodged Cortina, and finally defeated him, at Rio Grande City, on the 27th of December. Cortina crossed over into Mexico and established himself there. Once more he crossed over to the American side on a raid. We close this account by another quotation from Major Heintzelman's report:

> Most of his arms, ammunition, and supplies to maintain his forces for so many months came from Mexico, and principally from Matamoras. Most of the men were "pelados" from the towns and ranches along the Rio Grande. On the Mexican side he always found a market for his plunder. He was styled in orders "General en Gefe," and he went about with a body-guard.
> The whole country from Brownsville to Rio Grande City, one hundred and twenty miles, and back to the Arroyo Colorado, has been laid waste. There is not an American, or any property belonging to an American, that could be destroyed in this large tract of country. Their horses and cattle were driven across into Mexico and there sold, a cow, with a calf by her side, for a dollar.

In a letter to the Mexican general commanding on the Rio Grande, who had taken exception to the troops of Major Heintzelman following Cortina across the river into Mexican territory, Major Heintzelman maintained the right to do so, and said:

> After his (Cortina's) defeat, as above stated, he fled for safety to the Mexican side of the river, and there found it. He was received with sympathy. He was then allowed to remain and recruit his forces, arm and equip them, and watch for a favorable opportunity to make another attack. This attack he made by firing across the river, mortally wounding a man of our troops, and by firing upon the steamboat.

We have quoted fully from this official report, because, although written sixteen years ago, in describing the opening scenes of this border warfare it gives all the characteristic features of what has been enacted on that field for the last ten years.

During the civil war of the United States, and until about the year 1866, there was a period of comparative peace on that border. The reasons were various. In the first place, the Rio Grande became the only open inlet into the southern confederacy, and an immense trade was established there. The towns were full of strangers. Cotton was exported in immense quantities, and vast stores of merchandise imported. Matamoros became an important mart for the commerce of the world, and the whole population had an exceedingly remunerative employment. The roads were covered with wagon-trains and travelers. Many of the Mexican merchants made large fortunes. A number of them had their business in Texas, and mutual profits and usefulness established a friendly feeling. Meanwhile the French invasion, and the establishment of Maximilian's empire, drove the liberal government north toward the border, and for some time the fugitive government of [Benito] Juárez was at El Paso, on the American line, one foot, so to speak, on American soil and the other on Mexican. Then followed the rallying of the liberal forces. Escobedo, the chief commander of Juárez' forces, made up his army on the border, and started from there on his campaign which closed with the final tragedy of Queretaro. His army and the other liberal corps operating against the forces of the empire absorbed and carried away all the loose population of that border.

But after the close of the war, and with the return of the soldiery, commenced the pillaging on the Texas border. Cortina, the old robber chief, had obtained the rank of brigadier-general in the Mexican army, and had risen to power and distinction. From that time forth he was the central figure of the robbing population which established itself on the Mexican side of the Rio Bravo. His power was despotic. The lawless men who, through him, enjoyed the advantages of organization and political power on their own soil, and unlimited license to plunder on the Texan side, supported him with enthusiastic devotion, and in turn gave him the power and position which, in such a country, naturally falls to the leader who can command the unhesitating services of a large body of warlike followers. He became individually far more powerful than any other power—national or state. It was known that he had made and unmade governors at his pleasure.[4]

When we now look upon the fearful history of rapine, murder, and wholesale robbery which from that day to this present date has desolated and is still desolating our border, the robber communities that have sprung up and are constantly increasing, a whole population living on what they plunder from their neighbors, and a set of local authorities conniving at and participating in the spoils of these notorious crimes, grown to be a regular means of livelihood, we cannot wonder at this result, when we reflect on the condition of a government which had to confer rank and position on a successful robber in order to avoid his hostility.

And when we consider that it is our own people who have been the constant victims of these crimes for the last ten years, and are now still more exposed to them than ever, we feel that every sentiment of manhood and of regard for the honor of our country, and its most sacred obligations to defend the life and property of its citizens, cry out against the criminal neglect which allowed this evil to assume its present formidable proportions. That a man like Cortina, who had left the territory of the United States, in open war with the United States troops and the troops of the State of Texas, and against whom numerous indictments for murder and other crimes are now pending in the State courts, should have been placed in high command immediately on our border, was a strange act for a government professing to be friendly; and it was as strange for our Government to suffer it for so long a time. Cortina has been arrested by the Mexican government, and, until lately, held in the city of Mexico. His return to the old theater of his crimes and insults against our people, some time since triumphantly announced in Matamoros, would be an act of open defiance. . . .

Meanwhile our people on the border are impoverished day by day, and their lives are held by a slender tenure. It is stated in the evidence before us that all the American stock-raisers, who could do so, have abandoned their ranches, and sought safety for their families in the towns. Business in the towns has almost ceased. No merchant dares to credit a country merchant or a stock-raiser, whose whole possessions are liable every day to be swept away, burned, or otherwise destroyed. Such is the insecurity of life that Captain McNally, who appeared before your committee, a man of known daring, and a bold leader in those border fights, declares upon oath that no compensation, however great, could induce him to incur the danger which every inhabitant of the country between the Rio Grande and Nueces incurs every day, and that he considers his life, as a man whose business is war, safer than that of any inhabitant of that district. Deliberately and with full conviction, as this opinion is stated by one who is familiar with that country and all the facts, as a perusal of his evidence will show, it is fearful in its weight, and should come home to the heart and mind of every American.

But it is not alone the danger incident to the life in a country overrun by robbers, which is the constant menace to our people, but there is, according to all the statements, a perfect terrorism established by the robbers. Every one who is suspected, by word or deed, to have taken part against them is doomed to death. Captain McNally says:

> Many of them have not nerve enough to take an active, decided stand against it, either by giving information or by personal assistance. Still, a number of them have done it since I have been out there, and some eight or ten, probably twelve, have been killed on that account. It has been the history of those border counties that when any man, Mexican or American, has made himself prominent in hunting those raiders down, or in organizing parties to pursue them when they are carrying off cattle, he has been either forced to move from the ranch and come into town, or he has been killed. Quite a number of Americans have been killed within the last year out there, and also quite a number of Mexicans, probably twelve or fifteen, for that offense alone. The men on the other side of the river threaten to kill them, and the fact is known publicly.[5]

They say, "We will kill that man within a week," and the report is heralded over the country, and if the man does not leave they usually carry their threat into execution. The same statement occurs in all the evidence. While the resident Mexican population, who have any property, are in sympathy with our people, there is a large floating population who have come over from the other side who have no permanent abode anywhere, and who are the spies and informers of the raiders. . . .

The protection of our border is a supreme duty, and we must take such means as will be efficient in giving that protection. Should Congress fail in this, there may be well-grounded apprehensions that the people of Texas will rise in arms in their last despair, and themselves cross the border and wage a war of retaliation. They want no war and no more territory. We are assured that they would consider a war as destructive to their interests, and that they want peace and immigration to fill up their own vast territory before they desire to see new fields opened to draw immigrants elsewhere. Their country offers them all the prosperity they desire, if they can only have peace and security for themselves, their families, and their property. But they are men and they are Americans, and there are limits to patient suffering. A war of retaliation, after what they have suffered, would not be confined to the punishment of the robbers alone, and would precipitate such complications upon this nation that we could not ignore them. A failure to act promptly may, and probably will, therefore, bring about the very thing we wish to avoid. As yet what has to be done can be done in regular order, justly, discreetly, and in proper bounds, and this Government will be able to know and direct how far to go and where to stop.

We beg leave to submit the following joint resolutions, and recommend their passage:

Resolved, [SEC. 1.] That for the purpose of giving efficient protection to the country between the Rio Grande and Nueces River, in the State of Texas, from the cattle-thieves, robbers, and murderers from the Mexican side of the river, the President of the United States be, and hereby is, authorized and required to station and keep on the Rio Grande River, from the mouth of that river to the northern boundary of the State of Tamaulipas, above Laredo, two regiments of cavalry, for field-service, in addition to such infantry force as may be necessary for garrison duty, and to assign recruits to said regiments so as to fill each troop to number one hundred privates, and they shall be kept up to that strength as long as they shall be required in that service.

SEC. 2. That in view of the inability of the national government of Mexico to prevent the inroads of lawless parties from Mexican soil into Texas, the President is hereby authorized, whenever in his judgment it shall be necessary for the protection of the rights of American citizens on the Texas frontier above described, to order the troops when in close pursuit of the robbers with their booty, to cross the Rio Grande, and use such means as they may find necessary for recovering the stolen property, and checking the raids, guarding, however, in all cases against any unnecessary injury to peaceable inhabitants of Mexico.

G. SCHLEICHER.

A. S. WILLIAMS.

N. P. BANKS.

S. A. HURLBUT.

Hon. L. Q. C. Lamar absent on account of sickness.

Notes

1. See Ex. Doc. No. 52, 36th Congress.
2. See Ex. Doc. No. 52, 36th Congress.
3. See Report of Mexican Commission, p. 129.
4. See Report of Mexican Commissioners, p. 150.
5. See testimony of Captain McNally, p. 9.

11 Juan Nepomucena Cortina ◆ Proclamation

Quintessential border bandit and champion of the oppressed, Juan Nepo-
mucena Cortina rebelled in 1859–60 against the power structure of South
Texas, charging Anglo-American exploitation, discrimination, and physi-
cal abuse against Mexicans. During the uprising, which endeared him to
the masses but made him a wanted man in official circles, he issued sev-
eral proclamations explaining his actions. One of these pronouncements
follows. Careful reading of this complex, flowery text reveals a thought-
ful man who yearns for justice.

COUNTY OF CAMERON,
Camp in the Rancho del Carmen, November 23, 1859

C OMPATRIOTS: A sentiment of profound indignation, the love and es-
teem which I profess for you, the desire which you have for that
tranquillity and those guarantees which are denied you, thus violating the
most sacred laws, is that which moves me to address you these words,
hoping that they may prove some consolation in the midst of your adver-
sity, which heretofore has borne the appearance of predestination.

The history of great human actions teaches us that in certain instances
the principal motive which gives them impulse is the natural right to resist and conquer our enemies with a firm spirit and lively will; to persist
in and to reach the consummation of this object, opening a path through
the obstacles which step by step are encountered, however imposing or
terrible they may be.

In the series of such actions, events present themselves which public
opinion, influenced by popular sentiment, calls for deliberation upon their
effects, to form an exact and just conception of the interests which they
promote; and this same public opinion should be considered as the best
judge, which, with coolness and impartiality, does not fail to recognize
some principle as the cause for the existence of open force and immu-
table firmness, which impart the noble desire of coöperating with true
philanthropy to remedy the state of despair of him who, in his turn, becomes the victim of ambition, satisfied at the cost of justice.

There are, doubtless, persons so overcome by strange prejudices, men
without confidence or courage to face danger in an undertaking in sister-
hood with the love of liberty, who, examining the merit of acts by a false
light, and preferring that of the same opinion contrary to their own, pre-

From U.S. Congress, House of Representatives, "Difficulties on the Southwestern Frontier," 36th Cong., 1st sess., House Executive Document no. 52,
April 2, 1860, pp. 79–82.

pare no other reward than that pronounced for the "bandit," for him who, with complete abnegation of self, dedicates himself to constant labor for the happiness of those who, suffering under the weight of misfortunes, eat their bread, mingled with tears, on the earth which they rated.

If, my dear compatriots, I am honored with that name, I am ready for the combat.

The Mexicans who inhabit this wide region, some because they were born therein, others because since the treaty Guadalupe Hidalgo, they have been attracted to its soil by the soft influence of wise laws and the advantages of a free government, paying little attention to the reasoning of politics, are honorably and exclusively dedicated to the exercise of industry, guided by that instinct which leads the good man to comprehend, as uncontradictory truth, that only in the reign of peace can he enjoy, without inquietude, the fruit of his labor. These, under an unjust imputation of selfishness and churlishness, which do not exist, are not devoid of those sincere and expressive evidences of such friendliness and tenderness as should gain for them that confidence with which they have inspired those who have met them in social intercourse. This genial affability seems as the foundation of that proverbial prudence which, as an oracle, is consulted in all their actions and undertakings. Their humility, simplicity, and docility, directed with dignity, it may be that with excess of goodness, can, if it be desired, lead them beyond the common class of men, but causes them to excel in an irresistible inclination towards ideas of equality, a proof of their simple manners, so well adapted to that which is styled the classic land of liberty. A man, a family, and a people, possessed of qualities so eminent, with their heart in their hand and purity on their lips, encounter every day renewed reasons to know that they are surrounded by malicious and crafty monsters, who rob them in the tranquil interior of home, or with open hatred and pursuit; it necessarily follows, however great may be their pain, if not abased by humiliation and ignominy, their groans suffocated and hushed by a pain which renders them insensible, they become resigned to suffering before an abyss of misfortunes.

Mexicans! When the State of Texas began to receive the new organization which its sovereignty required as an integrant part of the Union, flocks of vampires, in the guise of men, came and scattered themselves in the settlements, without any capital except the corrupt heart and the most perverse intentions. Some, brimful of laws, pledged to us their protection against the attacks of the rest; others assembled in shadowy councils, attempted and excited the robbery and burning of the houses of our relatives on the other side of the river Bravo; while others, to the abusing of our unlimited confidence, when we intrusted them with our [land] titles, which secured the future of our families, refused to return them under false and frivolous pretexts; all, in short, with a smile on their faces, giving the lie to that which their black entrails were meditating. Many of you have been robbed of your property, incarcerated, chased, murdered, and hunted like wild beasts, because your labor was fruitful, and because your industry excited the vile avarice which led them. A voice infernal said, from the bottom of their soul, "kill them; the greater will be our gain!" Ah! this does not finish the sketch of your situation. It would appear that justice had fled from this world, leaving you to the caprice of your oppressors, who become each day more furious towards you; that, through witnesses and false charges, although the grounds may be insufficient, you may be interred in the penitentiaries, if you are not previously deprived of life by some keeper who covers himself from responsibility by the pretense of your flight. There are to be found criminals covered with frightful crimes, but they appear to have impunity until opportunity furnish them a victim; to these monsters indulgence is shown, because they are not of our race [mestizos, or people of Spanish-Indian blood], which is unworthy, as they say, to belong to the human species. But this race, which the Anglo-American, so ostentatious of its own qualities, tries so much to blacken, depreciate, and load with insults, in a spirit of blindness, which goes to the full extent of such things so common on this frontier, does not fear, placed even in the midst of its very faults, those subtle inquisitions which are so frequently made as to its manners, habits, and sentiments; nor that its deeds should be put to the test of examination in the land of reason, of justice, and of honor. This race has never humbled itself before the conqueror, though the reverse has happened, and can be established; for he is not humbled who uses among his fellow-men those courtesies which humanity prescribes; charity being the root whence springs the rule of his actions. But this race, which you see filled with gentleness and inward sweetness, gives now the cry of alarm throughout the entire extent of the land which it occupies, against all the artifice interposed by those who have become chargeable with their division and discord. This race, adorned with the most lovely disposition towards all that is good and useful in the line of progress, omits no act of diligence which might correct its many imperfections, and lift its grand edifice among the ruins of the past, respecting the ancient traditions and the maxims bequeathed by their ancestors, without being dazzled by brilliant and false appearances, nor crawling to that exaggeration of institution which, like a sublime statue, is offered for their worship and adoration.

Mexicans! Is there no remedy for you? Inviolable laws, yet useless, serve, it is true, certain judges and hypocritical authorities, cemented in evil and injustice, to do whatever suits them, and to satisfy their vile avarice at the cost of your patience and suffering; rising in their frenzy, even to the taking of life, through the treacherous hands of their bailiffs. The wicked way in which many of you have been oftentimes involved in persecution, accompanied by circumstances making it the more bitter, is now well known; these crimes being hid from society under the shadow of a horrid night, those implacable people, with the haughty spirit which suggests impunity for a life of criminality, have pronounced, doubt ye not, your sentence, which is, with accustomed insensibility, as you have seen, on the point of execution.

Mexicans! My part is taken; the voice of revelation whispers to me that to me is entrusted the work of breaking the chains of your slavery, and that the Lord will enable me, with powerful arms, to fight against our enemies, in compliance with the requirements of that Sovereign Majesty, who, from this day forward, will hold us under His protection. On my part, I am ready to offer myself as a sacrifice for your happiness; and counting upon the means necessary for the discharge of my ministry, you may count upon my coöperation, should no cowardly attempt put an end to my days. This undertaking will be sustained on the following bases:

First. A society is organized in the State of Texas, which devotes itself sleeplessly until the work is crowned with success, to the improvement of the unhappy condition of those Mexicans resident therein; exterminating their tyrants, to which end those which compose it are ready to shed their blood and suffer the death of martyrs.

Second. As this society contains within itself the elements necessary to accomplish the great end of its labors, the veil of impenetrable secrecy covers "The Great Book" in which the articles of its constitution are written; while so delicate are the difficulties which must be overcome that no honorable man can have cause for alarm, if imperious exigencies require them to act without reserve.

Third. The Mexicans of Texas repose their lot under the good sentiments of the governor elect of the State, General Houston, and trust that upon his elevation to power he will begin with care to give us legal protection within the limits of his powers.

Mexicans! Peace be with you! Good inhabitants of the State of Texas, look on them as brothers, and keep in mind that which the Holy Spirit saith: "Thou shalt not be the friend of the passionate man; nor join thyself to the madman, lest thou learn his mode of work and scandalize thy soul."

JUAN N. CORTINA.

12 Congressional Investigative Board ◆ El Paso Troubles in Texas

This selection summarizes a report issued by a U.S. military board charged with investigating disturbances that occurred in 1877 in San Elizario, Texas, about twenty-five miles southeast of El Paso. The incident became popularly known as the "Salt War" because the conflict stemmed in part from the greedy appropriation by Anglo-Americans of salt mines that had long been used by local Mexicans in communal fashion. Tension over politics and ethnic relations also contributed to the rebellion. Several people lost their lives, while many suspected participants escaped prosecution by fleeing to Mexico. Although it contains errors and racial slurs, the report provides a good overview of the Salt War.

Summary

The Board finds that at San Elizario, in the latter part of September (September 29, 1877), Charles H. Howard, Gregoria [*sic*] N. García, the county judge and a justice of the peace, were, for causing the arrest of two Mexicans, citizens of that town, named Maadonia [*sic*] Gandara and José María Jaurez [*sic*], for saying they intended to go and get salt from the salt lakes (as charged in affidavits), themselves arrested, confined in durance, and threatened by an armed mob numbering about fifty or sixty men, of whom ten were from the Mexican side of the Rio Grande; they were led by Cisto [*sic*] Salcido and León Granido, at that time citizens of Texas. It is believed that even then Howard's life was in danger, but at the earnest and united petitions of the Rev. Pierre Bourgad [*sic*], the priest of the parish, and Louis Cardis, as stated in their own words, it was spared, and both he and the two officials were released, but on condition that the first should bind himself in the sum of $12,000, with good security, to relinquish his interests in the salinas, and then to leave the county never to return, nor yet to prosecute them for their action in the matter. As for the county judge and the justice, they were released on tendering the resignation of their respective offices.

In the beginning of November following, Howard returned to the county, notwithstanding the pledge he had given to remain away, whereupon the Mexicans became incensed and gathered together again, some with arms in their hands, to the number of about two hundred, of whom

From U.S. Congress, House of Representatives, 45th Cong., 2d sess., House Executive Document no. 93, March 16, 1878, pp. 13–18.

about twenty were citizens of Mexico, living on this and the other side of the river, and threatened the lives of the bondsmen to enforce the payment of the bond which they declared was rendered forfeit by Howard's return. But the timely arrival of an officer of the State of Texas, Maj. John B. Jones, who came before their junta accompanied by the parish priest as interpreter, prevented their half-matured plans from culminating into any overt acts of disorder. They expressed themselves satisfied with the interview, and as a result of his visit promised to disband and disperse and await the decisions of the courts. But their professions and promises must have been insincere, for as found, the people, early in December, that is to say, December 12, 1877, rose *en masse* and armed themselves for the mischief that ensued. Yet with imperfect organization and little discipline they were speedily joined by friends and sympathizers who came, some to fight and others to steal, from across the river in squads of a few at a time, until their numbers grew to formidable proportions. Their exact force is difficult to compute. Their leaders who know are in foreign parts, and the estimate of those who have testified differs widely, but there could not have been far from 400, of whom not less than one-third were Mexican citizens, the remainder being from El Paso County, Texas. All were under the leadership of Francisco (*alias* Chico) Barcla [*sic*], with Desiderio Apodaca as second in command, and these were assisted by Ramón Sambrano, León Granido, Cisto Salcido, Anastasio Montez, and Acaton Porras, all residents of Texas, except Montez, who was from Mexico. They assembled in the town of San Elizario and made no secret of their intentions to kill Charles H. Howard (who had gone there under escort of a small company of the Texas Battalion of Rangers), but disavowing at the same time, so it is said, any purpose to become involved with the United States Government. Here the mob remained in possession from the 12th to the 17th of December. They surrounded and besieged the house and corral where the rangers were quartered, and, after some casualties on both sides, compelled their surrender and disarmament. They plundered stores and warehouses of goods and provisions, and carried the booty across the river. They killed on the 12th Mr. Charles E. Ellis, whose store and mill they afterward robbed. On the 13th they shot down in the street Sergt. C. E. Mortimer, of the Frontier Battalion of Rangers, and on the 17th, after the surrender, in broad daylight and in cold blood, they murdered Charles H. Howard, John G. Atkinson, and John E. McBride; the last-named was one of the rangers, the other two were quartered in the building for protection. The death of Mortimer was the only loss suffered by the rangers during the siege. The number and extent of the casualties on the side of the mob is not known and probably never will be. It must have been large.

It is impracticable as yet to fix the true value of the property destroyed and stolen, as the principal losers are dead, but it is believed that the amount is rather more than instead of less than $12,000.

No evidence taken substantiates the report heretofore prevalent, that the people coming from Mexico and taking part in these criminal proceedings were an organized body previously drilled and disciplined by officers of the Mexican army. One Ferris Lermo, or, as known by the Mexicans, Teniente Lermo, who was formerly a lieutenant in the Mexican army, but not connected with it for many years, and now an old man, did assist the mob of November by written advice and personal instruction in tactics, but finding they were disposed to adopt extreme measures, which he could not second and from which he would have dissuaded them, he incurred their dislike, and went or was driven away before the rising, and there is nothing to show that he returned.

The inhabitants of the adjacent towns on both sides of the river have hitherto, for many years, lived in a state of amity, and are intimately connected by the bonds of a common faith, like sympathies and tastes, and are related in numerous instances by marriage; hence each would naturally support and defend the other, if occasions real or fancied demanded their aid, to any sacrifice. In the words of one who ought to know them well, if they have a good man to lead them, there is not a more pacific, easily governed, and loyal people on the face of the earth; if they have a bad one they will be just as bad as he would have them. The statements of reliable citizens, showing the character of the people, in this view are important and worthy of consideration.

The Causes

The causes which led to these disturbances are, it is believed, local in their character, directly issuing from a disagreement or personal feud long subsisting between two prominent and influential men in the community, one Charles H. Howard, the other Louis Cardis, which grew into deadly hatred, culminating in the violent death of Cardis at the hands of Howard, on the 10th of October, 1877, in this town. Cardis, although an Italian by birth, could speak the Spanish language most fluently, and possessed the entire confidence of the Mexican population, who had elected him to represent them in the legislature, and whom they reverenced as their leader, adviser, and friend. So it was but natural that when their favorite was slain by one whom they distrusted and hated, they should feel the blow thus aimed at them (so they reasoned), and prepared, as they did, after the fashion of an ignorant and hot-blooded-race, to take vengeance upon his

slayer. But the avengers of blood brought in their train a mongrel following of thieves and robbers, birds of prey scenting the quarry from afar,
whose deeds of rapine entailed most serious consequences.

One ground of disagreement between the two men, and the parties
whom they respectively represented, was a claim to certain salt deposits
or salinas, asserted by Howard (as agent) and denied by Cardis, who,
believing he understood the law bearing upon the matter, had interpreted
it to his friends, the Mexicans, adversely to Howard's interests. These
salt deposits or salinas, which are believed to be the primal cause of all
these disturbances, are very valuable, on account of the abundance and
purity of the salt yielded by them. They are situated . . . about 90 miles
. . . [eastward] from San Elizario. They were discovered and utilized many
years ago, as evinced by cattle-trails leading to them, but not until about
1863 were they accessible by wagon-road; this was opened up to them at
that time, and the expense defrayed by public subscription. At present a
portion of the people recognize the claims of the locator of the lakes by
paying him a certain established rate for each fanega hauled away. . . .

Action Taken by Mexican Authorities

No Mexican troops have for many years been quartered nearer this neighborhood than the State of Durango, and the action taken by the civil authorities, being unsupported by the military arm, was, although pacific
and conciliatory, yet ineffective and powerless to prevent all bloodshed.
On the 14th of December, the gefe [*sic*] político, the chief civil officer of
the district of the Brazos, issued an aviso warning the people that a riot
was in progress at San Elizario, and prohibiting them under penalty from
crossing the river to take any part therein. He also directed the captain of
the town guards of Paso del Norte to so station the men at his command
as to enforce this prohibition, along the right bank of the river, as far
down as San Elizario, and turn back all who should attempt to cross with
arms in their hands.

Action Taken by the United States

But as soon as news of these lawless proceedings reached his ears, the
district commander, Col. Edward Hatch, Ninth Cavalry, hastened in person to the county, and promptly made such disposition of the troops at-
tainable as stopped all further violence therein, and tended in large measure

to restore the confidence of the people, many of whom had fled into Mexico.

The State and County

No immediate action beyond that of the sheriff, presently to be mentioned, was taken, so far as has transpired within the knowledge of the Board, by the civil authorities of the State of Texas or county of El Paso.

The district attorney, whose duty it is to prosecute in the name of the State, had tendered his resignation, and its acceptance lay under advisement. The district judge, the only person empowered to make requisitions under the extradition treaty on the authorities of Mexico, for persons charged with crime and fugitives from justice, was, according to his own statement, absent from the neighborhood from about September 25, 1877, to about February 3, 1878. He held his last court in Tom Green County, and adjourned the same about November 30, 1877. On February 28, 1878, the judge who was *ex-officio* extradition agent, made a formal demand on the authorities of Mexico, under the extradition laws, for 17 persons, citizens of Texas, charged with murder and robbery, and then in hiding; but at the date of this present writing (March 14, 1878), none have been delivered up.

The county judge and the local justices of the peace, four in number, are Mexicans, the latter unable to speak the English language, and by no means well versed in the law. In any other community, more civilized than this, they would be regarded as ignorant men.

The county judge, though an educated man, is addicted to drink, and is frequently unfitted for business by reason of intemperance. At San Elizario, the Board, at its first visit, learned that he was drunk, and could not have appeared before it had he been summoned, and at its second visit failed to secure his attendance, although it remained there three days, the assigned cause being drunkenness.

The county commissioner from this precinct is known to have taken part in the mob, and is now a fugitive from justice. All of them were reported, at the last session of the district court, for diverting a portion of the public funds into an irregular channel, by the grand jury, which pronounced their action as meriting the severest penalty of the law, but that it resulted more from ignorance than from any deliberate design, and that they were not competent to discharge in a strictly legal manner the responsible duties devolving upon them. There is no county jail here, and the county has no money nor yet credit to build one. If criminals in numbers should be arrested they would escape, as there is no way to make provision for their custody and keeping. But without arraigning any official, either State or county, or reflecting upon their professional conduct, which the Board does not wish, even if authorized, to do, it is within its field of duty to say that civil law in this section is very loosely administered.

Soon after the death of Cardis, already mentioned, a body of troops, amounting to about twenty men, was hastily enrolled by Maj. J. B. Jones, under the authority of the governor, with Lieut. John B. Tays in command, to assist the local authorities in the maintenance of order and the enforcement of the law, and on December 22 another small force of about thirty men arrived from Silver City, who had been called into temporary service by Sheriff Charles Kerber, under telegraphic instructions from the governor. But, unhappily, as was natural and according to experience in raising volunteers along the border, when the exigencies of the occasion do not permit that delay which a wise discrimination in the choice of material would cause, the force of rangers thus suddenly called together contained within its ranks an adventurous and lawless element, which, though not predominant, was yet strong enough to make its evil influence felt in deeds of violence and outrage matched only by the mob itself. Notable among these atrocities should be classed the shooting of two Mexican prisoners, who were bound with cords when turned over to the guard at Ysleta, ostensibly to bury the bodies of Howard, Atkinson, and McBride, then lying in the fields of San Elizario, and when next seen, about an hour after, were pierced with bullet-holes, their appearance giving rise to grave apprehension in unprejudiced minds that their death was "neither necessary nor justifiable." Another was the killing of the Mexican and the wounding of his wife in a house in Socorro, through the door of which a shot had, it was said, been fired, and, being a spent-ball, had struck without hurting one of the rangers belonging to Lieut. Tays's company. On a personal examination by the Board of all the outside doors of the house, there could be found no marks of a bullet-hole, but through an inner door, across the *sala*, behind which the unfortunate victim had received his death and his wife a serious wound, were counted no less than fifteen bullet-holes, piercing the door from the outside, and none merging from the inner side. These are regarded by the Board as wanton outrages.

In this connection the Board cannot refrain from commenting on the fact that, as shown by the record herewith presented, the death of Cardis at the hands of Howard seems to have been premeditated murder, a crime for which there is no bail provided by law. Yet Howard, after its commission, and without being confined, or examined in the presence of a prosecuting officer, either on the part of State, district, or county, was suffered to give bail and go free.

Recommendations

The Board recommends, as a measure likely to prevent a recurrence of these evils, the establishment of a permanent post somewhere in this vicinity, to be garrisoned by about two hundred men, of whom fifty should be cavalry; a portion of this force to be retained at San Elizario as long as the department commander may deem it necessary to restore confidence to the well-disposed people now residing there. In the judgment of the Board, there is no doubt that if a small force of United States troops had been stationed here the late deplorable events would not have transpired; hence the danger of neglect, for similar causes might easily occasion similar uprisings. This done, the salt-war is probably ended. But, in addition to the questions likely to spring from the present constitution of society, that of water, as to its division and distribution, the Board regards as serious. The Rio Grande, at this season of the year even an insignificant stream, its channel often shifting and always erratic, but during the heats of summer sometimes dry, affords, by being directed into acequias on either bank, a scant and variable supply of water to the people of both nationalities, but is utterly insufficient to irrigate this extensive valley, where the yearly rain-fall measures but a few inches. As time progresses and the country is opened by accessions to its populations, sure to come—for it is a most fertile region and gloriously rewards the labor spent in irrigation—the question must grow in importance, and may occasion trouble beyond the reach of diplomacy to settle. This sad result, so serious to these people, so injurious to all, might be warded off, at least delayed, by the moral effect of a single battalion.

In conclusion, should the Republic of Mexico, after a reasonable time allowed for legal process, fail or refuse to surrender the persons for whom requisition has been made in due form under the provisions of the treaty of extradition, it is recommended that the demand be urged and pressed by the United States, and reparation claimed and exacted for our citizens in such an amount as shall be by the losers from the riots fully substantiated as just and equitable.

There being no further business before the Board, it then, at 8:30 P.M., adjourned *sine die.*

JOHN H. KING,
Colonel Ninth Infantry, President of Board.
W. H. LEWIS,
Lieutenant Colonel Nineteenth Infantry, Member of Board.
LEÓNARD HAY,
First Lieutenant and Adjutant Ninth Infantry, Recorder.

III The Rise in Transborder Interaction

By the 1880s the borderlands were less geographically isolated, and lawlessness had declined in the region as a result of expanded modernization in both Mexico and the United States, paving the way for increased binational interaction. The governments of the dictator Porfirio Díaz (1876–1880 and 1884–1911) succeeded in bringing about greater political stability and economic growth throughout Mexico, especially in the northern states. Foreign investment poured into critical sectors such as the railroads, mining, ranching, and agriculture. Towns and cities in the boundary region emerged as important trade, transportation, and migration centers. To meet the demands of the border population, the Mexican government stimulated commercial activity by creating a free trade zone that functioned from 1885 to 1905. Along the U.S. borderlands, population growth accelerated with the arrival of the railroads, which, by the turn of the century, penetrated deep into the resource-rich zones of the U.S. Southwest and of Mexican states such as Sonora and Chihuahua. Demand for Mexican labor picked up north of the boundary, initiating a process of international migration that continues today.

The essay (Selection 13) included in this section explores United States-driven cultural change in the Sonora borderlands, while the controversy surrounding the *Zona Libre* (Free Zone) is highlighted in two of the section's documents. Selections 14 and 15 present both sides of the debate that the *Zona Libre* spawned in Mexico: Chamber of Deputies member C. Perales, a borderlander, argues for the preservation of free trade, whereas Secretary of the Treasury Matías Romero gives the arguments against continuing that privilege. The last document, Selection 16, which informs the reader about the social and cultural dilemmas faced by border Mexicans who are in close contact with the United States, is drawn from José Vasconcelos's autobiographical work *Ulises criollo*.

13 Miguel Tinker Salas ◆ Sonora:
The Making of a Border Society, 1880–1910

Following the signing of the Gadsden Treaty in 1853, Anglo-American merchants, miners, farmers, and ranchers penetrated the Arizona-Sonora frontier in search of new opportunities. By the late nineteenth century, Sonoran society had developed deep ties with the U.S. economy, and these ties led to increased cultural interaction as well. Historian Miguel Tinker Salas examined these cross-border links in great detail in his doctoral dissertation, "Under the Shadow of the Eagle: Sonora, The Making of a Norteño *Culture, 1880–1910."* In the following article, based on his larger work, Tinker Salas summarizes major changes experienced by Sonorans.*

Before 1848, a confining geography and the presence of a large hostile Indian population shaped the modern history of Sonora. Besides California, Sonora represented Mexico's remote northwestern border. During this early phase of Sonora's history, a frontier way of life took shape as settlers struggled to eke out an existence on the periphery of the Mexican nation. After 1848, social and economic relations with the United States conditioned Sonora's history. This shift shattered Sonora's previous isolation and transformed it from a desolate frontier within Mexico to an international border with the United States. Attracted by its mineral wealth, North American entrepreneurs and miners flocked to the region. In Sonora, contact between two countries, two cultures and two people generated both conflict and accommodation. Opportunities in mining and agriculture also attracted significant numbers of Mexican emigrants to the north, prompting further exchanges. A border lifestyle emerged as the Sonoran *norteño* incorporated new norms and customs. . . .

Moving to Center Stage

From a relative backwater in the Mexican republic, Sonora by the turn of the century had become one of the most prosperous states in Mexico as well as the largest recipient of United States mining investments. By 1902, Americans had invested "$37,500,000 in Sonora, of which over three quarters or $27,800,000 was in mining." By contrast, in the other north-

From *Journal of the Southwest* 34, no. 4 (Winter 1992): 429, 434–41, 443–46, 448–49. Reprinted by permission of Joseph Wilder.
*(University of California, San Diego, 1989).

ern states American investments in mining totaled $21,300,000 in Chihuahua, $13,900,000 in Coahuila, and $11,400,000 in Nuevo León.[1] The presence of German, French, American, British, Spanish, and even Guatemalan consular offices in Hermosillo attested to the state's newfound international importance.[2] Within a few short years, Sonora underwent a visible social transformation, abandoning traditional agriculture and rural life and appearing to embark on the path toward modernization.

For many *norteños*, progress and modernization became synonymous with commercial ties to the United States. This characterization of progress facilitated the rapid diffusion of North American values and customs. The previous frontier life, marked by extreme hardships and a weak economy, offered little attraction. Most elites willingly jettisoned traditional economic ties with European interests and embraced contact with the north. Upper classes readily accepted American customs, utilizing them to augment their traditional cultural repertoire. They saw no contradiction in the incorporation of American foreign customs and norms as part of their Sonoran lifestyle. In everything from education, language, luxury and consumer goods, and even dress, this group looked north. Gradually, common folk also became exposed to foreign influences. The public purchased low-priced American goods, drank St. Louis beer, and developed an interest in playing sports such as baseball. But beyond these limited activities, the material conditions for the widespread dissemination of American culture were not present among the lower socioeconomic stratum of the population. Mexican and Indian labor confronted a labor hierarchy and a dual wage system dominated by Anglo-Americans. As elites sought to differentiate themselves from the common population, cultural preferences increasingly masked social and class differences. Over time the infusion of American norms and customs increased the social distance between northern elites and the common folk.

Completion of the Sonoran railroad in 1882, built by the Atchison-Topeka, linked the port city of Guaymas in the south to the Arizona border in the north, partially ending Sonora's isolation. After years of desolation, many heralded this event as the beginning of a new era in the state. Sonorans, one commentator observed, were being "pushed by the forces of civilization arriving from the north," not from Mexico in the south.[3] As had been predicted, the railroad invigorated the economy by stimulating large-scale mining and commercial agriculture for export to the United States. The arrival of the railroad also turned the tide in the war against the Indians, as it facilitated the movement of government troops through the state.

The construction of the railroad was the culmination of social and economic changes taking place along the Arizona-Sonora border since the 1850s. Beginning in that decade, Sonora initiated the gradual process of economic integration with California and later Arizona. Sonoran merchants and hacendados profited by exporting wheat and other products to the new American territories while laborers migrated to these areas to work. As Mexicans went north, Americans looked south. Attracted by legends of mineral wealth, growing numbers of Americans moved to Arizona and Sonora as word of "untold mineral treasures, vast grazing ranges bathed in sunshine and a new frontier" spread throughout the United States. One miner, Robert Ekey, for example, settled in the area when news of the "opening of a border empire along the Mexican-Arizona border reached California."[4] As had occurred earlier in California, hundreds of Americans now saw Sonora as the new land of opportunity.

As Americans moved in, the state underwent rapid economic changes, forcing its people to grapple with new social issues. The survival of Sonora's regional customs and traditions became a hotly contested subject. In 1881, an editorial in *La Constitución*, the state's official newspaper, summarized Sonora's predicament: "We are in the presence of a great and powerful race, that although friendly tends to absorb us. Without realizing it, we have fallen into the terrible dilemma faced by Hamlet: "To be or not to be."[5] Many Sonorans feared that American economic forces and customs would eventually dominate their state and undermine its culture.[6] To counter the American-sponsored railroad, opponents retraced Sonora previous experience with American filibusters. Consequently, the Sonoran railroad, the principal stimulus of these changes, had many critics. Fierce debates over the implications of a railroad were common in the local press and in the state assembly.[7] Mexico City also feared the implications of Sonora's close ties to the United States. They expressed concern about the political and cultural repercussions of constructing a railroad between an isolated and distant Sonora and its powerful neighbor to the north. President Sebastián Lerdo de Tejada had underscored this concern when, in reference to a railroad between Sonora and the United States, he said that "between a strong nation and a weak one, the best defense is a desert."[8] With [Porfirio] Díaz in the presidency, proponents of the railroad triumphed over their military opponents in Mexico City and commercial adversaries in Sonora.

La Frontera

Prior to 1882, Sonora had no permanent settlements in the area of the future border. Even its *aduanas* (customs houses) were inland at Magdalena and Fronteras. Along the banks of the Río Grande, by comparison, some Mexican settlements dated from the eighteenth century.[9]

These early villages attracted population, evolving their own set of customs and traditions prior to the establishment of an international border.[10] In contrast, border settlements in Sonora developed as a direct consequence of economic exchange with the United States. As the railroad neared completion, new towns, such as Nogales, Sonora, and Nogales, Arizona, appeared along the once unpopulated border. Nogales, Sonora, flourished and within two years it had a population of over one thousand residents, formally becoming a state municipality.[11] From their inception, life in these new communities revolved around their roles as border cities. "Ambos Nogales" prospered as links in the thriving copper mining and commercial trade between Sonora and Arizona. Each settlement depended on the other for its existence. In describing their interdependence, the *Oasis*, a Nogales, Arizona, newspaper, asserted that "we speak of the two towns as one, for they are really such, being divided by an imaginary line only, which passes along the center of the international strip, or more properly speaking street."[12]

Mexican businessmen in Nogales took full advantage of the interdependent border and the *Zona Libre*, which by 1884 included most of the northern states. They imported American fabrics and manufactured clothing in the border region. Afterwards, much to the chagrin of merchants to the south, these products were resold as Mexican goods.[13] Sonorans living on the border also enjoyed the benefits of the *Zona Libre*. They preferred purchasing the bulk of their consumer goods on the American side. Americans walked across to the Sonoran side to buy Parisian fashions at "La Moda," an emporium owned by merchant José Camou, as well as vegetables, fruits, and other foods. Bakers, butchers, and grocers from one side sold their products on the other.[14] Saloons, dance halls, and other establishments of ill repute proliferated in both towns. First-time American visitors to Nogales were urged to "eat and sleep on the Arizona side and drink and smoke on the Mexican side. The purchasing power of the American two-bits doubles on the Mexican side of the line."[15]

Despite the many vicissitudes they faced, out of practical necessity the early residents of "Ambos Nogales" learned to cooperate with each other. Reflecting their mutual interdependence, retailers on both sides formulated an agreement to regulate the hours that stores would be open in order to avoid undue competition and "the mid-day heat."[16] By closing during the noon hour, American businessmen incorporated a Mexican custom. American and Mexican merchants also freely accepted either the peso or the dollar in commercial transactions, a practice frowned upon elsewhere in Arizona.[17] This mutual rapport extended to the government of both cities. Mexican and American leaders, such as A. L. Peck, George Marsh, Edward Titicomb, Anton Proto, Ignacio Bonillas, and Manuel

Mascareñas belonged to the same Masonic lodge and other social clubs, thereby contributing to the social harmony.[18]

Town leaders sought to resolve local matters on a personal basis without involving outside officials from their respective governments. In so doing, they adopted an informal, less structured approach to conducting politics and business affairs. A letter from the leadership of the Masonic lodge of Nogales, Arizona, to Mascareñas, then president of the Nogales, Sonora, city council, recognized:

> that petty international questions are almost unavoidable owing to our peculiar international situation. We believe that such questions, not affecting the dignity of either nation can best be settled among ourselves without involving our respective governments in vexatious international controversies.[19]

As the population grew, border life became more complex. It was not always possible to maintain harmonious relations between "Ambos Nogales." Notwithstanding their collective existence, the two Nogaleses possessed distinct cultures. Although commonly described as "twin sisters," according to the *Arizona Graphic*, a Phoenix magazine, "Ambos Nogales" maintained different public identities, "one blonde and the other brunette."[20] Despite a shared locale, Nogales, Sonora, still represented the traditions of Mexico and Nogales, Arizona, those of the United States.

Border life involved an intricate balance of diverse cultures and interests. With no physical obstacle to bar contact between the two towns, conflicts between individuals frequently spilled over the border. Clashes along the border included arguments between estranged couples, common fistfights, disagreements between business partners, and on occasion, even major international confrontations such as those that occurred during the Mexican Revolution. Local government officials, Mexican and American, repeatedly interceded in disputes between Sonorans and Arizonans. If not resolved quickly, petty personal clashes between Mexicans and Americans could easily escalate into international incidents.

As friction persisted, Sonoran officials proposed various solutions to lessen the likelihood of direct contact between Americans and Mexicans. In the aftermath of one 1887 fracas involving a Mexican colonel and his disaffected mistress, the governor of Sonora, Luis Torres, proposed to President Díaz that the federal government establish a special vacant zone of approximately 100 meters, on the Mexican side, between the two towns, in order to prevent future confrontations.[21] In the wake of another "border incident" at Naco in 1899, Mexican consul Mascareñas proposed the construction of a "steel fence between neighboring border cities" in order to prevent potential conflicts.[22] According to Mascareñas, in addition to limiting conflict, the fence would end "jurisdictional problems on the border, deter contraband, and prevent cattle rustling."[23] President Díaz rejected any unilateral proposals indicating that it was ill advised to cede any land which Americans might later claim as theirs.[24]

The construction of a fence along the border would not have impeded the spread of cultural norms between these towns. American customs became common practice on the Mexican side, while traditional Sonoran ways of life soon became part of the culture of Anglo-Americans living in Arizona. Americans adopted a host of social and national celebrations common in Sonora.[25] In 1898 large numbers of Americans attended a Mexican circus performance in Nogales, Sonora.[26] During Christmas, Americans frequented events such as dances and posadas which were held on the other side or "el otro lado."[27] With little previous tradition in Arizona to rely upon, many Anglo-Americans willingly adapted to Mexican culture.

Having arisen simultaneously, neither town had a long history of established conventions. "Ambos Nogales" borrowed from each other, but they also created a cultural fusion where new practices emerged. In 1895, for example, "Ambos Nogales" jointly celebrated a Latin American carnival. Promoters on the American side compared the border carnival to New Orleans' Mardi Gras and launched a campaign to attract tourists from throughout the southwest United States. Accordingly, they announced that "the fiesta will be remarkably successful and will draw a large concourse of people from all parts of Arizona, New Mexico, and Sonora . . ."[28] The sight of Americans and Mexicans dressed in costumes, riding on "carros alegóricos" or floats and "throwing flour on each other" even attracted the attention of the *New York Times*, which described the event as "an international episode of the most commendable sort."[29] For Nogales elites, the maintenance of amicable relations between both towns provided the foundation for continued economic prosperity.

Besides Nogales, mining and business development along the border led to the founding of other towns, such as Naco and Agua Prieta. American counterparts to these settlements soon followed. Opposite Naco, Sonora, appeared Naco, Arizona, and alongside Agua Prieta, Sonora, sprang up Douglas, Arizona. These towns underwent similar modifications in the organization of everyday life. For instance, during a *visita* (official inspection) in 1901, the district prefect reported that in Naco few people used the metric system, lots for houses had been measured in feet, and merchants sold goods by the pound, not the kilo. Signs in stores, cantinas, and hotels appeared in English, not Spanish. Merchants charged for their goods in *oro* (American dollars), not Mexican pesos.[30] Fearing a loss of sovereignty and foreign cultural dominance, the prefect ordered that all tracts be remeasured in meters and that English signs be taken down. The situation at Agua Prieta paralleled that of Naco. . . .

Culture and Language

In areas where Americans concentrated, such as Cananea in the north, La Colorada in the central region, and Empalme (called Junction City by Americans) in the south, they sought to recreate their former lifestyle. In these economic and cultural enclaves, they organized baseball teams and celebrated holidays such as Thanksgiving and the Germanic version of Christmas. The Guaymas newspaper, *El Nacional*, reported that "in Empalme, American families are hosting a magnificent feast to which many people have been invited. Turkeys, ready to go into the oven, are on their way from Kansas, Los Angeles, and Phoenix in refrigerated cars."[31] In Cananea, the mining company observed Thanksgiving as an official holiday. The *Cananea Herald* announced that "Thursday and Friday of this week will be observed as Thanksgiving holiday."[32] Celebrations of this sort included primarily Sonoran middle and upper classes.

Thanksgiving continued to be totally foreign to most Mexicans and never gained a strong following in the state. The American rendition of Christmas, however, which included the evergreen tree and the sharing of gifts on December twenty-fifth, touched a sympathetic chord in Sonora. Americans invited Mexican notables and officials to their celebrations and slowly this group imitated these customs. In border communities such as Nogales, the evergreen tree became a symbol of the Christmas spirit for broader segments of the population. In 1894, for example, residents of Nogales, Sonora, held parties to raise funds to purchase a Christmas tree to display at the city's central plaza.[33] Hoping to take advantage of the new spirit, stores on both sides of the line held special Christmas sales. According to the *Imparcial*, a Guaymas newspaper, northerners celebrated Christmas "in the American fashion."[34] By emphasizing the American practice, the Latin American tradition of exchanging gifts on January 6th, the Feast of the Epiphany, slowly lost its traditional popularity.

In addition to adopting new and different holidays, Sonorans developed an affinity for American sports, in particular, baseball. The origins of baseball in Sonora are traced to American sailors who played the game while on leave in the port city of Guaymas in the 1870s. Reportedly, Mexican children who watched the sailors began to play it themselves. Gradually, the game spread to the major towns in the state, especially to those where Americans lived, such as Nogales and Cananea. In Empalme and Guaymas, railroad workers formed teams that included Americans and Mexicans.[35] Travel by railroad facilitated games between cities and gradually a statewide league took shape. The language of the game soon developed a decidedly Spanish intonation. Spanish adaptations of terms such as *un honron, un picher, un strike, el manager*, and *un cacheo* became commonplace. The popularity of baseball contributed to the social cohesion of many Sonoran communities. It provided a common bond and increased the opportunity for interaction between different social classes.

For aspiring groups, Sonoran economic and social ties with the United States made learning English an imperative and the number of schools offering it soon increased.[36] Private schools had previously offered English instruction, although it had not been given a priority, being taught along with French and, to a lesser extent, Latin.[37] The practical benefits associated with English caused Sonoran upper and middle classes to frown upon the learning of Romance languages. The Guaymas newspaper *El Noticioso*, for example, argued that learning English was for the "fronterizos [people of the border] a real avocation, because young people who speak it are assured good paying jobs in any business."[38]

Depending on their financial status, families eager to have their children learn English sent them off to Catholic boarding schools in the United States and Mexico City. Schools in California, such as the Santa Catalina Girls School, regularly advertised their services in the Sonoran press.[39] In 1888, Mascareñas, while a city councilman of Nogales, Sonora, sent his children to school in Los Angeles in order to further their education and, above all, for them to learn English.[40] The merchant José Camou of Hermosillo and Alejandro Ainslie, the editor of the state's official newspaper *La Constitución*, sent their children to Mexico City for an education and to master English.[41] Many parents, unfamiliar with the north, preferred sending their children to Mexico City where business associates or relatives could look after them. Those who did not have ties in Los Angeles or Mexico City enrolled them in the recently established University of Arizona at Tucson, or in one of the many public and private institutions which taught English in the state.

In Sonora, English became the language of business, and elites incorporated it into their vocabulary.[42] Correspondence from Cristina Camou in Mexico City to her father José in Hermosillo contained a smattering of English, while his letters to her began "Dear Chamaca."[43] Knowledge of English opened doors, improved employment opportunities, and, many believed, raised one's social standing. The ability to speak French and Latin offered no such practical advantages. When a priest at a Los Angeles school, for example, attempted to teach councilman Mascareñas' children Latin and Greek, he objected, saying that these "dead languages . . . were of no use in Sonora." According to Mascareñas, time spent learning

Greek or Latin could be put to better use learning "accounting or other matters of importance to their careers."[44]

By the 1880s, English had become common within business circles. Its use in commercial transactions and mining contracts became a concern for Sonoran officials worried about the legal and cultural ramifications that foreign language dominance could produce in the state. In 1881 the governor of the state prohibited its use in official documents and private contracts. To add teeth to the decree, the state government refused to recognize the legality of contracts not written in Spanish. Also due to growing American influence, the state in 1884 established "the metric system as the only valid measurement in commerce and real estate."[45] Yet English steadily gained popularity, gradually permeating the Spanish vocabulary, ensuring its commonplace use. Government officials, at all levels, continued receiving correspondence in English and had to either learn the language or employ translators.[46]. . .

Language was only one expression of the broader changes taking place in this northern Mexican society. The incorporation of language also led to the modification of values and patterns of doing business. Many firms, for example, began to publicize that they conducted business in the "American style." Bakeries represented their establishments as "Panaderías Americanas," that sold *quekis* (cakes), a word still heard in Sonora today.[47] Butchers purported to be "Carnicería Estilo Americano" (American style) and offered thick American cuts of beef rather than thinly sliced Mexican steaks. Hotels, such as the California in Guaymas, managed by a young Plutarco Elías Calles, advertised "Modern American style," which meant private lavatories, showers, a pool hall, a dining room, and a bar.[48] Similarly, many restaurants claimed to serve American-style food. Ironically, one establishment, a drugstore with a very patriotic name, the "Botica de México de Benito Juárez," advertised American, English, French, and German remedies, though not Mexican drugs.[49] Although on the surface these changes appear minor, their accumulative effect began to reshape the tastes and customs of middle- and upper-class *norteños*. For many Sonoran social groups, the United States rather than Mexico became their cultural point of reference.

Changes in language and manner of conducting business were not without their critics. The constant use of English, according to some commentators, corrupted the Spanish language and the culture of Sonora. For instance, a columnist for *El Imparcial* promised his readers that in his articles "you will not find phrases such as chic, sports, creme and other foreign words which are used by pedantic persons who want to appear well versed in three or four languages, but who in reality wind up butchering their own."[50] The writer for *El Imparcial* pledged to use only Spanish. Such ridicule, however, did not seem to carry much weight among notables, and the use of English continued to spread. When Sonoran caudillo Luis Torres decided to rent his home in Hermosillo, the ad in the local newspaper appeared in English.[51] As the use of English became popularized throughout Sonora it underwent modification and increasingly developed a Spanish intonation. In keeping with Spanish grammar, English words were written the way they sounded. For example, names such as Hughes, became "Hugues," words like thrift store became "trist store," discount became "descount," and fancy, "fancey."[52] Sonorans' Spanish adaptation of English guaranteed its permanent place in the state's vocabulary.

Notes

1. *Annual Report of the Commercial Relations between United States and Foreign Nations*, North America: Mexico (Washington, DC: Government Printing Office, 1903), pp. 436–39. Reporting Year 1902.

2. Archivo del Boletín Oficial (hereafter A.B.O.), *La Constitución*, August 3, 1883 n.32, p. 4. Notice regarding opening of new consulates. Archivo Histórico del Gobierno del Estado de Sonora (hereafter A.H.G.E.S.), Carpeton 13. Don León Gutiérrez named Spanish consul in Guaymas, April 14, 1879, Sec. Relaciones Exteriores.

3. A.B.O., "La prensa en Sonora," *La Constitución*, August 15, 1881, n.4, p. 3.

4. Arizona Historical Society, Tucson (hereafter A.H.S.), Biographical File, Ada E. Jones, ms-389, p. 2, folder 9.

5. A.B.O., *La Constitución*, June 4, 1881, n.27, p. 4, "Quien vencerá siempre es el progreso." "To be or not to be" appeared in English.

6. See A.B.O., "Gacetilla, El Ferrocarril," *La Constitución*, April 29, 1880; Tomo II, n.17, pp. 3–4.

7. See for example, A.B.O., "Profecía del diputado Lemus," *La Estrella de Occidente*, December 10, 1869, p. 4.

8. Sebastián Lerdo de Tejada, cited in David Pletcher, "The Development of Railroads in Sonora," *Inter-American Economic Affairs* 1, 4 (1948): 15.

9. See Gilberto Miguel Hinojosa, *A Borderlands Town in Transition: Laredo, 1755–1870* (College Station: Texas A & M Press, 1983) and Arnoldo de León, *The Tejano Community* (Albuquerque: University of New Mexico Press, 1982).

10. For Paso del Norte see Oscar J. Martínez, *Border Boom Town: Ciudad Juárez since 1848* (Austin: University of Texas Press, 1978), p. 12.

11. A.B.O., *La Constitución*, July 11, 1884, Tomo VI, n.29, p. 3. Publication of law which decreed Municipality of Nogales, Sonora.

12. *Oasis*, May 13, 1899, p. 2.

13. A.H.G.E.S., Tomo 1625, May 19, 1900. Petition from the residents and merchants of Santa Cruz, in opposition to the *Zona Libre*.

14. A.H.G.E.S., *La Justicia*, March 29, 1914, Tomo I, n.121, p. 1. During the revolution, the border was periodically closed. The newspaper lamented the effects of the closure on Sonora's border merchants, in particular, grocery stores who depended on this trade.

15. A.H.S., *Arizona Graphic*, October 7, 1899, Vol. I, n.4, p. 2.

16. *Oasis*, July 9, 1909, Vol. III, n.9, p. 4.

17. A.H.G.E.S., *El Monitor*, Nogales, Arizona, May 13, 1899; Año VIII, n.1, p. 2.

18. Pimeria Alta Historical Society, Ephemeral Collection, "Societies, Mormons," Records of Nogales, Arizona, Masonic Lodge II, charter August 6, 1892.

19. Special Collections, University of Arizona (hereafter S.C.U.A.), ms-14, box 5, folder 3, August 21, 1893. Free and Accepted Order of Masons, Nogales Lodge 11 of F.A.M. to Manuel Mascareñas.

20. A.H.S., *Arizona Graphic*, Phoenix, Arizona, October 7, 1899, Vol. I, n.4, p. 1.

21. Archivo Porfirio Díaz (hereafter A.P.D.), L12, C5, n.002452, March 25, 1887. Luis Torres to Porfirio Díaz.

22. S.C.U.A., Manuel Mascareñas, ms-14, box 5, folder 6, December 21, 1899. Mascareñas to Ignacio Mariscal, Foreign Relations, Mexico. Also in A.H.G.E.S., Tomo 1567, March 1, 1900. Consul of Nogales to Governor of Sonora.

23. Ibid.

24. A.P.D., L12, C5, n.002452, March 25, 1887. Díaz to Torres.

25. *Oasis*, May 15, 1899, p. 2.

26. *Oasis*, April 18, 1898, p. 2.

27. *Oasis*, December 6, 1894, p. 5.

28. *Oasis*, January 19, 1895, p. 4.

29. *New York Times*, March 24, 1895, 29:6.

30. A.H.G.E.S., Tomo 1695, March 22, 1901, exp. 1. District Prefect of Arizpe Ramón Cardena to Governor of Sonora.

31. *El Nacional*, Guaymas, November 12, 1912, n.18. "Thanksgiving Day Announcement."

32. A.H.G.E.S., *Cananea Herald-Heraldo*, November 25, 1907, Vol. VI, n.13, p. 1. Also *El Correo de Sonora*, November 19, 1901, Año IV, n.1075, p. 3. The American Proclamation of Thanksgiving appeared in the Sonoran press.

33. *Oasis*, December 6, 1894, p. 5.

34. *El Imparcial*, Guaymas, December 27, 1909, n.1209, p. 3.

35. See Miguel S. Durazo, *El beisbol en Sonora* (Hermosillo: Durazo, 1956), p. 10.

36. A.B.O., *La Estrella de Occidente*, January 15, 1869, p. 4. The paper carried an ad for a "new" English school run by Carlos F. Gompertz in the home of Florencio Monteverde. In Alamos, to the south, another English school opened later that same year.

37. Biblioteca Central de la Universidad de Sonora, Colección Pesqueira, Tomo III, 1851–1856, November 18, 1852. Announcement of classes offered by the Colegio de Sonora.

38. A.H.G.E.S., Periódicos, *El Noticioso*, Guaymas, July 27, 1910, Año XI, p. 1.

39. A.B.O., *La Constitución*, Several, November 11, 1880, p. 3, and February 11, 1887, Tomo IV, p. 4.

40. S.C.U.A., Manuel Mascareñas ms-14, n.14, August 7, 1888. Manuel Mascareñas to Rafael Ruiz.

41. Archivo Histórico del Museo Regional de la Universidad de Sonora (hereafter A.H.M.R.U.S.), Cartas Camou, n.44–46, November 16, 1888. José Camou

to his children Eugenio and Ernesto in Mexico City. A.H.G.E.S., Periódicos, *La Libertad*, Guaymas, July 2, 1902, n.105.

42. S.C.U.A., Manuel Mascareñas, September 18, 1888, ms-14, n.39. Mascareñas congratulated his children for their letters in English.

43. See A.H.M.R.U.S., Cartas Camou, April 4, 1906.

44. S.C.U.A., Manuel Mascareñas, ms-14, n.472, December 14, 1890. Mascareñas to Don Mariano Roman in San Francisco, California.

45. A.B.O., *La Constitución*, January 25, 1884, Tomo VI, n.4, p. 1. The actual decree was promulgated on December 14, 1883.

46. See for example, A.H.G.E.S., Carpeton 454, July 30, 1856. Letter from Charles P. Stone to Governor Pesqueira, translated and certified by Tomas Robinson.

47. A.H.G.E.S., *El Heraldo de Cananea*, February 1, 1903, Vol. I, n.2, p. 2, and *El Heraldo de Cananea*, October 28, 1905, Vol. IV, n.8, p. 2.

48. A.H.G.E.S., Periódicos, *La Libertad*, Guaymas, April 26, 1902, n.95. Advertisement Hotel California "Estilo Moderno Americano" or Modern American Style. Also see Gilberto Escobosa Gamez, *Cronicas, cuentos y leyendas sonorenses* (Hermosillo: Gobierno del Estado de Sonora, 1984), p. 33.

49. A.H.M.R.U.S., Periódicos, *El Hogar Católico*, Hermosillo, January 1, 1903, Tomo I, n.1, p. 1.

50. A.H.G.E.S., Periódicos, *El Imparcial*, Guaymas, October 22, 1892, Tomo III, n.159, p. 1.

51. A.H.G.E.S., Tomo 2559, *La Constitución*, December 12, 1910, Tomo XLI, n.5, p. 3. The ad reads: "For Rent, A very beautiful home on the outskirts of town, seven rooms and kitchen, fine garden, roses, apply to Luis E. Torres."

52. A.H.G.E.S., *Sonora Moderno*, March 11, 1905, p. 1. Advertisement for a "Thrift Store" in Magdalena used: "Staples and Fancey Groceries, Descounts."

14 C. Perales ◆ Why the Border Needs the Free Zone

Free trade began on the border in 1858, when the state of Tamaulipas created a Zona Libre, *or Free Zone, along its boundary with Texas. In 1885 the central government in Mexico City sanctioned free trade along the entire border, but opposition led to the zone's demise in 1905.*

Early in its existence the Free Zone came under attack from Mexicans living in the interior. Merchants resented the advantages enjoyed by their border competitors, and government officials complained of lost revenues in uncollected tariffs. C. Perales, a borderlander and member of the Chamber of Deputies (Mexico's House of Representatives) defended free trade in a debate in 1869. In his statement he reflects on the difficult conditions that prevailed on the Tamaulipas frontier between 1848 and 1858 and on the beneficial changes that occurred after the creation of the Zona Libre.

The Congress will not be surprised to hear me speak on the important matter of the Free Zone. As a son of the border, my duty obligates me to be an advocate on behalf of that part of the nation. . . .

The Free Zone is a question of life or death for the border population, and especially for the people who live adjacent to the Rio Bravo [Rio Grande] in the state of Tamaulipas. This has been so since 1848, when our usurping neighbors advanced to the Bravo, when the military camps established by Generals Zachary Taylor and Winfield Scott opposite our towns of Matamoros, Reynosa, Camargo, and Mier spawned American settlements which were later adjudicated to the United States by the famous Treaty of Guadalupe Hidalgo. This has been so since the government of the United States announced that the products of the whole world would be free of any tariffs merely by touching the ground that the United States had conquered. From that moment on the cities and towns on the Tamaulipas border found themselves in an exceptional situation relative to other centers in the Mexican republic.

The city of Brownsville blossomed as if by magic. What was formerly a deserted beach overnight became a flourishing area intent on swallowing, with its boa-like breath, the Mexican towns which, because of [unfavorable Mexican] fiscal policies, could not participate in the progressive and civilizing commercial feast. Brownsville and the other American towns received life from robust commercial privileges, enjoying the

From statement to Chamber of Deputies, September 13, 1869. Reprinted in Ulises Irigoyen, ed., *El problema económico de las fronteras mexicanas*, 2 vols. (Mexico City, 1935), excerpted from 1:39–43, trans. Oscar J. Martínez.

vigor of youth and possessing all the necessary things to become centers of population.

Free commerce in Brownsville attracted thousands of fortunes and thousands of individuals. Those Mexicans who sought a comfortable life went to live under the pavilion of the north by crossing into the left bank of the Rio Bravo; and those who, because of love of country did not wish to abandon their homeland, chose to starve or to survive as smugglers. There was a time when patriotic Mexicans seeking to feed their families were shot by customs guards from Matamoros, who had been placed there by the government to prevent smuggling. I am against criticizing those departed officers who abused the people, but this body needs to remember the horrible inequities produced by the commercial restrictions that were imposed on our northern border.

During the span of ten sad years, from 1848 to 1858, our border became depopulated. All the hard-working people who had given life to industrial activity disappeared completely because of the miserable situation to which they were subjected in their homes. Those Mexicans who did not reside in Brownsville or other American towns lived a nomadic life in the mountains as smugglers, eluding the customs guards. The rest, those who remained in their homes, lived under miserable conditions and were constantly under surveillance. They were not worthy of being classified as a social entity.

Crossing into the United States to buy pieces of cloth with which to make clothes for a family was considered a perverted act, even if one had a permit for doing so. Importing sugar, flour, lard, potatoes, and other basic necessities without paying the appropriate Mexican duties was a grave offense. While Brownsville allowed unobstructed trade, Matamoros and other Mexican towns had all kinds of restrictions and inconveniences to prevent their development. In Brownsville shopping could be carried out with complete freedom, without having spies and censors checking what servants and laborers bought for the subsistence of their employers or their families. The people of Matamoros could not even buy a bowl of lentils in Brownsville without having to pay duty on it when crossing the border. If they failed to declare it they were labeled as smugglers and sent to prison. The choice for my countrymen during those ten years was to leave Mexico or become smugglers.

In 1858 we had a governor [in Tamaulipas], Licenciado Guerra, who was willing to be labeled a criminal to prevent the ruin of our border area. He established free trade on the right bank of the Rio Bravo. After the creation of the Free Zone, smuggling [into the Mexican border zone] ceased to exist because there was nothing left to encourage it. Goods sold in Brownsville lost their appeal because they could be purchased in Mexico at the same or even lower price. Before the advent of the Free Zone, poverty, depression, and low spirits prevailed on the right bank of the Rio Bravo, but afterward there was activity, well-being, and progress. Mexican businessmen used to cross into the United States to make their purchases and then avoided paying ever-rising tariffs in Mexico; after the Free Zone they had no need to spend their fortunes in American establishments or to defraud the Mexican treasury.

With equality in commerce, truly a necessary thing in that part of the nation, emigration of Mexicans to the United States ceased, poverty ended, and a state of well-being was reestablished. The customs house in Matamoros collected more revenues. Traffic to Brownsville declined because of the inconvenience of crossing the Rio Bravo and making transactions in a different language and culture. Matamoros became the most dynamic commercial center along the border. As if by magic, Matamoros grew from ten thousand residents in 1858 to twenty thousand today (1869).

Do we need better evidence to judge that the Free Zone is not injurious to honest commerce? I do not think that is necessary. Free trade has destroyed smuggling, has caused our border towns to flourish, and has increased customs' revenues. Ten years of experience justifies what I say. The Free Zone is not only convenient for the progress of a few border communities but also useful and necessary for the whole country.

15 Matías Romero ◆
Why the Free Zone Should Not Exist

*Matías Romero, Mexico's secretary of the treasury, led the opposition to
the Tamaulipas* Zona Libre, *and to its possible extension to other border
areas, during the 1869 debate in the Chamber of Deputies. In his statement, Romero expresses concern about smuggling in the interior and its
harm to legal commerce. He also offers alternative means of dealing with
border economic conditions should the government decide to eliminate
free trade. Nevertheless, the* Zona Libre *continued to exist and was even
expanded borderwide in 1885. It was finally abolished in 1905
following prolonged internal as well as external opposition.*

It is difficult for me to be here to oppose an institution that has constitu-
encies, that seems to enjoy the support of a considerable number of
deputies, and that is grounded in considerations that are worth noting.
The president has studied the issue of the Free Zone in detail, and after a
long assessment he believes it is his duty to inform you, through me, that
in his judgment there are many serious and grave problems, not only in
terms of extending the Free Zone [to other border areas], as has been
proposed, but even to maintain it where it exists now.

It is necessary to keep in mind, above everything else, that the
Tamaulipas Free Zone is a privilege, and that the constitution prohibits
all privileges. It seems doubtful that if it were extended along the entire
border it would cease to be a privilege. But there is no doubt whatever
that, as constituted now, in only one part of the border, it would continue
to be a privilege.

If, confined as it is now to the state of Tamaulipas, it has created so
many problems, what would happen if we were to extend it to Coahuila
and Chihuahua, as some are proposing? What about if the Free Zone were
extended to Sonora and Baja California, as it necessarily would be since
its representatives would of course request it. Congress would not find a
reason to deny some states what it had conceded to others.

Congress well knows that the smuggling that goes on on the
Tamaulipas border in the shadow of the Free Zone is unnecessary. Goods
imported into the Free Zone make their way to San Luis Potosí, where
they compete with goods imported through the [Mexican] Gulf ports,

From statement to Chamber of Deputies, September 13, 1869. Reprinted in
Ulises Irigoyen, ed., *El problema económico de las fronteras mexicanas*, 2 vols.
(Mexico City, 1935), excerpted from vol. 1:43–46, trans. Oscar J. Martínez.

bringing ruin to honest commerce and to [the collection of] public revenues. Such [nontaxed, smuggled] products even reach Mexico City, where they compete with goods imported through Veracruz.

It is true that by increasing our customs enforcement this contraband could be made more difficult and even curtailed in part, and the administration has requested the necessary authorization to bring that about. But the results of greater enforcement will never be totally satisfactory. That was tried in the past, and smuggling continued on a great scale. The vast length of the Tamaulipas border and the sparseness of the population would make it necessary to deploy so many agents that the costs would exceed the ability of the nation to cover them.

If the Tamaulipas Free Zone continues to function, it is certain that the competition between smuggled products and those imported legally will continue. Such competition serves to convert honest importers into smugglers, reduces public revenues, and creates many inconveniences and problems. And if all this is happening now in one Free Zone confined to only one border state, in what proportion would these dangers and problems increase if it should be granted to the other border states? If preventing smuggling in Tamaulipas is so difficult now, how much more difficult would it be once the Free Zone was extended the length of the border? How large would our defenses need to be?

I would not communicate completely the ideas of the president on this matter if I did not say that he is the first to understand the precarious situation that our border residents face and the necessity of the federal government to protect them. If the tariff law is declared in force on the Tamaulipas border, it is true that the people on the Mexican side will find themselves in worse conditions than their counterparts across the border. The former will have to pay duties in cash [on the spot] on their imported merchandise, while the latter will have the benefit of delayed payment and bonded warehouses where such merchandise can be temporarily deposited. On the other hand, residents on the Mexican side will have the advantage of paying lower tarrifs [extant on the Tamaulipas border] than residents on the other side.

Perhaps the simplest way to solve the problem would be to equalize conditions between our side and theirs by establishing points of deposit [i.e., bonded warehouses] in Mexico such as exist in the United States. Further, the president certainly would authorize the free importation of some basic necessities like livestock, foodstuffs, and other items destined for consumption by the border population. In this manner, residents on the border will get the protection they desire without harming the interests of other Mexicans. Anything else beyond that would increase considerably the evils that exist now.

16 José Vasconcelos ◆ A Mexican Schoolboy's Experiences in Eagle Pass, Texas

Despite the improved relations between Mexico and the United States in the late nineteenth and early twentieth centuries, national and ethnic rivalries remained deeply embedded in both societies. Anglo-Americans continued to believe themselves to be superior to Mexicans and to act on that belief; that attitude exacerbated the bitterness felt by Mexicans over the territories they had lost to the United States in the midnineteenth century as well as over other American acts of aggression. Animosities surfaced with regularity in schools in the U.S. borderlands, as José Vasconcelos eloquently relates in this excerpt from his autobiography, Ulises criollo. Vasconcelos (1882–1959) was a prominent educator, philosopher, author, and politician in Mexico.

Piedras Negras [Mexico, opposite Eagle Pass, Texas] was a prosperous town, but it lacked a good school. On the other side of the border, the Yankees matched their concern with material progress with careful attention to education. Because of that my family moved to Eagle Pass when I was about ten years old.

It was not a time of official espionage or strict border inspections. It cost a coin to cross the international bridge, and the guards from both countries would merely look at the packages carried by border crossers without inquiring about their identities. [When the bridge first opened many official] reciprocal visits took place. But the ordinary people kept their distance. Those in Piedras Negras declined to visit Eagle Pass and those in Eagle Pass didn't venture into the land of the "greasers." At that time there were real fights between the rabble who lived adjacent to the river. Racial hatred and the memory of the war of 1847 kept the rancor alive. Yelling "greasers" or "gringos" was enough to produce bloody clashes.

My first experience in the Eagle Pass school was a bitter one. I saw American and Mexican children seated in front of a teacher whose language I didn't understand. Suddenly the kid seated closest to me, a bilingual *tejanito*, said to me, "Hey, how many of these guys can you beat up?" I didn't understand what he was talking about, and he continued, "Can you take on Jack?" and he pointed to a red-haired boy. After looking at him I replied modestly that I couldn't. "What about Johnny, and

From *Ulises criollo*, 2 vols. (Mexico City: Ediciones Botas, 1945), 1:22, 24–27, 29–33, trans. Oscar J. Martínez.

Bill?" Irritated at his persistence, I riskily said yes. The targeted one was a freckled boy more or less my size. I thought there was nothing else I could do.

When we went to recess a circle formed. Some students came close to take a look at me, others shook my hand, and several of them pushed me. Then my neighbor the *tejanito* yelled, "This guy says he can lick Tom." They immediately brought us face to face and drew a line between us. Whoever stepped on it first was the braver one. We lunged forward, not at the line but at each other, and we started hitting. Then we paused and observed each other, then started fighting again. Finally we were separated.

A few weeks later, a small and chubby new boy who didn't want to fight was pushed and slapped around by the group until they made him cry. The incident angered me, and, being shy and sad by nature, I withdrew.

As soon as we found an acceptable place to live we moved to Piedras Negras. My family was glad to get away from Eagle Pass. To get to school [in Eagle Pass] I now had to cross the international bridge and walk an additional two or three blocks. It was almost a kilometer. There were moments when it seemed the bridge would collapse when the wind hit it. I thought I might be swept out into the emptiness.

Recesses at school often degenerated into field battles. We would scatter into the ravines by the river and march through the thicket. We would play "follow the leader." When rival groups encountered each other rock fights would follow. The idea was to aim at the feet, but invariably there would be someone who would get hit on the head. Confrontations became worse if by chance rival bands consisted entirely of Mexicans and Yankees.

School won me over gradually. I came to like it better than the best recreation. I never missed class. One of the teachers would test our mental quickness by giving us math problems, and the first one to figure out the answer would yell it out. We had similar spelling exercises. Periodically we would have competitions. I won a spelling contest on geography, but there was a certain guile. My Anglo classmates could not spell "Tenochtitlán" [ancient Mexico City] and "Popocatepetl" [major volcano]. When they complained, I replied, "Don't you think spelling 'Washington' is hard for me?"

The teacher's equanimity manifested itself in the arguments that erupted when the history of Texas came up. We discussed issues in a democratic manner; the teacher confined herself to directing the debates. Texas independence and the war of 1847 divided the class into rival camps. We constantly talked about the Alamo, the cruel executions carried on by

Santa Anna, and the [treatment of] prisoners of war. There were only a few Mexicans in the class, but we were determined [to defend Mexico]. When I refer to Mexicans I include many who, despite their residence in Texas and their parents' U.S. citizenship, sided with me because of ethnic affinity. Had they done otherwise they would have still been considered Mexicans because Anglos labeled them as such. Full-fledged Mexicans rarely went to that school. For years I was the only one.

I never felt obligated to make excuses [about Mexican history or Mexican society]. But when it was affirmed in class that one hundred Yankees could chase off one thousand Mexicans, I would rise and say, "That isn't true." I would get even more angry when someone would assert, "Mexicans are a semicivilized people." At home I always heard the opposite, that it was the Yankees who were the newcomers to culture. I would rise and say, "We had a printing press before you did." The teacher would intervene, remarking [to the other students], "But look at Joe [José Vasconcelos]. He is a Mexican. Isn't he civilized? Isn't he a gentleman?" For the moment, that just observation would reestablish cordiality. But that would last only until the next lesson, until we would again read in our textbook phrases and judgments that drove me to ask for permission to refute them. Passions would rise anew. We would make challenging signs to each other. At first I would only have to remain alert in class and be ready to launch my verbal defenses. The other Mexicans would support me and take care of my rivals; during school holidays they would fight with them.

But the conflict grew and became personalized. A sanguinary, aggressive, blond gringo took a dislike toward me. The predictable argument over Mexican valor ended up with the remark, "We'll see about that outside." As soon as school finished we headed to the adjacent field. A large group followed, forming a circle. We started hitting each other with rage. From the beginning I got the worst of it. In order to keep his fists away from my face I grabbed him and tried to knock him down. He bloodied my nose. I lost control and started kicking and scratching. But he kept punishing me systematically.

It was customary that the loser would say, "That's enough." At that point the fight would end and the adversaries would shake hands, just like in the ring. My friends were shouting, "Give up, that's enough." But my ire made me forget my wounds; I didn't feel the pain, even though I was bleeding. Finally the teacher arrived and separated us. Because there was no shaking of hands, the matter was not resolved. I was in terrible shape. My face was excoriated, scraped, and swollen.

As I crossed the bridge on my way home I thought of the story I would make up to explain my condition. I decided to say I had fallen off a cliff. My mother took care of me and accepted my story, or pretended she did. But when my father arrived all hell broke loose. He said, "Surely it was someone much bigger than you. This is a savagery. I will complain to the consulate. You will not return to that school." The following morning, however, no one said to me, "Don't go to school." I followed the same route as always, alone.

At lunchtime, as I thought bitterly about my defeat the day before, one of my Mexican friends handed me a big knife, saying, "I'll lend it to you. Save it for this afternoon. These gringos are afraid of 'iron.' " We returned to the classroom. The teacher gently avoided any reference to subjects that might incite anger. The class returned to normal. I kept touching the instrument in my pocket. When school was over, Jim, the guy who had defeated me, stood in front of his group. Accompanied by my group, I approached him and gave him a sign, inviting him to fight, simultaneously flashing the knife I held in my right hand. "No, not that way," said Jim. I said, "You go look for one." He replied, "No, Joe, not like that. If you want to, let's fight like yesterday." I said, "No, not like yesterday, like now." My friend then came over for his knife, saying, "You see, you see. . . . Buy yourself one of these, and make sure they know that you always carry it with you. These gringos will never bother you again."

It was a good thing that I [finally] won their [the gringos'] respect, because the classes fascinated me. One of the books that we read that especially caught my interest was *The Fair God*, a novel that dealt with the conquest of Mexico. It was very interesting that the North Americans, who so jealously guarded their privileges as a white caste, when it came to Mexico . . . always sympathized with the Indians and never with the [white] Spaniards. The thesis of the barbarous Spaniard and the noble Indian was not only taught in Mexican schools; it was also taught in Yankee schools. At that time I didn't suspect that our own textbooks were nothing but paraphrases of Yankee texts and instruments for introducing new influences [into Mexico].

IV The Mexican Revolution

The 1910s stand out as one of the most tumultuous periods in the history of Mexico. Revolution swept the land, resulting in considerable restructuring of society. Northern Mexico, especially the border region, witnessed many battles that brought to it physical destruction, economic disruption, and displacement of population. Communities such as Ciudad Juárez became prime targets for the contending factions because control of an international port translated into access to tariff revenues and armaments from the United States. Much of the national revolutionary leadership hailed from El Norte, including Francisco Madero, Venustiano Carranza, Alvaro Obregón, Pascual Orozco, and the famous rebel-bandit Francisco "Pancho" Villa. Through abundant press accounts, Americans became well acquainted with these men and with the revolution itself. The Mexican borderlands, then, along with key communities north of the boundary that were used by rebels for asylum, to organize new campaigns, and to enlist Mexican Americans in revolutionary activity, played a highly significant role in the drama that unfolded in Mexico in the early years of the twentieth century.

Essay Selections 17 and 18 focus on events in El Paso-Ciudad Juárez and along the Arizona-Sonora border, respectively. Documents incude the story of a political activist (Selection 19), a seditious plan that urged border Mexicans and Chicanos to take up arms against U.S. authorities (Selection 20), and a denunciation by a Chicano lawyer of the modus operandi of the Texas Rangers (Selection 21).

17 Mardee Belding de Wetter ◆
Revolutionary El Paso, 1910–11

Because of its strategic location on the border and on the most important
railroad line between the United States and Mexico, the El Paso-Ciudad
Juárez area was highly valued by both government troops and revolu-
tionaries. Thus, these twin cities held the spotlight in the initial phase of
the Mexican Revolution and were abuzz with activity in 1910 and 1911.
In May 1911 the insurgent forces, led by the major figures Francisco
Madero, Francisco "Pancho" Villa, and Pascual Orozco, invaded Ciudad
Juárez in the first important battle of the civil war. Their victory led to
the downfall of the Porfirio Díaz regime and the ascendancy to the
presidency of Madero. Mardee Belding de Wetter narrates events during
this decisive period, giving us an excellent local perspective on the
revolution. She drew this essay from her master's thesis, "Revolutionary
El Paso, 1910–1917," completed at the University of Texas-El Paso.

It was in 1911 that El Paso achieved its first revolutionary importance.
The city became the hotbed of activity, since Juárez was the largest
port of entry on the Mexican border and its capture was essential to the
revolutionists. On January 1 circulars printed in El Paso were distributed
in the streets of Juárez, calling upon Mexicans to sacrifice their last drop
of blood in a supreme effort for liberty or death. "The circulars were printed
on yellow paper in red ink and recited that for the last thirty years the
Mexican government had been in the hands of usurpers."

Reports of *insurrectos* surrounding Juárez continued to reach the papers. Nevertheless, on January 3 the [*El Paso*] *Times* reported that "all
was quiet on the Rio Grande last night including . . . Juárez. . . . The
mounted policemen in Juárez were suffering with the cold and were more
busily engaged in keeping the hoods of their overcoats about their heads
than in watching for elusive *insurrectos*." The whole state of Chihuahua,
under the governorship of Alberto Terrazas, was watching for *insurrectos*.
Governor Terrazas stated that the bands of men who were fighting the
government were mostly outlaws and that their complete subjection was
inevitable. But this surety was soon removed.

Meanwhile, the U.S. Secret Service officials in El Paso were not idle
in their search for revolutionary plotters but these neutrality-lawbreakers

From *Password* (publication of the El Paso County Historical Society) 3,
no. 2 (April 1958): 52–59. Reprinted by permission of the El Paso County Historical Society.

proved very elusive. They constantly shifted their meeting places to avoid being caught and continued their work of spreading revolutionary literature. These men were not entirely welcome in El Paso. As Tom Lea said:

> There were many Mexican spies in El Paso working for various factions. Also there were the refugees. Most of the men refugees were cowards who would not fight. These people set up myriads of little Mexican newspapers in the south of the town. . . . They wrote terrible things about the United States and yet they enjoyed American security.[1]

Rumors of advancing bands of *insurrectos* continued to spread and Juárez prepared for a siege. General Juan Navarro, a veteran soldier, was placed in command of federal headquarters in Juárez. Federal troops were camped on the river across from Washington Park. Reinforcements for the Juárez garrison arrived—two hundred cavalrymen and their women, the camp followers, who were nearly all barefooted and nearly all carrying infants in their arms. Correspondingly, as Juárez bulged with soldiers, the civilian population began to migrate en masse to El Paso to stay with friends and relatives. El Paso boomed.

The Federal Government became alarmed over the border situation and continued to ask the United States for effective patrol of the boundary. The Mexican Secret Service reported to the U.S. Secret Service in El Paso that forty armed men had crossed the river into Mexico a few miles below El Paso to join the *insurrectos* and that more were planning to do so. Smuggling, too, was a problem. The Mexican Central passenger train that left the Union Station at six forty-five P.M. on January 28, arrived in Juárez where it was searched. As soon as the train stopped at the Mexican Central Depot, Mexican Secret Service officials looked under the car "Sagamore" and found four cases of ammunition. It was Mexican ammunition, labeled in Spanish, and the Secret Service men seemed to know exactly where it was. Much speculation followed in El Paso, for it seemed to be an attempt by the Mexican agents to make a reputation for themselves.

Be that as it may, the United States endeavored to comply with Mexico's requests. The secretary of war issued orders to triple the number of soldiers guarding the border and the secretary of the treasury authorized the collector of customs at El Paso to appoint ten additional deputies. At the same time Major Nathan Lapowski, commanding the Second Battalion, Fourth Infantry, Texas National Guard, received notice from Sheriff Peyton J. Edwards to have his forces in readiness to cooperate with the sheriff's office in case of eventualities. And the number of soldiers on guard on the American side of the international bridge was increased by forty men.

Much more serious trouble than smuggling now faced the border, however. Passengers on a Mexican train reported that twenty-three miles below Juárez they had passed Pascual Orozco, the insurgent chief from the Guerrero district, and that his troops numbering fifteen hundred men were engaged in unloading horses and a carload of dynamite in preparation for their march on Juárez. Consequently, "Colonel R. G. Martinez ordered everything in Juárez closed in the way of keno games, dance halls and saloons. A large crowd of Americans who were attending the various places made a rush for the streetcars." At the same time the Banco Mínero and the branch bank of the Banco Nacional were moved to El Paso where they continued to transact business. Their cash reserves were deposited in El Paso banks. The Juárez post office was likewise moved to El Paso.

Meanwhile, on February 3, announcement was made by Señor Abraham González that he had engaged Dr. I. J. Bush to organize a hospital corps and establish a hospital for the care of the revolutionists. Of this Dr. Bush later wrote:

> About daylight February 3, 1911, Abraham González roused me out of bed and told me that a courier had made his way through the Federal lines with a message from Pascual Orozco who was at Samalayuca, twenty-five miles south of Juárez. He had fought a battle at Sierra Mojino Ranch and wanted a doctor to treat the wounded.[2]

Dr. Bush established his *insurrecto* hospital at 410 South Campbell Street where he treated many of the wounded rebels. He also trained a number of Mexican girls to be nurses.

The following day, February 4, the U.S. Consulate in Juárez reported that notice had been received from Pascual Orozco that he would attack the city within twenty-four hours. Immediately several hundred young men fled to El Paso because they feared that the authorities would impress them into service. But Orozco did not attack. Instead, Juárez was reinforced with Federal troops. But El Pasoans did not know of the changed situation and by eight A.M. on February 6 thousands of people had made their way to the tops of tall buildings and to the Franklin and Krazy Kat mountains. When no battle took place, "the disappointment of the public was something tremendous."

El Paso, with a swollen population estimated at sixty-five thousand, watched and listened. Mexican Federal infantry patrolled the border. They kept a sharp lookout and in the still night air their cry of "*sentinela alerta*" could be clearly heard across the Rio Grande. Orozco, meanwhile, moved north and located his camp on the Mexican bank of the river opposite the El Paso smelter where it was in full view of El Paso. Immediately *insurrecto* sympathizers flocked to the river and, until stopped by American authorities, threw silver dollars across to the Orozco troops. Within a few days, however, Orozco moved his camp down the Rio Grande to Guadalupe, thirty-five miles south of Juárez, and for a little while at least excitement abated in El Paso.

Now for the first time El Paso felt the pinch of the revolution. The smelter officials announced that the smelter would have to close within five days unless a supply of ore was received from Mexico. The smelter received eighty percent of its ore from that country but it had not received so much as a ton in five weeks. If the smelter closed, several hundred men would be thrown out of work.

But El Paso made the most of what she had. Newspapermen from all over the country flocked to her. The Sheldon Hotel became their headquarters as it was also the headquarters for the U.S. Secret Service, *insurrecto* officers, and others interested in the revolution. The revolutionary junta in El Paso was besieged by soldiers of fortune. Among the newcomers were Willis E. Taylor of Redlands, California; General Benjamin Viljoen; A. W. Lewis, a Canadian captain of artillery in the Boer War; the "Triplets," Mahoney, McDonald, and Charpentier, Irish, Scotch, and French, respectively; Giuseppe Garibaldi, grandson of "Red Shirt" Garibaldi; and "Death Valley Slim" from Arizona. Anglo volunteers of lesser importance were organized into "El Falange de los Extranjeros." At the same time the ladies of the Mexican colony opened a restaurant on San Antonio Street, serving Mexican national dishes. They had so many patrons in one evening that they had to turn away more than five hundred. The proceeds were to be used for Red Cross doctors and nurses for the *insurrectos* in Mexico. Colonel Pascual Orozco also visited the city and almost started a riot. When he emerged from a restaurant on San Antonio Street where he had been dining, he was recognized by a crowd which enthusiastically surrounded him. He had come to El Paso, he said, to spend a few luxurious hours.

But all was not going well with the *insurrectos*. Madero was defeated at Casas Grandes and with the remnants of his army joined Giuseppe Garibaldi's battalion at Bauché. The combined forces marched up the Rio Grande and camped opposite El Paso where Orozco had camped in February. The camp was not more than a mile from the Federal *cuartel* in Juárez but it was not molested by Federal troops.

It was at this time that a famous revolutionist made his first appearance on the Rio Grande. "Major Francisco Villa, in command of seven hundred *insurrectos*, one hundred of them mounted, arrived at Madero's camp." W. H. Fryer was at the camp at the time and he later described the "motley crew" as "walking commissaries." Mr. Fryer stopped to talk with one of the men who was scooping water from the river to make coffee. He asked if the water was not dirty and the man replied, "If I drink much of this I'll have a 'dobe brick in my stomach."[3] Thousands of El Pasoans visited Madero's camp to take pictures of the mustachioed warriors. El Paso merchants used the presence of the troops to advertise their goods. One advertisement read: "Whether bloodshed or peace in Mexico we don't know; we hope for the best. We do know that the Bazaar has revolutionized the clothing business in El Paso."

On April 23 the El Paso junta announced that a five-day armistice to discuss peace was to begin that day at noon. Señor Don Venustiano Carranza, provisional governor of Coahuila, arrived from San Antonio to take part in the conference, and Abraham González arrived shortly thereafter. To celebrate the armistice a concert was given by the Madero army band and several hundred armed *insurrectos* were in attendance as were also Francisco and Raoul Madero, Colonel Garibaldi, Pascual Orozco, Francisco (Pancho) Villa, General Blanco, and many other officers of lesser importance. There was also a number of El Pasoans present. Between the Madero camp and the smelter was a swinging foot bridge belonging to the brick plant. United States soldiers were stationed at each end of the bridge to check the crowd and to prevent too great a strain on the structure.

When the armistice came to an end without a satisfactory understanding, a five-day extension was agreed upon. During this time *insurrecto* officers were allowed in El Paso on pass. This was excellent for business and Chihuahuaita was crowded until a late hour each night with *insurrectos* buying khaki campaign uniforms, underwear, and shoes. The men, however, showed no inclination to discard their large sombreros for American hats. It was estimated some five hundred men outfitted themselves in one day.

While the men were enjoying their shopping in El Paso, the peace commission continued in session. According to the *Times*:

> A prettier or more picturesque spot for holding the Mexican peace conference than the one selected opposite Hart's Mill could not have been found elsewhere on the border. It is a miniature valley carpeted with green grass and shaded by a luxuriant growth of cottonwood trees. The restless murmuring waters of the Rio Grande rushing over Hart's dam, sweep along at the foot of the valley, lying within the shadow of Orozco Hill. The place will hereafter be known as Peace Grove.

The *insurrectos* presented their demands to the Federal negotiators. These included participation in government affairs, representation in the cabinet, and twelve state governors to be chosen from Maderistas. Although the demands do not seem radical, they were rejected. Madero then demanded the resignation of President Díaz. Díaz agreed to resign but insisted that he remain in office until the peace had been restored. This the Maderistas refused to accept and the conference became deadlocked. Both sides then prepared for all out war. And the first objective of the war was Juárez.

The battle of Juárez began very suddenly and without the knowledge of the Federals, El Pasoans, or Francisco Madero. Against Madero's orders a fairly large body of *insurrectos* attacked the border city. The group was led by Pancho Villa and Pascual Orozco and was joined by most of the foreign legion. The *insurrectos* followed the irrigation ditch leading into Juárez and thus were not detected by General Navarro's men. The rebels fell upon the Federals and by the afternoon of May 8 began a general assault on the city. On the second day the battle was fought almost entirely in the center of the city and by nightfall the rebels held all of Juárez except the bullring, the *cuartel*, and the church. On the third day the rebels captured all of Juárez and General Navarro surrendered with five hundred men. Colonel Garibaldi received Navarro's sword.[4]

The casualties for a Mexican battle were heavy. About fifty Federals and fifteen *insurrectos* were killed. Among the dead was Colonel Tamborrel, one of Navarro's officers. The day before the battle he had called Madero's men a "bunch of cowards" and they had not forgot. After the battle he was found lying on a bed in a hotel with his hands tied behind him and a bullet hole through his head. Above the bed on which he lay was a large picture of Porfirio Díaz.[5]

The *insurrectos* also sought to kill General Navarro but Madero, realizing Navarro's danger, gave him permission to leave for El Paso. The general gave his word of honor he would return to Mexico to stand trial when Madero called him. Navarro then plunged his horse into the Rio Grande and escaped. No one knew his whereabouts until editor T. G. Turner was called to the phone at the [*El Paso*] *Herald* and a voice said: "This is A. Schwartz speaking. General Navarro is here and he asks me to tell you to please come to see him. He is in Chinaware in the basement." Turner went to the Popular Dry Goods Store and arranged for Navarro to enter the Hotel Dieu [hospital] under an assumed name where he remained as a patient until the feeling against him had subsided.[6]

Immediately after the battle El Pasoans surged to Juárez. The streetcars resumed service and carried loads of sightseers. A large ad appeared in the *Times*, "When you go to Juárez today things of interest are to be seen now that the town is in the possession of the insurrectos." El Paso physicians went for a different reason, to care for the wounded. Much amputation work was done without anesthetics. The stoicism of the mestizo who held out a finger to be amputated and, biting his collar, did not whimper, was not an unusual story. The bravery of the Mexicans was supreme. They knew how to die. As the rebels brought in their prisoners to be shot the doomed men shouted to the last, "¡Viva Don Porfirio Díaz!"

The news of Madero's victory reached Mexico City where it was received with open enthusiasm. Cheers for Madero rang out and the people demanded Díaz's resignation. On May 15 a conference was held across from the El Paso smelter between representatives of the Díaz government and those of Madero. A protocol of peace was drafted and signed on May 21. Díaz agreed to resign within two weeks. Francisco de la Barra[7] was to serve as interim president and his cabinet was to be filled with Maderistas. Madero bade his army farewell in Juárez and left for Mexico City. On May 26 ex-president Díaz left the capital for Vera Cruz where a French cruiser awaited to take him to France.

After Madero left for Mexico City a plot to assassinate him was discovered by General Viljoen. A Boer named Villiers was arrested on the charge of conspiracy, indicted, and released on bond. Little was actually known of the plot except that it was instigated by three *científico* agents in El Paso and that Orozco and Villa were used as tools. The *científicos* endeavored to implant suspicions of Madero in the minds of these two chieftains and almost succeeded. The plot was the first against Madero and it failed.[9]

With the coming of peace the citizens of El Paso realized the great service the newspapermen had performed for their city. El Paso was now a widely publicized spot, known all over the United States and, in fact throughout the world. To show the city's appreciation the Chamber of Commerce gave a banquet at the Hotel Sheldon for the correspondents.[10]

Another pleasant prospect for El Pasoans was the arrival of the Fourth U.S. Cavalry. Hopes were beginning to bud that Fort Bliss might be made a regimental post. A few months later their dream seemed near fulfillment when the secretary of war Henry Stimson said, "El Paso is a highly strategic point."

It was inevitable that commercialism should raise its head to take advantage of El Paso's unusual relation to the revolution. The A. D. Foster Company manufactured revolutionary spoons which sold for two dollars and fifty cents each. There was the Madero spoon, Blue Whistler spoon, Juárez spoon, McGinty Cannon in Action at Ojinada spoon, and the Orozco spoon. They proved to be very popular.

But the peace that had come to Mexico was an uneasy one and was not to last for long; but it was peace nevertheless. Díaz had been overthrown and the Electoral College on October 16 had elected Madero president and Pino Suarez vice president. Then in December the peace was threatened. El Pasoans learned that Bernado Reyes, a supporter of Díaz, was heading a counterrevolution and had organized a junta in their city, and that the junta had deposited seventy thousand dollars in an El Paso bank. But the threat to the peace was soon ended, at least temporarily. Fourteen Reyistas were arrested and a carload of .30-30 rifles shipped from Chicago was confiscated. Reyes himself was captured in Mexico by Madero's troops and placed in prison in Mexico City.

Thus ended the eventful year of 1911, a year of intense excitement for border residents who were beginning to realize the potency of Mexico's upheaval. "It has not ended," they told themselves, as they looked forward to a prosperous and exciting New Year.

Notes

1. Interview with Tom Lea, March 7, 1945. Mr. Lea was a prominent lawyer and mayor of El Paso from 1915 to 1917.

2. I. J. Bush, *Gringo Doctor* (Caldwell, UT, 1939), 171.

3. Interview with W. H. Fryer, November 9, 1945. Mr. Fryer has been a well-known attorney in El Paso for many years.

4. Bush, *Gringo Doctor*, 210. Garibaldi wore a special plushy hat which became very popular in El Paso. It was known as the "Garibaldi hat."

5. Interview with Mr. Fryer, November 9, 1945.

6. Timothy G. Turner, *Bullets, Bottles, and Gardenias* (Dallas: Southwest Press, 1935), 68–70.

7. De la Barra was identified with the Díaz regime and, although he admitted into his cabinet some Maderistas, he retained the Díaz bureaucracy and army and attempted to disband the revolutionary troops.

8. *Científicos* was the term adopted by the "insiders" of Díaz's government, because they claimed to be scientists in government. Their enemies claimed they were scientists only in graft and scoffingly called them "*cien tisicos*," the "hundred consumptives."

9. Carlo de Fornaro, *Carranza and Mexico* (New York, 1915), 56, 132–34.

10. Turner, *Bullets, Bottles, and Gardenias*, 70.

18 Linda B. Hall and Don M. Coerver ◆
The Arizona-Sonora Border and the Mexican Revolution

The close economic and social ties that had developed between Arizona and Sonora since the 1850s were disrupted by the Mexican Revolution. Border battles and disturbances in 1913, 1915, and 1918 raised tensions and resulted in the militarization of the frontier. Conflicts between American companies and Mexican politicians interrupted economic activity in Sonora, and labor troubles polarized the two societies. Sensing danger from the rise in Mexican nationalism, many U.S. citizens left Sonora. Linda B. Hall and Don M. Coerver, who are well known for their works on Mexico and the borderlands, discuss these developments.

The Arizona-Sonora border was significantly affected by the events of the Mexican Revolution. Though Arizona was less troubled by raids across the frontier than was South Texas, it nevertheless suffered from dangers to its citizens and their property along the border and experienced considerable disruptions of the cross-border economy. The decade of the revolution also saw Arizona emerge from territorial status to statehood, while Sonora moved from its position on the periphery of national power to place one of its sons, Alvaro Obregón, in the Mexican presidency. These two states—coping with similar problems of geography, environment, resources, and isolation from the political centers of their respective nations—developed along quite different lines. Their symbiotic relationship, despite occasional clashes, was of major importance in determining the course of historical events.

In both states, the major industries were mining, cattle, and irrigated agriculture. Both were influenced by the considerable development of the copper mining industry, especially in response to World War I; by the growth and development of large land companies, which frequently also served as construction companies that created irrigation facilities; and by the continual problem of insufficient water, which led to disputes over water rights and to the eventual development of a policy of public works designed to deal with this shortage.

Further, the border between Arizona and Sonora was just as permeable as other parts of the frontier. North Americans had been present in Sonora in considerable numbers at least from the 1880s, when the closing

From *Revolution on the Border: The United States and Mexico, 1910–1920* (Albuquerque: University of New Mexico Press, 1988), 28–43, 171–73. © 1988 University of New Mexico Press. Reprinted by permission of the University of New Mexico Press.

of the U.S. frontier led the adventurous to seek new opportunities to the south. By the same token, Mexican laborers had been migrating, temporarily or permanently, from Sonora into the territory of the United States from the time of the Treaty of Guadalupe Hidalgo in 1848. Many of these migrants had been prospectors, drawn by the California gold rush, and many continued to prospect in Arizona. As the copper mining grew to be a major industry in Arizona, more workers were needed. A large number of Sonorans, attracted by the economic opportunities afforded by this industry, moved across the line, returning to Mexico should the desire or the necessity arise. Thus, economic, social, and even family ties bound the two areas. Further, coping with similar problems and the similarity of economic development led in turn to similarities of technology and business practice in the two areas; engineers and businessmen, such as the prominent mining engineer Louis D. Ricketts, worked in both Arizona and Sonora.

The development of the border area until 1910 had not been entirely peaceful. As in Texas, the presence of the border itself had created major problems of law enforcement, with rustlers running cattle back and forth across the line, Indian raids a constant menace, smuggling an everyday occurrence (as it still is), and ordinary barroom shootouts far from unusual. Order was enforced on the Sonora side of the line in the Díaz period by the Federal police force known as the Rurales, led by Emilio Kosterlitzky, and in 1901 Arizona established its own force, the Arizona Rangers. In existence only nine years at the beginning of the revolution, the Rangers performed their duties of patrolling the border, enforcing the law, and keeping the labor force, particularly Mexican, in line. This latter function they pursued on both sides of the border. The Rangers' first captain was Burt Mossman, formerly superintendent of the Aztec Land and Cattle Company. He recruited men noted more for their toughness and willingness to take action than for their judgment. In fact, some sources report that some Rangers had formerly served on the wrong side of the law. In any case, they were violent and effective in what they saw as their duty. Mossman soon resigned, following some irregularities, to take a position with William C. Greene, cattle baron and mine owner in the Arizona-Sonora area.[1]

The Rangers came into constant conflict with Mexican migrants, with the most flagrant outbreaks occurring during mine strikes. In 1903, a strike of the Mexican, Italian, and Slavonian workers at the mines of the Arizona, Detroit, and Shannon copper companies operating at Clifton, Morenci, and Metcalf, Arizona, was broken by fifteen Rangers, the sheriff, and fifty deputized civilians, later joined by national guardsmen and several troops of regular cavalry. A number of Mexicans were ultimately arrested for inciting a riot, although in fact no riot had occurred. Three years later the Rangers, under Capt. Thomas Rynning, along with a number of Arizonan volunteers, went into Sonora to put down a strike at the Cananea Copper Company, owned by Greene and heavily staffed by U.S. citizens. After the U.S. group had scattered the strikers, Kosterlitzky and the Rurales arrived to take over, but the Rangers were apparently loath to leave the scene. Eventually persuaded that the situation was under control, they went back to Arizona. This incursion was followed by considerable outrage on the Mexican side of the line, despite the fact that the Rangers had been invited by Gov. Rafael Yzabal. Theodore Roosevelt, who had served as Rynning's commanding officer in the Spanish-American War, was more pleased than the Mexicans and commented with delight, "Tom's all right, isn't he?" The last captain of the Rangers was Harry Wheeler, who was later sheriff of Gila County and responsible for the deportation of more than one thousand striking workers from Bisbee, Arizona, in 1917.[2]

The year 1910 saw the beginning of Arizona's final and successful drive for statehood. While Arizona's delegates were meeting to draw up a constitution, the rumblings of revolution were beginning to the south. The young Mexican presidential candidate, Francisco Madero, who was running against Díaz, had made a campaign visit to Sonora in December 1909. After repeated harassment by Sonoran authorities, he left the state through Arizona. He was arrested in June 1910; and in October of that year he fled to San Antonio, Texas, at almost exactly the same time that the Arizona constitutional convention began meeting.

Simultaneously, Sonoran landowner José Mariá Maytorena, who later supported the Maderista revolution, made his way to Tucson, where he helped direct revolutionary forces crossing back into Mexico. Chihuahua, however, not Sonora, became the major scene of the battles against Federal forces during this stage of the revolution, and intense problems between the two states did not arise at this time. Nevertheless, the situation was watched with interest in Arizona, which achieved statehood on February 14, 1912.[3]

The state of Arizona was politically controlled by Anglos from the outset. Indeed, one historian has concluded that a major problem in the long drive for statehood was that Arizona needed to acknowledge its Spanish-speaking population in order to make the territory eligible, but did not want Hispanics to vote. When, in 1902, a committee headed by Sen. Albert Beveridge had visited the territory, Marcus A. Smith—Arizona territorial representative to Congress—angrily accused committee members of trying to prove that so many of its people were non-English-speaking that it did not merit statehood. The Mexican-born population was indeed significant—29,542 in 1910 according to the census count, as compared with a total of 294,353 residents in that year. Other estimates place the number of Mexican-born at double or triple that figure.

In any case, the problem was resolved to some degree by a bill introduced in the territorial legislature in 1909 by the future governor of the state, George W. P. Hunt. This bill provided that only those who could read and write English would be eligible to vote. Even before that time, though, Anglos had been preeminent in politics, with only eight individuals with Spanish surnames appearing on the rosters of the territorial Council and House of Representatives between 1864 and 1909.[4]

From statehood on, however, Arizona was increasingly affected by the revolution developing on its southern borders. Though Sonoran fighting in the initial stage of the revolution had been minimal, the assassination of Francisco Madero in February 1913 and the refusal of the Sonorans to accept his successor, Victoriano Huerta, made Sonora a major focus of revolutionary violence. Further, Sonorans and other Mexicans of all factions moved back and forth across the border, and Arizona "hardware" and "sporting goods" stores began to do a land-office business in the arms trade, both legal and illegal.[5] Another complicating circumstance was the large number of Mexican laborers who came into Arizona during the decade, pushed by the danger of Mexico's revolutionary violence and unstable economy and pulled by jobs in the rapidly developing Arizona copper industry. Thus, the histories of Arizona and Sonora between 1910 and 1920 were deeply intertwined.

The most spectacular encroachments of the revolution on the populace of Arizona were the border battles. Immediately upon receipt of the news of Madero's death in February 1913, plans were made by Sonoran leaders to gain control of a border town, which would permit supplies to come freely into the state. Contingents of the Federal Army, controlled by Huerta, occupied the border towns of Naco and Nogales and also had troops in the mining town of Cananea. The Federal Army also controlled the southern part of the state, and most important, the port of Guaymas, the only major port on the Sonoran coast. The Sonoran revolutionaries were effectively isolated and rather than attack through the Federal forces in the south and face the Federal gunboats in Guaymas, they decided to move against Nogales, which was guarded by four hundred well-armed and well-trained men under Colonels Reyes and Kosterlitzky.[6]

The battle began on March 13, 1913, and was observed from the Arizona side by the citizens of Nogales, Arizona, and the sightseers who had come from all over the state. In fact, Nogales, Arizona, and Nogales, Sonora, are physically one town, separated only by a street, and stray bullets from the Mexican side continually fell onto the U.S. side. The commanders for the Constitutionalists, as the Mexicans who had refused to recognize Huerta were calling themselves, were Juan Cabral and Alvaro Obregón, the latter a farmer from the area of Huatabampo who became the most successful general of the revolution and eventually president of Mexico.

The battle began at 5:15 A.M., and continued all day, many bullets striking the Arizona side. The fighting accelerated toward nightfall as the Constitutionalists pushed the attack. At about the same time, a company of U.S. soldiers set up a machine gun at the top of the hill on the Arizona side and ordered the Federal troops to stop firing, which they did immediately after seeing the machine gun. Soon, Mexican Federal troops began crossing over to the U.S. side of the line, leaving their uniform coats and caps in a heap at the Mexican customs house and stacking their guns. Many of these men were Rurales, who were confined with their commander, Kosterlitzky, for several months in the army camp on Cavalry Hill before being returned to Mexico. Crossing in the other direction at the same time were two hundred Chinese residents of Sonora who had come over to the U.S. side earlier and had been held under guard at the Masonic Hall all day for their own protection. Shortly after their departure, trains began coming into Nogales, Sonora, from the south for the first time in two weeks. Some 1,200 to 1,500 Constitutionalist troops had arrived by evening on four trains, including a construction train that was rebuilding bridges damaged by the Federals.[7]

The loss was costly for the Federals, not so much in casualties, as in men crossing the line and being taken prisoner by U.S. troops. Obregón reported that his opposition had lost 250 men in that way and also claimed that the damage and injuries on the Arizona side had not been caused by his troops. At 7:00 P.M. he had received word from the North American commander in Nogales that U.S. troops were pulling back from the line because order had been restored. The U.S. commanding officer, according to Obregón, exonerated the Constitutionalists from any responsibility for the shots that fell on the Arizona side, though it is difficult to imagine who else might have fired them.[8]

Within two weeks, the Constitutionalists controlled the northern part of Sonora, and with it the border.[9] The fighting, however, was far from over. By August 1914, Constitutionalist troops had taken Mexico City, but within Sonora, factional fighting among Constitutionalists had already broken out. Maderista Gov. José María Maytorena, who had fled to Tucson in February 1913, returned several months later when the danger was past. He had, however, became jealous of Obregón, who had won victories with his Army of the Northwest all the way to Mexico City and stood high in Carranza's favor. Pancho Villa, fighting in Chihuahua, had likewise become jealous of Obregón and for various reasons was on the verge of a rupture with Carranza, whom he neither liked nor trusted. As early as July 1914, Maytorena had broken with Plutarco Elías Calles, then military commander in the state, over control of the town of Cananea, where the copper mines were still operating and continuing to provide a major source of revenue for the Constitutionalists. Thus Maytorena looked to Villa, who had not yet broken openly with Carranza, for support against Calles, who supported Carranza and Obregón. Calles then controlled the north, and Maytorena remained dominant in Hermosillo. Meanwhile, the main body of Constitutionalist forces had moved far into the interior of the country, and in August 1914, Constitutionalists under Obregón took over Mexico City. Huerta had already fled the country. Even this victory, however, could not prevent the Sonorans from fighting each other.

In October 1914, while representatives of the various revolutionary factions were meeting in Aguascalientes to try to preserve peace among themselves after the defeat of Huerta, open warfare again broke out in Sonora. Villa and Obregón had met with Maytorena earlier to try to resolve the difficulties, but they had been unsuccessful. By late September, Maytorena was besieging the forces of Calles and Obregón's close friend and associate, Benjamin Hill, at the border town of Naco, just north of the copper mining town of Cananea. The siege lasted for more than two months, and the number of casualties from stray bullets falling on the U.S. side led the U.S. border population to clamor for military action. The siege was replete with bizarre incidents, including the desertion of a black trooper, who, apparently disgusted with the United States, joined Hill's forces and occasionally used his machine gun to strafe the North American side of the town.[10] Another incident was the Villistas' arrest of several gringos. Charged with high treason, they were accused of having attempted to dynamite one of Maytorena's troop trains en route from Del Río to Nogales and of having tried to steal Maytorena's private airplane. One of the men was actually arrested on the U.S. side of the line. Some of these men were released after a month's confinement, but the fate of the others remains unknown.[11]

In any case, by December 1, forty-one residents of Naco, Arizona, had been injured by the fighting on the other side, and on December 4, two more were killed by snipers. At this point, Pres. Woodrow Wilson at last responded to the outraged demands of the citizens of Arizona, and authorized the secretary of war, Lindley M. Garrison, to send Hugh L. Scott, the Army chief of staff who was experienced in border negotiations, to try to resolve the situation. Though Garrison told Scott that "the President wants you to go down and drive those armies away," it was clear that Scott's duties were to be diplomatic rather than military.[12]

His recommendation to both factions was that they pull out of Naco, with Calles and Hill taking control of a port of entry to the United States at Agua Prieta to the east and Maytorena at Nogales to the west. Calles and Hill agreed immediately, since they were losing, a fact that Scott noted, but Maytorena proved more intransigent. He eventually agreed, however, after Scott went directly to Villa, who had at last broken openly with Carranza and Obregón. Villa agreed to put pressure on his subordinate, and Maytorena finally evacuated Naco in January 1915.[13]

Estimates made in a report by the U.S. Army in April 1915 of troops belonging to the two factions had rated them somewhat higher for the Villistas: 5,230 as opposed to the Carrancistas' 3,500. However, the Carrancistas had 2,000 more troops in Mazatlán, just down the Pacific Coast, making the totals in or near the state approximately even. The Villistas under Maytorena, however, had a considerable advantage in armament and ammunition received during the preceding months: 15,568 rifles and 8,542,470 rounds of ammunition, as opposed to 5,282 rifles and 5,195,160 rounds of ammunition for Calles and Hill. Much of this, of course, had been expended in the battle. Nevertheless, it is fair to assume that the Carrancista forces were at a disadvantage.

The same report assessed the commanders as well. Calles was reported as "a man of some executive ability," but "not very friendly to Americans." Further, it was claimed that he was using his position for personal economic gain, sending $1,000 to $2,000 every week or so to his brother-in-law, Fernando Chacón, in Nogales, Arizona, for deposit to his personal account. Maytorena was described as from a "very old and aristocratic Mexican family." The report went on to say that "he is well educated and possesses some little executive ability, though his lack of knowledge of the military art is pitiable." His greatest weakness, it was pointed out, was in "the poor quality of material selected for his officers. They are ignorant, of exceeding intemperant [sic] and low moral habits; due to jealousies among them, coordinated action in any direction is impossible."[14]

In July, Calles began driving westward along the border, taking Naco and attacking Nogales, as Obregón moved northward from Mexico City against the main Villista force in the center of the country. Apparently Maytorena's problems with his officers had virtually undercut his ability to deal with Calles.

Villa was poised to come into Sonora. Embittered by his losses to Obregón at Celaya in April and León in June and by the United States' de facto recognition of the Carranza government in October 1915, his depredations throughout the state were particularly brutal. During the months that Villa had been fighting Obregón in the center of the country, Calles had fortified himself at Agua Prieta, opposite Douglas, Arizona, where he was threatened by Maytorena to the west and Villa from his Chihuahuan base to the east. When it was reported that Villa would move against Calles at Agua Prieta, President Wilson, to aid the de facto government he had recognized, permitted the reinforcement of the town through the United States. Calles had surrounded Agua Prieta on three sides with deep trenches behind barbed wire and had placed machine guns in positions to sweep the entire front. Since the Villistas frequently attacked at night, Calles had prepared for this by installing a huge searchlight to illuminate potential areas of attack.

The number of border raids had accelerated in the months just before the battle at Agua Prieta, and U.S. officials, hoping that a quick defeat of Villa might end them, cooperated as much as possible with the Carrancistas, who were even allowed to move troops along the railroad on the U.S. side from El Paso to Arizona. The Carrancista troop train was joined in El Paso, on October 29, 1915, by several U.S. infantry companies assigned to guard the train along its route from El Paso to Douglas, Arizona. A number of U.S. troops remained at Douglas during the fighting at Agua Prieta, the trenches being manned for three days by units of the Seventh, Eighth, Eleventh, Twentieth, and Twenty-second Infantry Regiments, Ninth Cavalry, and Sixth Field Artillery.[15]

The Villistas did not wait long, mounting a massive attack at 1:30 A.M. on November 1, 1915. The searchlight did its job, and the Villista ranks, running into the barbed wire, were cut down by the machine-gun cross fire. Hundreds of bullets fell on the North American side, but the U.S. commander, Frederick Funston, reported that, though authorized, he had not fired across the border, since both Mexican commanders were already trying to "prevent injury to Americans," and that the only effective way to control firing into Arizona was to cross the line and drive the Mexicans southward. The fighting was soon over, however, and to everyone's surprise Villa took his troops and turned south, to make an unsuccessful attack on Hermosillo, the Sonoran capital. It was some weeks before he reappeared, defeated and frustrated, on the border.[16]

When Villa returned, he was full of anger, as were his troops. In late November, shortly before Obregón's arrival on the border, Villa took the town of Nogales from the Constitutionalists, but then decided to abandon it before he could be challenged. As the Villistas pulled out of Nogales, looting of the town began. With trouble expected, five companies of the Twelfth Infantry were placed on the street dividing Nogales, Sonora, from Nogales, Arizona. About noon on November 26, the last Villista train pulled out of Nogales, but broke in two because of the heavy load of loot. As a result of the accident, part of those troops returned to join the three hundred Villistas who were still in town, drinking, smashing, and burning. One drunken soldier deliberately fired at least two shots at the U.S. troops, who immediately returned the fire. The Villista fell dead with some dozen bullets in his body. Villa's troops then opened up on the Twelfth Infantry, most of whom were in the street without cover. With the Villistas in houses, on roofs, or in automobiles, a fierce but brief battle took place. No American casualties resulted, but some fifty Villistas were killed and many wounded.[17]

Shortly thereafter, the Carrancistas began to fire on Company "L" of the Twelfth Infantry, believing them to be Villistas. One U.S. trooper was killed in the firefight that followed and two wounded. Estimates were that the Carrancistas suffered more than one hundred casualties before the error was discovered by a Carrancista officer, who then quickly notified the North Americans.[18] General Obregón himself arrived in Nogales a few days later to take over the northern army. He was successful in quickly running the Villistas from Sonora, and border problems of this nature subsequently shifted eastward, culminating in Villa's raid on Columbus, New Mexico, on March 9, 1916. The Arizona-Sonora border entered a new, if not more relaxed, phase.

The Villista attacks at Santa Ysabel, Chihuahua, and Columbus terrified U.S. citizens returning to Sonora's mining zones after Obregón had promised on November 23, 1915, that the de facto government would guarantee the safety of employees and their properties.[19] The Columbus raid and subsequent threats by Villa led to a general evacuation of North American employees from Nacozari, where Phelps Dodge had extensive mining operations, and North American soldiers were sent in to guard the copper smelters on the Arizona side.[20]

The Carranza government was completely opposed to the Punitive Expedition under Gen. John J. Pershing sent into Mexico in pursuit of Villa's band. Talks between Obregón and Gen. Hugh L. Scott, the Army chief of staff, in April and May failed to bring about U.S. withdrawal. It began to seem possible and even likely that war would break out between Mexico and the U.S., and, as troop movements began on both sides of the Arizona-Sonora border, more North Americans began to leave. Concern was especially high that Cananea, which had a large number of Villa sympathizers among the workers, might be endangered.[21]

In an attempt to avoid problems, General Calles, well aware of the economic importance of the Cananea mines to the Sonoran economy, telegraphed the presidente municipal of Cananea to "maintain a prudent attitude" and protect Americans residing in Cananea.[22] Despite the telegram, there was an immediate demonstration against the U.S. citizens at Cananea, but major violence was averted by careful patrolling of the streets and guarding of the houses by "responsible citizens."[23] Evacuation of the women began the following morning. Reports from the border led Chief of Staff Scott to write to his friend, Col. H. J. Slocum, in Columbus, New Mexico, that:

> It seems to me we are verging rapidly toward war. I told the President to look out for an attack upon Pershing by the national forces of the Mexican government; that there will be no way to stave off war, and that we should at once seize all the border towns—Cananea, El Tigre, Nacozari, etc.—and shove the Mexicans into the desert beyond.[24]

It is interesting that Scott mentioned areas that were not, in fact, "border towns," but mining camps in which there were major U.S. copper concerns. On the same day, L. D. Ricketts, the American mining engineer mentioned earlier who had now become the manager of the Cananea mine and an important official in the Amalgamated Copper Company, wrote Scott that all but thirty or forty Americans had been evacuated and that Calles had promised to send a troop train to bring them to the border. One American had come hurriedly down from Arizona at 2:00 A.M. in Ricketts's car to bring out the mine records. Nacozari, site of the Phelps Dodge mines, was reported completely evacuated, with the mines running under Mexican direction.[25] Calles meanwhile had promised to send in troops to protect the towns, but as of June 21 they had not arrived.[26]

Scott replied that the situation did indeed seem very threatening, but that he had instructed Frederick Funston, commanding general of the Southern Department, to watch over the mines and "try to save the large amounts of money invested there before the properties are destroyed by Mexicans." He went on to say that troops were very thinly distributed, but that National Guard units were being moved in along the border "just as fast as we can get hold of them," freeing the regular Army to enter Mexico across the length of the border in the event that Pershing were attacked.[27]

By June 27, virtually all U.S. mining employees had left the state, though food was being shipped in to the Mexican employees still on duty, and mining properties, including railroads, were being operated by Sonoran authorities. Calles was reported to have brought a force of between six thousand and seven thousand troops south of Agua Prieta, presumably to attack Douglas should hostilities ensue.[28]

In the midst of the excitement, Ricketts, a friend of Scott, sent him a handwritten note about the Sonoran leaders. He described Calles as "a pretty good man—a good organizer and disciplinarian and a *poor fighter*. On the whole he is among the best of the Mexicans." Ricketts dismissed Gen. Benjamin Hill as "not personally brave and not personally honest." As for Obregón, he was "not particularly able—very stubborn and narrow-minded."[29] Scott replied that Ricketts's views coincided exactly with his own.[30] Perhaps he was still exasperated by talks he had conducted earlier with Obregón that had failed to legitimize the North American military presence in Mexico. In any case, both were at least partially wrong. Obregón was particularly able, both militarily and politically, and emerged later as the consensus candidate for president of Mexico in 1920.

Although war was never declared, Calles kept the mines safe while the Americans took refuge across the border and rose a great deal in the good opinion of Walter Douglas, the general manager of Phelps Dodge, and Ricketts. Douglas already thought well of him, indicating to the U.S. Army commander at Douglas, Arizona, that he believed that Calles would do everything possible to protect U.S. lives and property, as long as "the integrity of the state is not seriously menaced." By July 3, the municipal president at Nacozari had ordered the Moctezuma Copper Company mines back into operation, though the Phelps Dodge management did not choose to send any of the North American personnel back at that time.[31]

By December 1916, the fear of war had receded, and Ricketts was again in communication with Scott about Calles. Ricketts commented that Calles, "while he may be severe to foreign interests," was an excellent administrator with a "pretty good head on him." Ricketts went on to praise Calles for adopting payment in silver for employees, since government-issue paper money was worthless, and for prohibiting the sale of alcohol, putting the mining camps on an "effective prohibition basis," an action pleasing to Ricketts both as an employer and as a witness to the violence of the area.[32]

Calles was elected civilian governor of the state in May 1917, but his term of office was more eventful than had been hoped. In fact, in the pre-Constitutional period, Calles had given indications that he might make life difficult for the companies, both because of his attitude toward labor and his taxation policies. Calles had served in 1915 as the Carranza-appointed governor of the state, and at that time he had ordered that all exports of metal be taxed and that payment be made in gold and silver. His stated rationale was that since metals were a resource of the state and usually exported, the state itself should realize some financial benefit.[33] In June 1916, he and Adolfo de la Huerta, whom Ricketts had referred to as "a young and inexperienced radical who has no judgment," had made attempts to cancel the concessions of the Cananea Copper Company and the Moctezuma Copper Company, presumably with an eye to renegotiation. The matter languished, however, and Calles was at least temporarily appeased by the Cananea Company's offer of $7,000 to improve the schools in that mining town.[34]

Further, he and de la Huerta were making considerable strides in improving the legal and actual status of labor in the state. De la Huerta had established a Cámara de Obreros, with one representative for each one thousand workers. The Cámara was to function as an official government body to study organizations and systems for improving workers' well-being, pass judgments on industrial accidents and award indemnities, act as arbiter in worker-employer conflicts, and arrange for the inspection of plants to avoid health hazards to workers.[35] At the time of the Mexican Constitutional Congress of 1916–17, Sonora already had an advanced labor code, providing for a minimum wage, the eight-hour working day, special protection for women and children, and a six-day work week.[36] Further, both Calles and de la Huerta had encouraged labor to organize, and a number of unions were emerging throughout the state, especially in the mining regions.[37]

When Calles assumed the constitutional governorship of Sonora in 1917, he immediately began to demand increased taxes from the copper companies, which were potentially the major source of income for the many social programs he hoped to put into operation, especially in the field of education. His tax demands, when combined with labor problems, forced shutdowns almost immediately in Cananea, Nacozari, and El Tigre, the three principal U.S. companies.[38]

Calles's initial reaction to the shutdowns was fury, and he rapidly took measures to resettle the miners on properties in Sonora and Sinaloa that the revolutionary government had taken over. His thought was that in this way, the workers would have work, the land would be cultivated, and the agrarian problem resolved. Given the critical nature of the situation, he announced that he was bypassing the usual red tape and taking immediate possession of these lands in order to colonize them. On the same day, he ordered a train to Cananea to transport the workers from the mines. By quick action, he hoped to prevent the migration of these workers to the United States, "where they encounter a difficult situation shameful to our race."[39] Two days later, he specified several properties that were to be divided, indicating that the resettled miners would be given the means to work the land, and announced that in this way, residents of Sonora would cease to be subject to the "whims of foreign capital." At the same time he sent a report of his actions to President Carranza, who had several months before forbidden such distributions of land without his prior approval.[40]

This sort of drastic action, however, failed to solve the economic problems of the state, and the commanding officer of the U.S.S. *Yorktown*, visiting Sonora in August, observed that the state was in economic chaos.

No money but fractional Mexican silver and U.S. currency was circulating, no banks were open, food was scarce and prices high, and neither industries nor mining camps were operating. He estimated that Calles's taxation policies had thrown ten thousand Mexicans out of work.[41]

Calles therefore moved to appease the copper companies and return them to operation. The U.S. consul in Nogales, E. M. Lawton, reported that Calles had abolished by executive decree the Cámara de Obreros "which has caused so much trouble in the mining camps of El Tigre, Cananea, and Nacozari." Lawton emphasized Calles's unfriendly attitude toward North Americans, however, and indicated that only the bankruptcy of the Sonoran treasury had caused Calles to back down.[42] At about the same time, Cananea representatives indicated that negotiations with Calles were promising.[43] By December 1917, the mines began to reopen and thereafter suffered no interruption of their operations. In 1918, production stood at 52,694,731 pounds, up from 16,333,081 in 1915.[44]

Calles's anger toward the copper companies had no doubt been exacerbated by the harsh crackdowns on striking laborers in Arizona during July 1917. In the most bizarre and flagrant of these incidents, Henry C. Wheeler, sheriff of Cochise County, had deputized two thousand men, including Phelps Dodge employees from Douglas, Arizona, to break the strike at the Copper Queen mines in Bisbee. Twelve hundred miners were rounded up, loaded in cattle cars, and shipped to the army post at Columbus, New Mexico. When the army refused to accept the "prisoners," the train carried them back to Hermanas, New Mexico, where the engine was unhitched and the cars containing the men were left standing in the rain with the doors unlocked. The strikers were first warned never to return to Bisbee, where many of them had families, and then abandoned. Eventually a detention camp was set up to provide for these men, and many of the Mexican citizens involved filtered back across the border. Nevertheless, as late as September, attempts were being made by a Sonoran committee to go to the aid of the Mexicans still at the camp to help arrange for their return and provide food and other provisions for them. In early October, ninety-one deported Mexicans entered Sonora at Agua Prieta, many still without word of their families in Bisbee.[45] This incident, and the many less glaring abuses to which Mexican citizens were subjected, strengthened Calles's resolve to reconstruct the economy of Sonora and to provide jobs for Mexicans in their own country.

The problems of the copper companies thus influenced the problem of agrarian reform, which Calles considered a key to economic recovery, particularly since Sonora was suffering widespread hunger in 1916 and 1917. The richest agricultural area of the state was the Yaqui Valley, which had been the site of extensive development by a U.S. corporation, the

Richardson Construction Company, since 1904. Irrigation works underwent a great deal of damage during the revolution, particularly from the Yaqui Indians, who had earlier been pushed out of their native homeland along the river and up into the mountains. As revolutionary factions fought one another, a group of Yaqui "broncos" took advantage of the opportunity and began to attack the new settlements sponsored by Richardson. By 1916, much company property had been abandoned, and the Sonoran government ordered Alfonso Echeverría to take over and administer the irrigation works so that the harvest would not be lost and new crops might be planted.

This action led to continual problems between Calles and the company, since Calles attempted to cancel the Richardson concession. Calles blamed the company for all delays in repairing the works, as well as any shortage of water, and the controversy became increasingly bitter. The Richardson Company's holdings were gradually eroded by state action, and several years later, the national government acquired rights to what remained. Although the company had made major advances in agricultural techniques and irrigation works during its short tenure in Sonora, the problems involved in the monopolistic development of a vast agricultural area by one company, particularly a U.S. firm, were made vividly clear to Calles and his associate, Alvaro Obregón, and were important in influencing their decision to invest heavily in nationally financed public irrigation projects after their rise to national power.[46]

The Yaqui problem had ramifications for the U.S. citizens living in the Yaqui Valley and on the border as well. The Richardson Construction Company had confined its sales of irrigated land almost exclusively to North Americans, and the raiding by the Yaqui "broncos" put these U.S. citizens in considerable peril. As early as June 1915, the United States was considering landing an expeditionary force at Guaymas, should it become necessary to evacuate Americans. The flagship *Colorado*, carrying three companies of the Fourth Regiment U.S. Marine Corps, along with the cruisers *Chattanooga* and *Raleigh*, sailed for the Sonoran coast, but the situation calmed down, and they were not required to take action. In the next two years, as the Yaqui raids continued, many U.S. citizens left the area, being replaced in some cases by German sailors whose ships had been interned in the area at the outbreak of the First World War.[47]

The Yaquis' principal source of weapons was the United States, and though they did not raid on the U.S. side, they made frequent trips into Arizona to acquire arms and ammunition. Some worked for a time in the cotton and citrus ranches and in the Arizona mines to acquire the money to purchase needed supplies. After Villa had been driven from Sonora, Calles was able to turn his attention to the Yaquis, declaring a war of

extermination against them in 1917. The Yaquis' efforts increased pro-
portionally. They had a certain advantage in that they had regular routes
for smuggling, whereas arms shipments to Calles's forces were held up
by the U.S. export laws. Nevertheless, Calles's appeal for help across the
border was heeded, at least to some degree, by the North American authorities, which led to the last Indian battle fought by the U.S. Cavalry.[48]

In the late fall of 1917, ranchers south of Arivaca in Arizona began to
discover the remains of partially butchered cattle, evidence that the Yaquis
were using the area for regular crossings of the Arizona-Sonora border.
The U.S. Army, therefore, increased its patrolling of that particular region. On January 10, 1918, Capt. Blondy Ryder and Troop E of the black
Tenth Cavalry spotted a column of Yaquis along a skyline ridge. The
majority of the Yaquis escaped safely, leaving behind a group of ten to
hold off the cavalry. Both sides used the natural cover of the boulders and
bushes, the Yaquis falling back gradually for protection. After about thirty
minutes the Yaqui rear guard was pinned down and quickly surrendered.
Only one Yaqui, the eldest and apparently the chief of the group, had
been seriously injured when a shot had hit and exploded one of the car-
tridges in his belt, laying his stomach open. Although he was given medical attention, he subsequently died on the way to the hospital in Nogales.
One of the nine remaining Yaquis was an eleven-year-old boy, the grandson of the chief, who had fought along with the others using a rifle reported to be almost as long as he was tall.

The Yaquis were held for some time by Colonel Ryder's command,
and such a cordial relationship developed between the prisoners and the
captors that the Yaquis asked to enlist in the U.S. Army. They were turned
down, however, and subsequently brought to trial for exporting arms without a license. Calles was eager for them to be returned to Mexico, where
they undoubtedly would have been executed. This eventuality was avoided
by the judge, who, by sentencing all but the boy to thirty days in the Pima
County jail, managed to avoid the possibility of deportation.[49]

Sporadic incidents on the Arizona-Sonora border continued, such as
the "little battle of Nogales," in which a confrontation at the customs
house led to an exchange of fire between the U.S. and the Mexican armies,
the latter taking up a position in Gen. Alvaro Obregón's home on the
Mexican side and firing out the doors and windows. Evidently the general was not in residence at that time, and in any case the fighting quickly
stopped when the superiority of U.S. firepower became clear. On the U.S.
side 2 officers, 3 soldiers, and 2 civilians died; reports indicated that the
Mexicans buried 129, possibly including 2 Germans.[50] In general, however, the border calmed down considerably.

By 1920, Arizonans supported General Obregón for president of Mexico, evidently holding no hard feelings over the use of his home in the 1918 Nogales fighting. For the most part, they had been impressed with his business talent in organizing the garbanzo growers of Sonora and Sinaloa into a productive and efficient cooperative, and his work as an import-export agent had led to many contacts with Arizona businessmen. Gov. Thomas Campbell of Arizona met with him several times after his election as president. A large Arizona delegation attended his inauguration in December 1920.[51]

Former Governor Hunt had become a strong admirer of Obregón, and Sen. Harry Ashurst recommended to the president of the United States that Obregón's government be officially recognized. The Arizonans had faith in his ability to control the country and to end the sporadic and sometimes continuous violence that had been going on since 1910. Further, they felt that he understood the role that foreign and particularly U.S. capital could play in the development of Mexico. In short, they found Obregón acceptable as president because they knew him, thought him to be a practical man, and believed they could deal with him. Thus, the view of the Arizona-Sonora border at the end of the decade was colored by considerable good feeling and optimism about the future relationship of the two nations.

Notes

1. Jay J. Wagner, *Arizona Territory, 1863–1912: A Political History* (Tucson: The University of Arizona Press, 1970), 383–95. Marshall Trimble, *Arizona: A Panoramic History of a Frontier State* (Garden City, NY: Doubleday and Company, 1977), 321–27.

2. Wagner, *Arizona Territory*, 384–92. Héctor Aguilar Camín, *La frontera nómada: Sonora y la Revolución Mexicana* (Mexico City: Siglo Veintiuno Editores, 1977), 119–21. Antonio Rivera, *La Revolución en Sonora* (Mexico City: Imprenta Araña, 1969), 142–60.

3. Charles C. Cumberland, *Mexican Revolution: The Constitutionalist Years* (Austin: The University of Texas Press, 1972), 92–93, 111, 117–18. Rivera, *La Revolución*, 200.

4. Rodolfo Acuña, *Occupied America: The Chicano's Struggle Toward Liberation* (San Francisco: Canfield Press, 1971), 94.

5. Penney and Robinson to Calles, 1916, Archivo de Gobierno del Estado de Sonora, Tomo 3809.

6. Alvaro Obregón, *Ocho mil kilómetros en campaña* (Rpt.; Mexico City: Fondo de Cultura Económica, 1970), 35–36.

7. Eyewitness account by Mrs. Ada E. Jones, "The First Battle of Nogales," manuscript, Mar. 14, 1913, Arizona Historical Society.

8. "Toma de la villa de Nogales," written Mar. 15, 1913, in Obregón, *Ocho mil*, 36–39.

9. Cumberland, *Mexican Revolution*, 25.

10. Dallas *Morning News*, Oct. 7, 1914.

11. Arizona *Daily Star*, Oct. 12, 1914; Oct. 13, 1914; Oct. 15, 1914; Oct. 20, 1914; and Nov. 26, 1914. Dallas *Morning News*, Oct. 13, 1914.

12. Hugh L. Scott, *Some Memories of a Soldier* (New York and London: The Century Co., 1928), 509.

13. See Villa to Maytorena, Jan. 9, 1915, and copy of accord signed by Calles and Maytorena, Jan. 11, 1915, in National Archives, Villa's Revolution #2212358, Box 7644. For a more detailed discussion of the Naco incident, see Linda B. Hall, "The Mexican Revolution and the Crisis in Naco, 1914–1915," *Journal of the West* 16 (Oct. 1977): 27–35.

14. See commanding officer, 12th Infantry, to department engineer, Southern Department, Apr. 23, 1915, in National Archives, Military Intelligence Division, Record Group 165, #8536-7. Archive cited hereinafter as MID 165, followed by document number.

15. Calvin W. Hines, "The Mexican Punitive Expedition of 1916" (Master's thesis, Trinity University, 1961), 45–47.

16. Clarence C. Clendenen, *Blood on the Border* (London: Macmillan and Company, 1969), 187–89.

17. Hines, "The Mexican Punitive Expedition," 47–48.

18. Hines, "The Mexican Punitive Expedition," 49–50.

19. Clarence C. Clendenen, *The United States and Pancho Villa* (Ithaca: Cornell University Press, 1961), 224.

20. Vice-consul Douglas, Arizona, to Foreign Office, Archive of the British Foreign Office, 371/2699, #68777.

21. For Villista sympathies, see Ricketts to Scott, Dec. 1, 1916, HLS [Hugh Lenox Scott Papers, Library of Congress].

22. Calles to presidente municipal, Cananea, June 18, 1916, HLS.

23. Kingdon to Allen, June 18, 1916, HLS.

24. Scott to Slocum, June 20, 1916, HLS.

25. Ricketts to Scott, June 20, 1916, HLS.

26. Ricketts to Scott, June 21, 1916, HLS.

27. Scott to Ricketts, June 21, 1916, HLS.

28. [Walter] Douglas to Scott, June 27, 1916; Ricketts to Scott, June 26, 1916, HLS.

29. Ricketts to Scott, June 27, 1916. HLS.

30. Scott to Ricketts, June 28, 1916, HLS.

31. Douglas to Davis, June 27, 1916; Douglas to Scott, July 3, 1916, HLS.

32. Ricketts to Scott, Dec. 6, 1916, HLS.

33. Calles Decree #3, Aug. 20, 1915, Roll Number 60, Patronato de la Historia de Sonora. Archive hereinafter cited as PHS, followed by roll number.

34. Ricketts to Scott, Dec. 1, 1916, HLS. Moreno to U.S. Consul, Nogales, June 5, 1916; Simpich to De la Huerta, June 5, 1916; and Acuña to Huerta, June 13, 1916, PHS/63.

35. Huerta Decree #7.1, Dec. 10, 1916, PHS/65.

36. Mexico, *Diario de los debates del Congreso Constituyente* (Mexico City: Cámara de Diputados, 1917), 1:719.

37. See lists of unions in Cananea in gobernador del Estado de Sonora to presidente municipal. Cananea, Nov. 14, 1918, PHS/70. A more general but in-

complete list is in "Las sociedades existentes en el estado de Sonora, 1918," PHS/71.

38. Commanding officer, *Yorktown*, to commander, Division II, Pacific Fleet, Aug. 18, 1917, RDS-IA [Records of the Department of State Relating to the External Affairs of Mexico, 1910–1929], 812.00/21271. Lawton, Report on Conditions in Sonora, Sept. 12, 1917, RDS-IA, 812.00/21282.

39. Calles to Aguirre, July 11, 1917; Calles to administrador de bienes intervenidos, July 9, 1917, PHS/66.

40. Calles to Aguirre, July 11, 1917; Calles to Carranza, July 11, 1917, PHS/67.

41. Commanding officer, *Yorktown*, to commander, Division II, Pacific Fleet, Aug. 18, 1917, RDS-IS, 812.00/21271.

42. Lawton, Report on Conditions in Sonora, September 12, 1917, RDS-IA, 812.00/21282.

43. Military report of conditions along the border, Sept. 29, 1917, RDS-IA, 812.00/21312.

44. David Pletcher, *Rails, Mines and Progress: Seven American Promoters in Mexico, 1867–1911* (Ithaca: Cornell University Press, 1958), 254.

45. Pamela Mayhall, "Bisbee's Response to Civil Disorder," *The American West* 9 (May 1972): 22–31. Military report of conditions along the border, Sept. 29, 1917, RDS-IA, 812.00/21312. Presidente municipal, Agua Prieta, to gobernador interino, Oct. 4, 1917, PHS/67.

46. De la Huerta to Echeverría, June 4, 1916, and July 5, 1916; secretario de gobierno de Sonora to Cruz, June 5, 1916; de la Huerta to Acuña, July 5, 1916, PHS/63. Calles to Carranza, Feb. 28, 1916, PHS/61. Claudio Dabdoub, *Historia de El Valle del Yaqui* (Mexico City: Librería Manuel Porrúa, S.A., 1964), 193–235, 293–327. Luis L. León, Interview with Linda B. Hall, July 30, 1974.

47. *San Antonio Express*, June 18, 1915, and June 20, 1915. Dabdoub, *Historia*, 320–21.

48. Congreso de Sonora a sus comitentes. Oct. 24, 1917, PHS/67. Washington to Carranza, Dec. 1, 1917; Castro to Carranza, Jan. 6, 1917, PHS/68. Sage to commanding general, Southern Department, May 28, 1915, MID 165, 8536/18.

49. Colonel H. B. Wharfield, "Yaqui Border Incident," manuscript, Arizona Historical Society. Colonel H. B. Wharfield, "The Yaqui Indian Fight," in *The Black Military Experience in the American West*, ed. John M. Carroll (New York: Liveright, 1973), 367–74.

50. Clendenen, *Blood*, 346–74.

51. John S. Goff, *George W. P. Hunt and His Arizona* (Pasadena: Socio Technical Publications, 1973), 82. *El Heraldo de Mexico*, Oct. 12, 1920; *Excelsior*, Oct. 9, 1920; *El Demócrata*, Dec. 1, 1920; *El Monitor Republicano*, Oct. 17, 1920, in *Campaña política del c. Alvaro Obregón*, ed. Luis N. Ruvalcaba (Mexico City: n.p., 1923), 5:261, 270, 297, 513–15.

19 Señora Flores de Andrade ◆
Conspiring against Porfirio Díaz

*Contrary to popular perception, Mexican women were directly involved
in the Mexican Revolution.* Soldaderas *(female soldiers and field supporters) accompanied their men into the battlefield, cooking, nursing,
providing companionship, and, often, engaging in combat. Some*
soldaderas *assumed leadership positions among the insurgent forces.
Women also agitated for change as labor activists, radical journalists,
and militant intellectuals. In this selection Señora Flores de Andrade, a
revolutionary living in El Paso, reflects on her involvement in the anti-
Porfirio Díaz conspiracy headed by Francisco Madero.*

I was born in Chihuahua, and spent my infancy and youth on an estate
in Coahuila which belonged to my grandparents, who adored me. My
grandparents liked me so much that they hardly allowed me to go to Chihuahua so as to get an ordinary education. At seven years of age I was
master of the house. My grandparents did everything that I wanted and
gave me everything for which I asked. As I was healthy and happy I would
run over the estate and take part in all kinds of boyish games. I rode on a
horse bareback and wasn't afraid of anything. I was thirteen years of age
when my grandparents died, leaving me a good inheritance, part of which
was a fifth of their belongings, with which I could do whatever I wished.

The first thing that I did, in spite of the fact that my sister and my
aunt advised me against it, was to give absolute liberty on my lands to all
the peons. I declared free of debts all of those who worked on the lands
which my grandparents had willed me and what there was on that fifth
part, such as grain, agricultural implements, and animals, I divided in
equal parts among the peons. I also told them that they could go on living
on those lands in absolute liberty without paying me anything for them
and that they wouldn't lose their rights to it until they should leave for
some reason. Even yet there are on that land some of the old peons, but
almost all of them have gone, for they had to leave on account of
the revolution. Those lands are now my only patrimony and that of my
children.

Because I divided my property in the way in which I have described
(and as a proof of which, I say, there are still people in Ciudad Juárez and
El Paso who wish to kiss my hand), my aunt and even my sister began to

From Manuel Gamio, *The Mexican Immigrant: His Life Story* (Chicago:
University of Chicago Press, 1931), 29–35. © 1931 by the University of Chicago
Press. Reprinted by permission of the University of Chicago Press.

annoy me. My sister turned her properties over to an overseer who has made them increase.

They annoyed me so much that I decided to marry, marrying a man of German origin. I lived very happily with my husband until he died, leaving me a widow with six children. Twelve years had gone by in the meantime. I then decided to go to Chihuahua, that is to say, to the capital of the state, and there, a widow and with six children, I began to fight for liberal ideals, organizing a women's club which was called the "Daughters of Cuauhtemoc," a semi-secret organization which worked with the Liberal Party of the Flores Magón brothers in fighting the dictatorship of Don Porfirio Díaz. We were able to establish branches of the woman's club in all parts of the state by carrying on an intense propaganda.

My political activities caused greater anger among the members of my family especially on the part of my aunt, whom I called mother. Under these conditions I grew poorer and poorer until I reached extreme poverty. I passed four bitter years in Chihuahua suffering economic want on the one hand and fighting in defense of the ideals on the other. My relatives would tell me not to give myself in fighting for the people, because I wouldn't get anything from it, for they wouldn't appreciate their defenders. I didn't care anything about that. I wouldn't have cared if the people had crucified me, I would have gone on fighting for the cause which I considered to be just.

My economic situation in Chihuahua became serious, so that I had to accept donations of money which were given to me as charity by wealthy people of the capital of the state who knew me and my relatives. My aunt helped me a little, but I preferred for her not to give me anything, for she would come to scold me and made me suffer. There were rich men who courted me, and who in a shameless way proposed to me that I should become their mistress. They offered me money and all kinds of advantages, but I would have preferred everything before sacrificing myself and prostituting myself.

Finally after four years' stay in Chihuahua, I decided to come to El Paso, Texas. I came in the first place to see if I could better my economic condition and second to continue fighting in that region in favor of the Liberal ideals, that is to say, to plot against the dictatorship of Don Porfirio. I came to El Paso in 1906, together with my children and comrade Pedro Mendoza, who was coming to take part in the Liberal propaganda work. I put my children in the school of the Sacred Heart of Jesus, a Catholic institution; they treated me well there and took care of my children for me.

With comrade Mendoza we soon began the campaign of Liberal propaganda. We lived in the same house and almost in the same room and as we went about together all day working in the Liberal campaign the American authorities forced us to marry. I am now trying to divorce myself from my husband for he hasn't treated me right. He goes around with other women, and I don't want anything more to do with him.

In 1909 a group of comrades founded in El Paso a Liberal women's club. They made me president of that group, and soon afterwards I began to carry on the propaganda work in El Paso and in Ciudad Juárez. My house from about that time was turned into a conspiratory center against the dictatorship. Messengers came there from the Flores Magón band and from Madero bringing me instructions. I took charge of collecting money, clothes, medicines, and even ammunition and arms to begin to prepare for the revolutionary movement, for the uprisings were already starting in some places.

The American police and the Department of Justice began to suspect our activities and soon began to watch out for me, but they were never able to find either in my house or in the offices of the club documents or arms or anything which would compromise me or those who were plotting. I was able to get houses of men or women comrades to hide our war equipment and also some farms.

In 1911, a little before the revolutionary movement of Sr. Francisco Madero became general, he came to El Paso, pursued by the Mexican and American authorities. He came to my house with some others. I couldn't hide them in my house, but got a little house for them which was somewhat secluded and had a number of rooms, and put them there. I put a rug on the floor and then got some quilts and bedclothes so that they could sleep in comfort. So that no one would suspect who was there, I put three of the women of the club there, who washed for them, and took them their food which was also prepared by some of the women.

Don Francisco and his companions were hidden in that house for three months. One day Don Francisco entrusted my husband to go to a Mexican farm on the shore of the Bravo River so as to bring two men who were coming to reach an agreement concerning the movement. My husband got drunk and didn't go. Then I offered my services to Sr. Madero and I went for the two men who were on this side of the border, that is to say in Texas territory, at a wedding. Two Texas Rangers who had followed me asked me where I was going, and I told them to a festival and they asked me to invite them. I took them to the festival and there managed to get them drunk; then I took away the two men and brought them to Don Francisco. Then I went back to the farm and brought the Rangers to El Paso where I took them drunk to the City Hall and left them there.

Later when everything was ready for the revolutionary movement against the dictatorship, Don Francisco and all those who accompanied him decided to pass over to Mexican territory. I prepared an afternoon party so as to disguise the movement. They all dressed in masked costumes as if for a festival and then we went towards the border. The river was very high and it was necessary to cross over without hesitating for the American authorities were already following us, and on the Mexican side there was a group of armed men who were ready to take care of Don Francisco. Finally, mounting a horse barebacked, I took charge of taking those who were accompanying Don Francisco over two by two. They crossed over to a farm and there they remounted for the mountains.

A woman companion and I came back to the American side, for I received instructions to go on with the campaign. This happened in May 1911. We slept there in the house of the owner of the ranch and on the next day when we were getting ready to leave, the colonel came with a picket of soldiers. I told the owner of the ranch to tell him that he didn't know me and that another woman and I had come to sleep there. When the authorities came up that was what he did; the owner of the ranch said that he didn't know me and I said that I didn't know him. They then asked me for my name and I gave it to them. They asked me what I was doing there and I said that I had been hunting and showed them two rabbits that I had shot. They then took away my .30-30 rifle and my pistol and told me that they had orders to shoot me because I had been conspiring against Don Porfirio. I told them that was true and that they should shoot me right away because otherwise I was going to lose courage. The colonel, however, sent for instructions from his general, who was exploring the mountains. He sent orders that I should be shot at once.

This occurred almost on the shores of the Rio Grande and my family already had received a notice of what was happening to me and went to make pleas to the American authorities, especially my husband. They were already making up the squad to shoot me when the American consul arrived and asked me if I could show that I was an American citizen so that they couldn't shoot, but I didn't want to do that. I told them that I was a Mexican and wouldn't change my citizenship for anything in the world.

The colonel told me to make my will for they were going to execute me. I told him that I didn't have anything more than my six children whom I will to the Mexican people so that if they wished they could eat them.

The colonel was trying to stave off my execution so that he could save me, he said. An officer then came and said that the general was approaching. The colonel said that it would be well to wait until the chief came so that he could decide concerning my life, but a corporal told him that they should shoot me at once for if the general came and they had not executed me then they would be blamed. They then told me that they were going to blindfold me but I asked them if their mothers weren't

Mexicans, for a Mexican isn't afraid of dying. I didn't want them to blind-fold me. The corporal who was interested in having me shot was going to fire when I took the colonel's rifle away from him and menaced him; he then ordered the soldiers to throw their rifles at the feet of the Mexican woman and throw themselves into the river, for the troops of the general were already coming. I gathered up the rifles and crossed the river in my little buggy. There the American authorities arrested me and took me to Fort Bliss. They did the same thing with the soldiers, gathering up the arms, etc. On the next day the authorities at Fort Bliss received a tele-gram from President Taft in which he ordered me to be put at liberty, and they sent me home, a Negro military band accompanying me through the streets.

At the triumph of the cause of Sr. Madero we had some great festivi-ties in Ciudad Juárez. The streetcar company put all of the cars which were needed for free transportation from one side of the border to the other.

Afterwards Sr. Madero sent for me and asked me what I wanted. I told him that I wanted the education of my six children and that all the promises which had been made to the Mexican people should be carried out. The same man told me to turn the standards of the club over to Villa who told me that they weren't good for anything. I afterwards learned that Don Francisco was trying to cajole Pancho by giving him those things which we wanted to give to Pascual Orozco.

During the Huerta revolution I kept out of the struggle, for I consid-ered that was treason, and little by little I have been separating myself from political affairs and I am convinced that the revolution promised a great deal to the Mexican people but hasn't accomplished anything.

20 Plan de San Diego

In the mid-1910s, as the revolution continued to rage in Mexico, the Lower Rio Grande Valley of Texas was the scene of much confusion and many cross-border raids. Some incursions became associated with the "Plan of San Diego," a mysterious manifesto that called for a full-fledged insurrection throughout the U.S. borderlands. Historians have not determined the precise authorship of the plan, but it seems clear that Mexican revolutionaries used it as leverage in their dealings with the U.S. government and that Chicanos utilized it against the Anglo power structure in South Texas.

We, who in turn sign our names, assembled in the revolutionary plot of San Diego, Texas, solemnly promise each other on our word of honor that we will fulfill and cause to be fulfilled and complied with, all the clauses and provisions stipulated in this document and execute the orders and the wishes emanating from the provisional directorate of this movement and recognize as military chief of the same Mr. ———, guaranteeing with our lives the faithful accomplishment what is here agreed upon.

1. On the 20th day of February, 1915, at 2 o'clock in the morning, we will rise in arms against the Government and country of the United States and North America, one as all and all as one, proclaiming the liberty of the individuals of the black race and its independence of Yankee tyranny, which has held us in iniquitous slavery since remote times; and at the same time and in the same manner we will proclaim the independence and segregation of the States bordering on the Mexican nation, which are: Texas, New Mexico, Arizona, Colorado, and Upper California, of which States the Republic of Mexico was robbed in a most perfidious manner by North American imperialism.

2. In order to render the foregoing clause effective, the necessary army corps will be formed under the immediate command of military leaders named by the supreme revolutionary congress of San Diego, Texas, which shall have full power to designate a supreme chief who shall be at the head of said army. The banner which shall guide us in this enterprise shall be red, with a white diagonal fringe, and bearing the following inscription: "Equality and Independence"; and none of the subordinate

From translated copy of Plan de San Diego, *Records of the Department of State Relating to the Internal Affairs of Mexico, 1910–1929*, 812.00/1583, U.S. National Archives Microfilm Publications, microcopy no. M-274, pp. 145–48.

leaders or subalterns shall use any other flag (except only the white for signals). The aforesaid army shall be known by the name of "Liberating Army for Races and Peoples."

3. Each one of the chiefs will do his utmost by whatever means possible, to get possession of the arms and funds of the cities which he has beforehand been designated to capture in order that our cause may be provided with resources to continue the fight with better success, the said leaders each being required to render an account of everything to his superiors, in order that the latter may dispose of it in the proper manner.

4. The leader who may take a city must immediately name and appoint municipal authorities, in order that they may preserve order and assist in every way possible the revolutionary movement. In case the capital of any State which we are endeavoring to liberate be captured, there will be named in the same manner superior municipal authorities for the same purpose.

5. It is strictly forbidden to hold prisoners, either special prisoners (civilians) or soldiers; and the only time that should be spent in dealing with them is that which is absolutely necessary to demand funds (loans) of them; and whether these demands be successful or not, they shall be shot immediately, without any pretext.

6. Every stranger who shall be found armed and who cannot prove his right to carry arms, shall be summarily executed, regardless of race or nationality.

7. Every North American over 16 years of age shall be put to death, and only the aged men, the women, and children shall be respected. And on no account shall the traitors to our race be respected or spared.

8. The Apaches of Arizona, as well as the Indians (redskins) of the territory shall be given every guarantee, and their lands which have been taken from them shall be returned to them, to the end that they may assist us in the cause which we defend.

9. All appointments and grades in our army which are exercised by subordinate officers (subalterns) shall be examined (recognized) by the superior officers. There shall likewise be recognized the grades of leaders of other complots which may not be connected with this, and who may wish to co-operate with us; also those who may affiliate with us later.

10. The movement having gathered force, and once having possessed ourselves of the States above alluded to, we shall proclaim them an independent republic, later requesting, if it be thought expedient, annexation to Mexico without concerning ourselves at that time about the form of government which may control the destinies of the common mother country.

11. When we shall have obtained independence for the Negroes we shall grant them a banner which they themselves shall be permitted to select, and we shall aid them in obtaining six States of the American Union, which States border upon those already mentioned, and they may from these six States form a republic and they may therefore be independent.

12. None of the leaders shall have power to make terms with the enemy without first communicating with the superior officers of the army, bearing in mind that this is a war without quarter, nor shall any leader enroll in his ranks any stranger unless said stranger belongs to the Latin, the Negro, or the Japanese race.

13. It is understood that none of the members of this complot (or any one who may come in later) shall upon the definite triumph of the cause which we defend, fail to recognize their superiors, nor shall they aid others who with bastard designs may endeavor to destroy what has been accomplished with such great work.

14. As soon as possible each local society (junta) shall nominate delegates, who shall meet at a time and place beforehand designated, for the purpose of nominating a permanent directorate of the revolutionary movement. At this meeting shall be determined and worked out in detail the powers and duties of the permanent directorate and this revolutionary plan may be revised or amended.

15. It is understood among those who may follow this movement that we will carry as a singing voice the independence of the Negroes, placing obligations upon both races, and that on no account shall we accept aid, either moral or pecuniary, from the government of Mexico, and it need not consider itself under any obligations in this, our movement.

EQUALITY AND INDEPENDENCE.

21 J. T. Canales ◆
A Chicano Lawyer Blasts the Texas Rangers

A long history of border troubles, persistent ethnic animosities, and virulent nationalism precipitated by cross-border raids combined to create an explosive climate in the South Texas-Tamaulipas region in the 1910s. Miscarriages of justice by poorly trained and bigoted U.S. law-enforcement authorities against Spanish-speaking people were common. In this document, J. T. Canales, a Texas lawyer and state representative, testifies concerning abuses perpetrated by the Texas Rangers.

I have lived in Brownsville and its vicinity since 1904 and am well acquainted with conditions there. I have known the Rangers since I was born; in fact, my home, La Cabra Ranch, has been a haven for the Rangers. They stayed there, were stationed there, came there at all hours, got our horses, got our meals there, and they got our services. I have known among the Ranger forces some of the noblest and best men that I know. Captain Hughes, Captain Rogers, Captain Wright, and various other individuals. At that time they gave us protection. They were a capable set of men, and did not need any restriction because their own conscience was a self-restraint and law. In 1915, so far as my recollection goes, is when the first general outrages perpetrated by Rangers began. The service began to degenerate since that time. I will describe the condition of my town and my country about that time.

Unquestionably what we call the bandit troubles had their origin in German propaganda. I have in my home in Brownsville letters written to clients of mine threatening their lives if they did not join in the band [of raiders] and stating that they [the raiders] were financed by the Germans, that they [the clients] need not be afraid because there were 70,000 German soldiers in Texas who would take up arms with them. This condition existed just immediately prior to the bandit trouble. I handed those letters to my sheriff, Captain Vann, and consulted with him. At that time they [the law officials] never believed there was any truth in the German propaganda. Since that time we have established beyond question that German propaganda was initiated for the purpose of forcing either an intervention or a war between the United States and Mexico, so as to prevent the United States from entering the European war.[1]

From *Proceedings of the Joint Committee of the Senate and the House in the Investigation of the Texas State Ranger Force* (Austin: Texas State Archives, 1919), 856–74.

There was a great deal of dissatisfaction in wages. Some Mexicans were not paid by men who employed them. Some of those Mexicans were beaten and mistreated by what I supposed, or who were reputed to be, good men in my country, who took advantage of the conditions so as not to pay them, and in that manner agitated the friction between the two races. There was nothing but general stealing—they [Mexicans] stole saddles, arms and ammunition, and horses, but no life of an American in any way was threatened. It was about the latter part of June 1915, or the first part of July, that the first trouble commenced. [On July 28,] Daniel Hinojosa, who is now in the Ranger Service, and Frank Carr, a deputy sheriff of Captain Vann, arrested a man by the name of Rodolfo Muñoz nineteen or twenty miles from Brownsville, at eleven o'clock at night. They could have taken Muñoz to Brownsville in the morning. They could have taken him on the noon train, or on the afternoon train; they could have taken him safely in an automobile in the afternoon, but they started with him about eleven o'clock. It was generally known that Muñoz was in concert with certain citizens, among them some leading citizens not only of San Benito but of Harlingen. [On the way they were met by a band who] took the prisoner from them and after torturing him, they hung him. That incident immediately had this effect: every person who was charged with a crime refused to be arrested, because they did not believe that the officers of the law would give them the protection guaranteed to them by the Constitution and the laws of this state. The immediate effect, then, was that all men who were charged with crime would refuse to submit to arrest.

The next incident took place about a week later. It was called the Las Teulitas fight. Jeff Scribner led a party of U.S. soldiers and deputies to the Pizaña Ranch, near Las Teulitas Ranch. They arrived there early in the morning. Scribner had it in for one of the Pizaña boys, and Aniceto Pizaña afterward became one of the leading bandits, but at that time he resided at his own ranch. The purpose the soldiers had in being there was not to follow bandits but with regard to some private matter, some private animosity between Jeff Scribner on the one hand and Pizaña on the other. They were there with a company of soldiers and surrounded the house. The Pizaña boys were there, some eating breakfast, others were in the corral getting their horses ready to go out and gather cattle. The fight immediately started. McGuire, a soldier, was killed, and Aniceto Pizaña, afterward bandit leader, was shot through the thigh. Ramón Pizaña, the leader, was arrested, tried, and given fifteen years. I represented him. That was the first reason leading to the bandit trouble and this undesirable conduct of the Rangers. In that particular instance I stated that the man was absolutely acting in self-defense. The Rangers arrived almost immediately after this incident.

The incident that followed happened at Paso Real, where people were killed in their own houses.[2] Then there was the killing of the Austins at Sebastian, for which two Mexicans were convicted and hung.[3] Then there was the Norias fight [on August 8], in which no Ranger participated. They were there, but they were out on a scout. Five Mexicans were killed, and not a single American was killed at that time; one was slightly wounded. The Rangers arrived about an hour after the incident. Captain Ransom was sent there, and they began to kill Mexicans without giving them absolutely no [sic] chance. On the mere *dicta* or information given by any man the Rangers would go over there and unceremoniously kill him.

The effect was that immediately every relative of that Mexican would go to Mexico with his tale of woe, and it aroused a strong feeling between them and the bandits. That feeling increased to the extent that practically the Mexican border on the other side was at war with us, sympathizing with the relatives of these men that had been wrongfully killed, taken out of their homes at night after the Rangers had said, "If you surrender your arms we can protect you." Yet after they surrendered their arms the Rangers would go into their homes afterward and shoot them at night. Ten men were killed right near San Benito, right near the house of the father of Miss Janes, my stenographer.

Now, matters got very bad, until it culminated in the wreck of the train October 18, 1915. I was in constant touch with the situation and I cooperated with the military authorities there and furnished evidence to them. Sheriff Vann, who had been only elected shortly before and didn't know the Mexican character very well, was adverse to putting in Mexican deputies. I insisted to Captain Vann to put in Mexican deputies, because they could get in touch with those other Mexican bandits and thereby trap them easily. After that wreck, he realized that the condition was serious. General Nafarrate[4] was openly cooperating with the bandits and helped them with money and ammunition. We knew that. I then suggested the means of establishing Mexican scouts to cooperate with the military authorities that had camps every five miles. I told him it was necessary to get the Mexicans that lived in there and had been farmers and tenants along that border to give out information and to act as guides. The suggestion was taken up by Captain Vann and endorsed by him.

I then went to Colonel E. P. Blockson, gave him my plan, and he endorsed it. He gave me a short letter, giving orders to every commanding officer along the border to admit into full confidence any Mexican that I would recommend to him. Those scouts were unarmed; they were not to arrest anybody; they were merely to give information and serve as guides for the soldiers in order to trap those bandits. They were organized about three days after the railroad wreck. I spent three months organizing, guiding, and supervising this system of scouts. They were especially to watch at night while the soldiers were in camp, and they were instructed how to come at night into the camp without any risk to their lives. The first bandits connected with the wreck of the train were arrested at San Pedro Ranch on information given by my scouts. Major M. C. Butler, who was afterward murdered at Alpine, was in command at that time. I have his own letter stating that since the organization of the Mexican scouts, not a single band of Mexican bandits crossed through his line through the efficient information given by these scouts. I also had on the other side of the border men whom I had represented and who were in close touch and would give me information. I would furnish that immediately to the authorities on this side.

In December 1915, by the time the raids had been minimized, General Carranza came to Matamoros, and I was a member of the committee who called upon him. We requested of him the removal of General Nafarrate because we had information and evidence that he was assisting the bandits. He soon gave us his word he would relieve him, and he sent his own nephew, General Ricant, who was stationed there, and from that time we had no further trouble with the bandits.

But the Rangers had established a precedent, that is, whenever a suspect was arrested they would unceremoniously execute him on the road to Brownsville or to the jail, without giving him any opportunity. Frequently we would find dead bodies, and the ranches burned. Relatives were intimidated to the extent that they would not even bury their own relatives. That condition existed until it was nauseating, nauseating. It was terrible. I wrote to Governor Ferguson and told him what Captain Ransom and his men were doing. I received no information or reply from him.

I went to Austin in 1917 and the special Ranger bill was passed in the first called session in May. I was openly against it, because I knew that the Rangers had not reformed, that they were living up to the reputation they had acquired of killing their prisoners without giving them a chance to be heard or to prove themselves innocent. I was called to see Governor Ferguson. By that time we had declared war against Germany. In his office he asked me, "Are you going to oppose this Ranger bill?" I says, "Yes, I am going to oppose the Ranger bill and I am going to oppose the appropriation." He says, "I understand Jim Wells is also here against it." I says, "I don't know, I think Judge Wells is a very strong friend of the Rangers but I don't care about Judge Wells. He does not control my conscience. I am going to fight this bill because these Rangers have adopted a policy that is a shame and disgrce to my native state and to my American citizenship." I related to him these incidents and the number of men that have been killed without any justification and without any opportunity to be heard. Then he said,

> Canales, I realize that that is true, but we have just entered into war. I have reliable information that the Germans are making propaganda on the other side among Mexicans. You are an American citizen and I appeal to you as an American citizen not to make that fight, because it will imperil the property and the liberties of American citizens. I will give you my word of honor, I will remove whatever undesirable men. I will remove any man you will tell me that does not demean [deport] himself as a humane and good officer.

With tears in my eyes I shook his hand, and I said,

> Governor, on that appeal, to show you I am a loyal American, I am going to take you on that. Although the crimes that have been committed are terrible and I know these have disgraced my state and my American citizenship, yet on that appeal, Governor, I am going to show you. I am going over there and champion that bill.

And I went there and helped to champion that bill and it became a law.

It was soon after the governor vetoed the University Bill. We called him in that matter, and we impeached him. Whatever good intention he had to comply with his promise to me, he had no opportunity. A new governor was elected and a new adjutant general was placed in there, and I thought the new administration would correct the faults of the old, so the matter remained that way. While there were occasional misdeeds committed by the Rangers, the wholesale slaughter had stopped.

After my services in the House in May 1917, I went to Brownsville, and there was a great exodus of Mexicans into Mexico. The charge was made that it was on account of the Rangers and also on account of the registration [for the draft]. General Morton asked me to make speeches with him in my country to explain to the Mexicans the registration law and to show them that Governor Ferguson had promised to put a stop to all this mistreatment of the Mexicans, and I did. It was printed and circulated; it was translated into Spanish and my name was signed to it. The exodus stopped.

In 1918 Captain Stephens was sent to my county, and so far as I know, he is a good and conscientious man, but I believe he was under the influence of men who had private reasons for disturbing conditions in my county. I mentioned names to General Harley, and I mentioned them to Captain Stephens when he came to my office. I told him not to be misled by those gentlemen, but to do his duty. He began to disarm our men. He would even take double-barreled shotguns along the river. I said then that

that should not be permitted. They were disarming Mexican deputies who had done loyal service to the government of the United States and had acted as spies at the risk of their own lives. They disarmed Pedro Lerma, who was the deputy sheriff, and they disarmed my own brother, who had made a trip with his family from my father's ranch in Jim Wells County to Brownsville and had a Winchester rifle .22. They took his rifle from him. He had to travel one hundred and twenty or thirty miles across open country. They took his rifle away from him and quite a number of other Mexicans who had only shotguns for the purpose of killing rabid dogs and coyotes. Those persons could not even have chickens because they had nothing to kill the coyotes who came stealing their chickens and the wildcats who would prey on them.

At that time the river was very dry and you could cross it anywhere. The various regulations and provisions were such that people across the river could not get anything to eat and they were hungry. They would come at night and would steal corn and cows, would steal everything from our tenants. My own tenants were left without absolutely a beast of burden to protect them. We could hear those people come from across the river. They would take our beasts of burden from our own yards, and we were afraid to go out because we didn't even have a shotgun. They disarmed us. That was the condition of affairs. The Rangers were not living there. They would go in the daytime and disarm the people, and at night sleep in good beds of ease at the hotels in Brownsville and Harlingen and San Benito. And there were our people disarmed and at the mercy of their countrymen on the other side who would come and steal everything they had. That was the condition in August 1918.

Notes

1. German revolutionary intrigue in the borderlands is the subject of Michael C. Meyer's article, "The Mexican-German Conspiracy of 1915," *The Americas* 23:1 (July 1966): 76–89.

2. On August 3, 1915, Rangers and deputy sheriffs attacked the Desiderio Flores ranch, north of Brownsville, killing Mr. Flores and his two sons, who were alleged to be bandits.

3. On August 6, 1915, a band of fourteen Mexicans killed Charles Austin and his son after robbing them.

4. The Carrancista commander at Matamoros.

V Boom and Bust

The period from 1920 to 1940 witnessed significant economic expansion and contraction throughout the borderlands. Prohibition in the United States (1920–1933) drove unprecedented numbers of Americans to such Mexican towns as Ciudad Juárez and Tijuana in search of liquor, gambling, and other amusements not readily or legally available north of the boundary. These visitors poured substantial amounts of money into the border communities, creating boom conditions in those sectors associated with tourism. Entertainment establishments contributed hefty taxes to all levels of Mexican government, making it possible for local officials to undertake needed improvement projects. American cities also profited from these activities in Mexico by hosting many of the tourists. In addition, they sold consumer goods to the Mexican borderlanders who now found themselves with more money to spend. Along with the benefits, however, borderlanders had to contend with epithets hurled at their communities by religious groups and reform-minded organizations outraged by the alleged "sinful" nature of border tourism.

The borderlands' economic boom began to dissipate with the onset of the Great Depression in 1929. The crisis brought major disruptions to business and industry on the U.S. side, causing trade and manufacturing to drop sharply. By the early 1930s thousands of Americans on the border were receiving welfare assistance, and many in the ranks of the unemployed were put to work on public projects. The hard times were felt with even greater force on the Mexican side, where spending by foreigners decreased as the number of tourists dwindled. Greater declines in the entertainment industry ensued when Prohibition ended in the United States in 1933. Furthermore, the Mexican government initiated a reform program that resulted in the closing of border casinos and related establishments. Large numbers of workers lost their jobs, and, as on the U.S. side, impoverishment set in for the *fronterizo* population.

Layoffs and poverty hit people of Mexican extraction living in the U.S. borderlands particularly hard. Most of these Mexican Americans already led marginal lives and were highly vulnerable to downturns in basic industries such as agriculture and mining. In the early 1930s, as economic conditions worsened and xenophobic pressures mounted, many Mexican Americans joined Mexican nationals in a massive "repatriation" movement back home. Most Chicanos, however, remained in the United States, weathering the crisis as best they could.

Essays in this section discuss the cycle of boom and bust in Ciudad Juárez-El Paso (Selection 22) and the hardships endured by Mexican Americans in the Tucson area (Selection 23). Conditions among migratory workers in Crystal City, Texas, are detailed in Selection 24, an official document of the U.S. government.

22 Oscar J. Martínez ◆
Prohibition and Depression in Ciudad Juárez-El Paso

Reflecting broad trends in many urban areas, Ciudad Juárez-El Paso experienced both good and bad times during the period from 1920 to 1940. What makes this area particularly interesting are the overwhelming impact that Prohibition had on the local economy and the disruptions that the Great Depression caused in cross-border economic and social interaction. During the crisis years, El Pasoans tended to blame the Mexican side for their economic woes, an attitude greatly resented by juarenses. This selection examines how the people of the "Pass of the North" coped with changing conditions.

Prohibition

"Juárez is the most immoral, degenerate, and utterly wicked place I have ever seen or heard of in my travels," stated American Consul John W. Dye in 1921. "Murder and robbery are everyday occurrences and gambling, dope selling and using, drinking to excess and sexual vices are continuous. It is a Mecca for criminals and degenerates from both sides of the border." "I would rather shoot my son and throw his body in the river than have him spend an hour in the raging inferno of Juárez," commented an American evangelist at about the same time. To Americans, as well as Mexicans from the interior, Juárez and other border cities represented blatant centers of sin and degradation during the Prohibition Era. Yet, as El Paso and the rest of Texas went dry in 1918 and as the federal Volstead Act (Prohibition's enforcement statute) took effect in 1920, gringos from all over the South, the Midwest, and the Southwest descended upon the Mexican frontier towns to quench their thirst for liquor and to enjoy pleasures not readily or legally available in the States. Being the largest of the border cities, Juárez quickly developed a variety of entertainment highly popular with the hordes of tourists.

Boom in Tourism

Juárez had unenviable fame before the Prohibition Era, but with the passage of the dry law this town achieved unprecedented notoriety. Bars, cabarets, gambling houses, brothels, honky-tonks, lewd shops, and dope

From *Border Boom Town: Ciudad Juárez since 1848* (Austin: University of Texas Press, 1978), 57–59, 78–87, notes omitted. © 1978 University of Texas Press. Reprinted by permission of the University of Texas Press.

parlors proliferated. One newspaper reported that the city's main street boasted more saloons than any other street in the world. Although a law forbade close crowding of liquor dispensaries, this same thoroughfare had a bar nearly every twenty feet for six long blocks. In addition to the ordinary tourists, the availability of liquor drew hundreds of bootleggers from Dallas, Kansas City, St. Louis, and Chicago. Smuggling contraband liquor became a prominent activity, and gun battles involving U.S. customs agents versus smugglers, rumrunners, hijackers, and other lawbreakers occurred frequently. Between 1928 and 1933, seventeen U.S. lawmen were killed along the Texas–New Mexico–Arizona portion of the border, seven in the El Paso area.

Wide-open conditions also prevailed at other locations along the international line. "Everything goes at Tia Juana," wrote the Board of Temperance, Prohibition, and Public Morals of the Methodist Church in 1920. "There are scores of gambling devices, long drinking bars, dance halls, hop joints, cribs for prostitutes, cock fights, dog fights, bullfights. . . . The town is a mecca of prostitutes, booze sellers, gamblers and other American vermin."

Tijuana drew large numbers of visitors from Southern California, including prominent personalities like Jack Dempsey, who acted as honorary race starter, and movie stars who regularly frequented the town, such as Charlie Chaplin, Fatty Arbuckle, Tom Mix, and Buster Keaton. On July 4, 1920, about sixty-five thousand people reportedly visited Tijuana. That day there were so many cars that San Diego exhausted its fuel supply and resorted to rationing.

Although wicked diversions remained the top enticements, the border towns offered the "respectability-conscious" visitor traditional "Latin" attractions. In Juárez, the famous old mission, the marketplace, curio shops, and just the plain feeling of having visited Mexico became strong magnets for many American vacationers or conventioneers. One writer estimated that 75 percent of all travelers on their way to California via the snow-free southern highway first became acquainted with the Mexican side of the border at Juárez.

Traffic became so heavy at the Pass that in a ten-year period two new international bridges replaced two old ones. The El Paso Electric Company, a subsidiary of Stone and Webster and owner-operator of an attractive $250,000 steel and concrete span, reaped a fortune in tolls. Motor cars using the bridge paid twenty-five cents (U.S.) each, and pedestrians two cents each. The *El Paso Times* likened the movement of people and vehicles to a "parade around the world." The monies collected from the toll bridges were sufficient to permit the Electric Company to profitably charge only six cents (U.S.) for a streetcar ride around El Paso and Juárez.

A route of similar distance in other American cities of like population required a fare of eight to ten cents, with the operators in other cities claiming that they were losing money.

Promoting Border Attractions

Anxious to make good use of Juárez for El Paso's advantage, Americans energetically publicized the attractions on the Mexican side. "Juárez is our greatest asset and we are just beginning to realize it," remarked R. Burt Orndorff, president of the Sheldon Hotel Company, in 1921. "High class tourists from the East on their way to California stop just to see Juárez. They have money to spend and they want to find a good time our neighbor across the river can give them—a dinner with liquor and other amusements." In 1923, the El Paso Chamber of Commerce launched a publicity campaign in major popular magazines and professional journals designed to reach fifty million people in the United States and elsewhere. This effort elicited twelve thousand inquiries annually between 1924 and 1930 from tourists and prospective settlers. "It is to El Paso's interest to cooperate most energetically with the people of Juárez and the government of Mexico to promote the legitimate development of the Mexican City," noted George E. Kessler of St. Louis, the most prominent city planner of the era and a consultant to the El Paso City Planning Department in 1925. The success of El Paso's advertising and the strong magnet Juárez presented to visitors is reflected in national and regional conventions held in the area during the Prohibition years, including the following: the American National Livestock Association, 1921 and 1924; the Panhandle and Southwestern Livestock Association, 1921; the Texas Hotel Men, 1921; B'nai B'rith (the national Jewish organization), 1923; the National Postal Clerks, 1924; the American Federation of Labor (AFL), in conjunction with the Mexican Federation of Labor, 1924; and the International Fair and Exposition of the Southwest, 1924.

Rail transportation companies also promoted El Paso-Juárez, allowing tourists ten-day stopovers to relax and take in the sights. Traveling salesmen in El Paso customarily took time to visit the famous town across the river. The El Paso Chamber of Commerce sought to make the visitors' stay comfortable and pleasant on both banks of the river, while Juárez officials issued identification cards to tourists, assuring them of good treatment and immunity from arrest except for serious crimes. . . .

Depression

The worldwide economic collapse of 1929 did not have an immediate effect on Juárez-El Paso. Newspapers on the American side reported healthy business during the Christmas following the Great Crash and through the early part of 1930. As the months wore on, however, local bank closings, business failures, and rising unemployment began to cause concern. In September 1931, the collapse of the First National Bank signaled the beginning of hard times in El Paso. During that same year three major developments plunged Juárez into the depression: tourism dropped sharply the entire length of the Mexican frontier; the Mexican peso was devalued by 38 percent in relation to the dollar; and the reverse migration of Mexicans from the United States back to their homeland accelerated greatly. In response to the deepening economic crisis, El Paso and Juárez each sought to employ certain self-protective measures, the effects of which were, of course, felt on both sides of the river.

El Paso Protectionism

As in other U.S. cities, the depression brought major disruptions to business and industry in El Paso, causing many stores to close their doors and manufacturing activity to plummet sharply. Between 1929 and 1939 the number of major manufacturing establishments (production valued over $5,000) declined by 21 percent in the city and 18 percent in the county, and the number of workers employed in such plants diminished by 63 percent and 50 percent respectively. By the end of 1932 an estimated seventeen thousand El Pasoans were receiving direct public relief, and thousands of homeless wanderers were getting aid from the Salvation Army. Another five thousand formerly unemployed men worked on improvement projects financed by the Reconstruction Finance Corporation. . . .

Greatly disturbed by their economic misfortunes, El Pasoans early in the crisis sought to prevent the flight of the city's resources. An area of concern was the border traffic, which many persons saw as a major drain of the town's wealth. By May 1931, the old issue of the closing time at the international bridge came to the fore again, and many business and professional people, troubled by the volume of dollars spent on Mexican soil, now joined reformers who wanted to stop their compatriots from drinking and gambling in Juárez.

Aided by the editorial arm of the *El Paso Times*, individuals and groups spoke out, passed resolutions, and circulated petitions, some destined for Washington, DC, asking that the bridge be closed at 6 P.M. or 9 P.M. A group known as the Businessmen's Protective Association ran a full-page ad in the *Times* notifying readers that arrangements were under way to make available to credit grantors the names of customers who gambled in Juárez. "These names will also be given to the employers of El Paso to determine who are the 'Gambling Suckers.' Gambling in Juárez is the curse of El Paso." The Baptist Workers' Conference of the El Paso Baptist Association, said to represent 4,000 persons, adopted a resolution which read in part: "We unanimously endorse by vote the vigorous fight . . . to close the international bridges at such hours as to prevent persons from going to Juárez to gamble at night." After expressing neutrality on the issue, the El Paso Chamber of Commerce reversed itself when a referendum among its members resulted in a vote of 368 to 91 in favor "of asking our government to change the hours of closing the international bridge."

Utilizing page 1 coupons, the *Times* conducted a straw vote asking readers about time preferences for closing the bridge. A total of 5,470 persons cast votes, with 83 percent favoring 6 P.M. and 6 percent midnight as the desired closing hours. The remainder of the votes were scattered. The *Herald Post* maintained neutrality until it was attacked by the *Times* for publishing a full-page ad from the Juárez Chamber of Commerce "which pointed out the advantages of Juárez to El Paso as a fun center for convention delegates." In response to the *Times'* charges that the ad constituted a defense of gambling and an attack on early bridge closings, among other things, the *Herald Post* wrote: "Instead of bickering over bridge hours and weakening our appeal to conventions—instead of attempting to use a club to force Juárez to operate as we think it ought to operate—the *Herald Post* insists that we . . . ought to capitalize on [other] advantages."

Other El Pasoans shared the opinion that the city, known as a "convention town," would lose business if access to the excitement of the other side was blocked. In addition, some felt that merchants would suffer if *juarenses* became discouraged from crossing into El Paso to make purchases because of possible bridge entanglements. These sentiments notwithstanding, apparently a great majority of the reading public desired the bridge closed at an early hour, if the *Times* balloting is an accurate gauge of such opinion.

Another matter which drew considerable attention involved the estimated one thousand seven hundred to three thousand five hundred aliens who crossed the border daily to work in El Paso. Dissatisfaction existed on the U.S. side with the classification of legal commuters as "immigrants," a definition which had been upheld by the U.S. Supreme Court in 1929. Widespread rumors circulated in Juárez early in 1931 that many commuters had been fired from their jobs in El Paso and had been replaced by Anglos. The Mexican consul in El Paso confirmed the reports, stating that the losses had occurred in industry and agriculture. He also noted that the so-called League of Unemployed Voters in El Paso was pressing merchants, industrialists, and immigration officials to curb the commuter traffic. The consul minimized the effectiveness of this latter effort, observing that the commuter issue was being used for political purposes in connection with approaching city elections, and noted that officials were not cooperating fully with the voter group.

The Record, a local tabloid bearing no publisher's name but probably printed by organized labor, proposed that commuters, apparently without regard to their legal or illegal status, be prevented from reporting for work on time each morning through utilization of a 10 A.M. opening time for the bridge. These commuters, whose ranks were said to include domestic servants and washwomen (40 percent), store clerks (15 percent), artisans (30 percent), and laborers (15 percent), were pictured as a "backward" and "docile" class of labor by *The Record*. Indicating the alleged negative effects of commuters on El Paso's economy, this organ made "An Appeal to Reason, Not an Appeal to Treason" to the public for support:

> If these aliens did not come over . . . many American citizens that are now walking the streets, would be earning a living for themselves, their wives, and babies. . . .
>   . . . We do not blame these Mexican workers. We have no malice toward them, but self-preservation is the first law of nature, and our first duty is to our own—those for whom we are responsible. . . .
>   . . . If these . . . workers were American citizens, they would pay rent to El Paso landlords, buy merchandise from El Paso merchants, attend El Paso places of amusement, and pay taxes to the city, state, and county.

Commuters, who ostensibly were paid only 25 to 40 percent of the American wage standards in El Paso, drew blame for many of the city's ills. Because of the presence of cheap labor, stated *The Record*, theaters and restaurants closed down, banks left town, stores lost trade, more businesses were "put to the wall," wages went down, taxes went up, the standard of living decreased, and the number of indigents increased. All these factors had brought El Paso "to a near wholesale bankruptcy of its general population." As a means of correcting such ills, *The Record* asked the public to sign petitions which had been distributed throughout town endorsing the proposal to close the bridge at 6 P.M. and calling for a late morning opening hour of 10 A.M. Eventually the bridge-closing campaign dissipated as the commuter traffic declined and as competition for El Paso jobs lessened with the return of many of El Paso's Mexicans to Mexico.

This, however, did not lessen the efforts of the U.S. immigration officials to keep Juárez residents out of the El Paso labor market. Prompted by pressure from labor organizations, the U.S. Immigration and Naturalization Service in 1934 started a campaign to round up *juarenses* who used their Local Crossing Cards to work in El Paso. The following year the El Paso Political New Deal called for a boycott of El Paso businesses which employed commuter aliens. This group claimed that some of its members had been fired from their jobs to make room for commuters, who received lower wages, and stated that these aliens spent all their money in Juárez.

The attitude toward alien labor resulted in harassment and sometimes mistreatment of many Mexicans who crossed the international bridge daily, with U.S. immigration officials routinely asking embarrassing and insulting questions. Often even legally admitted Mexicans who lived in El Paso found themselves unable to reenter the United States. For a time the initials *A. C.* were stamped on passports to identify El Pasoans receiving aid from the Associated Charities. On their return to the United States after a short visit to Juárez, such persons were refused admittance under the pretext that they constituted public charges. Hopeful immigrants also encountered severe difficulties. In Juárez, the American consul followed the contemporary policy widely implemented in U.S. consulates throughout Mexico of withholding visas even from persons entitled to receive them. In El Paso, the U.S. Public Health Service doctor remarked that he had "proof" that venereal disease afflicted 95 percent of the Mexican people, and promptly instituted a vigorous campaign to limit their entry into the United States.

These practices prompted the Juárez mayor to call for a boycott of American commerce, a response which disturbed the El Paso Chamber of Commerce considerably because of the loss of business and the negative image the American city was projecting throughout Mexico. A statement issued by the Chamber declared that Mexicans had always been treated with respect and dignity by El Paso's merchants, and that the reports of abuses at the bridge were exaggerated. The Mexican consul in El Paso concurred with the first claim, but he found validity in the charges of misconduct by the Border Patrol and sanitation personnel at the bridge. American businessmen arranged meetings between El Paso and Juárez officials to discuss matters. Subsequently the U.S. immigration office denied that its officers had behaved improperly and promised that no abuses would occur in the future.

A short time later the NCWC [National Catholic Welfare Conference] reported better treatment of Mexicans at the bridge, crediting their local representative, Cleofas Calleros, with pressuring border agents to curtail unwarranted and illegal actions against aliens, pressing the Associated Charities to stop stamping passports, and helping to persuade the U.S. Public Health Service doctor to adjust his pronouncements on the incidence of venereal disease among Mexicans to conform with those of other doctors in El Paso. In 1934, El Paso hosted a Migration Conference to develop better methods of dealing with problems at the bridge. *El Continental* editorialized and the NCWC confirmed that progress had resulted from this meeting.

Hard Times in Juárez

Difficulties at the international bridge compounded the economic woes faced by Juárez as a result of the decline in other major forms of border traffic. All along the frontier the total number of crossings, including the all-important tourist movement, fell sharply after 1930. The 27 million crossings of 1928 plummeted to a low of 21 million by 1934, and the traffic levels of 1928–1930 were not equaled again until 1944. The largest drop occurred between 1930 and 1931, with U.S. citizen crossings down by 1 million and those of aliens down by 2 million. In Juárez, tourist spending declined from $3.5 million to $2.3 million during those two years. Absence of data prior to 1935 precludes knowing when El Paso-Juárez regained the crossing levels of pre-depression times; yet it can be said that by mid-decade slow but steady recovery was under way.

In addition to the depression itself, a wave of reform on the part of the Mexican government, especially during the Lázaro Cárdenas administration, further dented the tourist industry. Such reform, however, came after the real blow had been struck with Prohibition's end in 1933. As municipal, state, and federal authorities pressed for the enforcement of new laws which banned disreputable diversions, the *Herald Post* reported "a startling transformation" in Juárez as mid-decade approached:

> Gone are the hundred-odd saloons, the downtown honky-tonks and brothels, and the open gambling. In the Tívoli Casino the visitor no longer can hear the click of dice, the riffle of cards, and the sing-song of croupiers at the roulette tables. The place is closed by presidential decree. The Moulin Rouge, once the home of nude dances, is closed. Part of the building is being remodeled for a grocery store. Calle Diablo [prostitution lane] is no longer the mecca for El Paso night life addicts. A few cabarets remain open in the restricted zone on Calle Diablo, but most of the girls have moved to El Paso's restricted zone. Juárez no longer has vice resorts on her downtown streets.

Reform efforts went beyond the mere closing of establishments. Police arrested scores of loiterers, thieves, criminals, drunkards, and prostitutes. Sixty-four men faced prosecution in October 1934 for exploiting women. That month *El Continental* noted that Juárez had become a "tranquil city.". . .

In Juárez, as in other towns along the frontier, employment opportunities diminished greatly. When the prominent gambling center El Nuevo

Tívoli closed down, 150 persons became jobless. Well-paid wage earners throughout the tourist district, such as bartenders and employees of cafés and restaurants, also lost their jobs. Taxi drivers, curio employees, ambulatory merchants, shoeshine boys, and the like were similarly affected.

These developments contributed to the reemergence of an old problem: the insufficiency of public revenues. The Ayuntamiento again faced the prospect of not being able to meet administrative obligations or to undertake needed public works. Juárez officials waged a continual battle with the state capital in an effort to secure more funds. Aside from the revenues from gambling and related operations, the Ayuntamiento had only one other major source of funds: the levies collected by the customshouse. With the former gone, local officials directed attention to the latter.

Under established policy, the federal government allotted 2 percent of the customs duties to the Juárez Junta Federal de Mejoras (Federal Board for Public Improvements), which made decisions independently of city officials on how money would be spent. In 1934 the Ayuntamiento expressed dissatisfaction with this arrangement, stating that the town's needs were not being met. It requested control of the board, so that critical projects such as installation of water pipes, paving of streets, and construction and maintenance of schools could be carried out promptly. *El Continental* endorsed the Ayuntamiento's stand, noting that public services in Juárez, especially the water system, had reached a critical stage. "The lack of water is frightening," this newspaper declared. "It can be said that the majority of the people . . . are dying of thirst and the situation will get worse." The water shortages became so serious that various groups from all social classes protested government inaction. Later, city officials petitioned the federal government for an increase from 2 to 5 percent in the share of the customs duties destined for the Ayuntamiento, arguing that Juárez deserved a larger portion and pointing out that without added funds public works would be seriously neglected. Toward the end of the year financial aid came from the state government, after a Juárez delegation journeyed to Chihuahua City to explain the crisis. . . .

As usual, the lower classes in Juárez suffered the most from the admixture of the various economic downturns. Begging became widespread, as full-time and part-time mendicants took to the streets in an attempt to supplement meager family resources. The many destitute Mexican migrants from the United States who were passing through Juárez on their way to Mexico's interior made the problem worse, causing constant irritation for local authorities. Police frequently undertook roundup campaigns to remove beggars from the downtown streets, particularly the tourist sector. On December 15, 1934, officers apprehended sixty indigent persons in just two hours.

Families of more means suffered less but still endured serious privations. Juárez historian Armando B. Chávez M. recalls that rationing, lack of agricultural products, reduction of commerce, inflation, and other hardships plagued *juarenses*:

> I remember as a young boy the anguish we endured during those years. Many things we were used to buying disappeared overnight. Then for many goods the price was extremely high. . . . Such basic items as food, shoes, dress clothes, and underclothes were hard to obtain. School supplies also became scarce when there was a shortage in the United States. We ran around after ink, pens, pencils, notebooks, and supplies for our technical classes. In those days students needed to buy wood, tools, instruments, paint, and screws for these courses. . . . We had a lot of trouble, but eventually we came out of the crisis.

Mexican Nationalism

In their search for solutions to the increasingly complex and difficult economic situation, Juárez leaders promoted a nationalist campaign early in the crisis. Partly as a reaction to the treatment of Mexican bridge-crossers by U.S. immigration officials and El Paso employers, and influenced by the growing nationalism in Mexico and throughout Latin America, municipal officials and other prominent citizens exhorted local residents in 1930 to "buy Mexican." Local prominent personalities also encouraged people to resist Anglo-American customs and to educate their children on Mexican soil. The Juárez Chamber of Commerce appealed to consumers' loyalties to their city and their nation, criticizing the prevailing preference for U.S. commodities and the seeming disdain for Mexican products. The difficulties encountered in changing attitudes were substantial, however, for Mexican stores had considerable distance to cover to provide the variety offered by U.S. merchants. That year *La Frontera* commented: "[On the American side] from a single teat of the same cow they offer us six different kinds of milk: certified, special, whole-cream, skimmed, 'whipping cream,' and 'table cream,' and from what is left over they give us 'buttermilk,' ten different kinds of butter, and a few more 'by-products.' Ours is simply 'milk,' and as a result we say that it cannot be good."

A year later *La Frontera* expressed satisfaction at some apparent successes of the campaign, noting that new businesses, particularly shoe and clothing outlets, had been established. "At last we can harbor the hope of once again being able to count on the respectable commerce that disappeared when the Free Zone was abolished many years ago," stated the business periodical. Readers were cautioned, however, that in order to carry the effort to complete victory the border region needed to manufacture more products. People demanded goods in sufficient quantity, of satisfactory quality, and at the right price. If such needs were not satisfied on Mexican soil, *juarenses* would understandably continue to shop in El Paso, warned *La Frontera*. The buy-at-home idea actually became a necessity after the devaluation of the peso. Concurrently the decreased demand for foreign goods gave small businesses on Mexican territory new impetus.

23 Thomas E. Sheridan ◆ *La Crisis*

Although located sixty miles from Mexico, Tucson, Arizona, has some
characteristics of a border community. Since the nineteenth century,
Tucson's economy has been linked with that of Sonora, Mexico, and the
city has experienced a steady influx of Mexican immigrants. As historian
Thomas E. Sheridan points out, the Great Depression brought large doses
of unemployment, poverty, and misery to Tucson's Chicano community,
prompting many people to become repatriates to Mexico. Among those
who remained, community-minded groups responded to the crisis with
fund-raising activities to aid the destitute, while many turned to religion
for solace and comfort.

On December 15, 1929, nearly two months after the New York Stock
Market crashed on Black Wednesday, the *Tucson Daily Citizen* assured its readers that all was well. "The year 1930 in Arizona will be
generally one of normal development and a continuance of conditions
which have for some time made the state a bright spot on all economic
survey maps," the newspaper reported. "A slight reduction in copper production is contemplated," the *Citizen* continued, but the Southern Pacific
was "looking forward to another banner year."[1] As the last Christmas season of what Leland Sonnichsen calls the "Gold-Plated Decade" rolled
around, the harsh economic winds blowing off Wall Street seemed very
far away indeed.

In retrospect such optimism appears touchingly naive. By summer of
the following year, depression winds were searing Arizona as well as the
rest of the country. Cotton and copper prices dropped, smaller banks
closed, and tax revenues fell precipitously. Transients and "automobile
gypsies" streamed into the state, while more and more Arizonans lost
their jobs as major industries trimmed their sails and tried to weather the
gale. *La Crisis*, as the Great Depression was known in Spanish, was settling like a summer dust storm across the state, choking mining, agriculture, and the railroad, forcing small businesses into bankruptcy and once
proud and independent families onto relief. Unlike a summer dust storm,
however, *La Crisis* did not pass quickly. The year 1931 was worse than
1930, and 1934 was rougher than 1932 or 1933. It wasn't until mid-
decade that the state slowly began to recover, and it took World War II to
end the depression once and for all.

Characteristically, *La Crisis* first rolled into Tucson by rail. The largest single employer in town was the "S.P.," as the Southern Pacific Railroad was called. But during the first half of 1930, the Southern Pacific transferred more than one hundred Tucson jobs to other cities, especially El Paso, Los Angeles, and Phoenix. It did so in a manner that was "neither abrupt nor sensational," but rather by means of a "slow whittling process" undoubtedly designed to reduce public anxiety and to prevent the outbreak of troublesome strikes. Furthermore most of these losses occurred in the "back shops" of the company's Tucson operations—the blacksmith shop, the car repair shops, the shops dominated by Mexican labor.[2] In other words, when the depression hit Tucson, it hit Tucson's Mexican railroad workers hardest and first.

Mexican Labor in Arizona

The laying off of Mexican laborers was not limited to Tucson, however. On the contrary, it quickly became a routine way to deal with the pressures of the depression throughout the Southwest and beyond. As unemployment soared to eleven million and farm and factory income dropped by nearly 50 percent, Mexican workers served as easy targets for politicians, government officials, and corporate executives who wanted to pacify their Anglo constituents. . . .

Unable to find jobs, swelling the relief rolls when they could get on them, Mexicans began to be viewed as a tremendous burden on an already ravaged economy. And so many people came to feel that there was only one solution to the problem—the Mexicans had to be deported, "repatriated" in the political language of the time. Policemen and government immigration agents consequently moved through major southwestern cities like Los Angeles, arresting undocumented aliens and transporting them by train to the border. In 1931, more than 124,000 Mexicans returned to their native land. Four years later, roughly half a million braceros had been repatriated, either voluntarily or by force. One of the major population movements of the early twentieth century was slowly being reversed. Men and women who had once been wooed by *enganchadores* (labor recruiters; literally, "hookers") south of the border were now being compelled to go back home.

Ironically, the repatriation movement represented a complete change in attitude toward Mexican labor from the one that prevailed during World War I and the 1920s. Prior to the depression, the U.S. economy greedily demanded more Mexican workers than the laws allowed. Hundreds of thousands of legal and illegal immigrants therefore poured across the border to labor in U.S. mines, ranches, farms, and factories. At a time when the Quota Act of 1924 was all but eliminating the flow of Asians and Eastern Europeans into the United States, powerful business interests made sure that Mexicans were not included under the restrictions. As California farmer Samuel Parker Frisselle told a Senate committee, "We must have labor; the Mexican seems to be the only available source of supply, and we appeal to you to help us in the matter. . . ." A spokesman for the American Mining Congress reiterated Frisselle's plea, arguing that braceros were the "backbone" of the U.S. mining industry, constituting 60 percent of the mining labor force. U.S. railroads were even more dependent upon Mexican workers, who made up from 50 to 90 percent of the employees in every company belonging to the Association of Railway Executives. In the words of pioneer Mexican anthropologist Manuel Gamio, "A large part of the commercial and industrial activity in the frontier cities and states developed by using Mexican labor, and it would now be impossible or exceedingly difficult to continue such enterprises without it."

Because of the commercial nature of its economy, Tucson did not host as many of these immigrants as other areas of the Southwest. Nevertheless, Tucsonenses watched as many of their *"paisanos"* passed through town on their way to the cotton fields of the Salt River Valley. Thousands of these farm workers, in fact, were recruited south of the border by *enganchadores* who promised them *"el oro y el moro"* ("gold and glory") to pick cotton in the hot Arizona fields.[3] Once "hooked" (*enganchado*), however, the immigrants were often abused and cheated by labor recruiters or cotton growers. As early as 1918, *El Tucsonense* was complaining about the mistreatment of Mexican farm workers.[4] At the end of the 1921 harvest season, an estimated twenty-four thousand Mexicans in the United States were thrown out of work, fifteen hundred of them in Arizona alone.[5] And since the cotton growers frequently failed to pay Mexicans their wages, many of the *enganchados* were forced to make their way back to Mexico as best they could, relying on charity for food, clothing, and shelter.[6] In a moving article written in 1922, *El Mosquito* described the large trucks "loaded with human flesh" (*"cargados de carne humana"*) passing through the streets of Tucson, carrying hungry, half-naked farm workers back to the border.[7] Like so many others, these unfortunate immigrants were victims of the *enganchadores*, those "slave traffickers for the cotton companies" who promised workers they could "gather up money with a broom."[8] More often than not, however, the workers were contracted to growers who refused to pay them the meager one and one-half to two cents a pound they were supposed to make.[9] In such fashion, the cotton industry in Arizona boomed, while the braceros were left to fend for themselves as soon as the fields were picked clean.

The depression compounded this misery by taking away the opportunity to make even a subsistence living on the cotton farms. In 1931, six thousand four hundred out of a total of forty-five thousand Mexican laborers in the Salt River Valley voluntarily chose to return to Mexico as Arizona agriculture declined. Many others were forced back across the border by immigration authorities or federal judges, occasionally because of the petitions of U.S. citizens.[10] In February of 1930, for example, twenty Mexicans were deported from Tucson after pleading guilty in federal court to charges of entering the United States illegally.[11] Ten more were convicted of the same charge in July, but they were sentenced to three hundred days in the Santa Cruz County Jail before deportation.[12] Even though Tucson never experienced the massive wave of arrests that swept across larger cities like Los Angeles, the town still witnessed the forced repatriation of some Mexican nationals living in its barrios. And these occasional deportations kept occurring at least as late as 1936, when Carmen Calderón and her six children were shipped back to Mexico despite the fact that four of the children had been born in the United States.[13]

La Crisis in Tucson

Of course, not all repatriates were forced to return to their native land. As work in the mines and railroads dried up, many chose to weather *La Crisis* in Mexico rather than the United States. In 1931, for instance, the Mexican consul in Phoenix reported that over 7,000 Mexicans had registered for repatriation at the border. Among these emigrants were a group of 117 miners from the Ray-Sonora area in central Arizona.[14] During the depression, *el otro lado* ("the other side"; the United States) no longer held the attraction it had enjoyed the decade before.

Most Mexicans, however, remained in the United States, hanging on as best they could in the mining towns and farming districts, or migrating to cities like Tucson in search of jobs. Some found employment. Others lived on the margins, adopting a number of different strategies to survive. . . .

In Tucson the poor and unemployed undoubtedly ate a lot of prickly pear along with other wild foods such as mesquite pods, cholla buds, saguaro fruit, and *quelites*, or wild greens. People also rummaged through garbage dumps or sold bootleg liquor. According to Henry García:

> During Prohibition, bootlegging was another occupation that the women were involved in. There was bootlegging all over Tucson, and in the barrio, the people who actually sold the liquor to the customers were usually women. A woman would set up a room, with tables and chairs

and everything, and the men would come in, have a few drinks, talk and socialize. They sold mostly corn whiskey, *maíz*, they called it.[15]

Typical of many families' experiences is the story of Teresa García Coronado, who fled to the United States with her husband during the Mexican Revolution. Before the depression, Teresa's husband labored in various mines across Arizona, including Oak Creek, Copper Queen, Silver Bell, and Baboquivari. "In those days a man worked from dawn to dusk," Teresa recalled. "We only worked in the mines and that's the reason I never learned English. Only Mexicans worked there."[16]

During *La Crisis*, though, many mines closed. Teresa and her husband occasionally found work in the cotton fields, but other times they were unable to get jobs no matter how hard they looked. When their daughter Concepción was stricken with a disease that resulted in paralysis, the little girl cried out for eggs. Since there were only beans in the house, Teresa's husband was forced to steal from the chicken coops of more prosperous barrio residents. Teresa herself resorted to desperate measures to bring her family through the hard times. In her own words:

> I was going around to gather up whatever there was. One time the men of the C.C.C. [Civilian Conservation Corps] threw out two dead cows, and I grabbed a quarter which a man cut into three portions for me. They [the C.C.C.] had thrown them out for the people who were scavenging in the garbage dump of Hollywood [a local westside Tucson barrio]. There were apples and rotten oranges. There were long lines to receive the food that they gave away. That which I did for my children gave me no shame.[17]

Teresa Coronado and her family represented one end of the economic spectrum. They were the people without regular jobs, without their own businesses, people who felt the depression full force. Another vivid if fictional account of depression life among poor Mexicans in Tucson can be found in Richard Summers's novel *Dark Madonna*, the story of the Salcido family's attempts to survive *La Crisis* in the barrios. *Dark Madonna* suffers from many of the cultural stereotypes of the time, its characters speaking a mixture of Spanish and pidgin English that often sounds dangerously close to the Mexican caricatures on the Hollywood screen. Nonetheless, Summers does manage to capture the desperation and grinding poverty of those times, especially in the character of the father, Anselmo, a proud working-class man who loses his job and is forced to make and sell bootleg liquor to feed his family. Arrested by the police, he is sent to prison while the rest of the Salcidos eke out a living during the worst days of *La Crisis*, surviving on odd jobs and charity. By the end of the novel, Anselmo, released from jail, gathers up his family and decides to leave Tucson for Mexico, disgusted at life in the United States. But after crossing the border, he remembers the hardships of revolutionary Mexico; he turns the car around and the Salcidos head for Los Angeles, part of the stream of Tucsonenses who began migrating to California during the 1930s.

Not all Mexicans in Tucson suffered so acutely, however. Carlos Jácome, for example, opened his new department store in downtown Tucson in 1931, the year before his death. Under the management of his son Alex, Jácome's soon became one of the finest emporiums in the city. Other prominent Mexican businessmen like Federico Ronstadt, Arturo Carrillo, and Perfecto Elías endured some rough times, but ultimately their enterprises prospered and expanded as the economic climate changed for the better. Yet no one completely escaped *La Crisis*. Even middle-class families had to tighten their belts and pull together during the lean years of the early 1930s.

Many of the town's middle-class Mexican businessmen and professionals, in fact, became leaders in the drive to help destitute members of their community. Numerous charitable organizations were being formed in Tucson, but resources were limited and Mexicans often were overlooked by Anglo institutions. Mexican leaders therefore sponsored their own efforts to give aid to Mexican families struggling to persevere in the barrios.

One of the earliest of these charitable endeavors was a series of Sunday night dances at the Blue Moon Ballroom. Organized by the elite Club Latino during the spring of 1930, the dances raised money for free lunches at Ochoa school.[18] The following August, Dora Munguía and other Mexican women in town formed a local chapter of the Mexican Blue Cross.[19] And toward the end of that bitter year, representatives of the Alianza Hispano-Americana, the Sociedad Porfirio Díaz, the Sociedad Mexicana Americana, the Leñadores del Mundo, the Unión Fraternal de Ayuda, the Club Azteca, the Club Latino, and the Club Alma Joven gathered together at the home of Arturo Carrillo to formulate a major plan of relief. The result was the Comité Pro-Infantil, which provided food for needy children at Drachman, Davis, and Carrillo schools.[20]

There were individual gestures of generosity as well, such as pharmacist José Canales's offer to fill prescriptions free of charge for unemployed Mexicans at the Botica Cruz Blanca.[21] These Mexican-led, Mexican-run charities were particularly important during the early days of *La Crisis*, when many sectors of the Anglo community were more interested in deporting than assisting Mexicans in the United States.

Not surprisingly, *La Crisis* also caused many people to seek supernatural solace. In Tucson, one of the most popular religious shrines was *El Tiradito* [the place of the fallen one], a refuge of crumbling adobe and flickering candles lit by people desperate for jobs or health or love. Located in Barrio El Hoyo near Carrillo school, *El Tiradito* was a barrio legend long before the depression arrived. Like many oral traditions, there were a variety of accounts about the origin of the place. One common version contended that the shrine marked the burial spot of a young man who came to Tucson to look for his long-lost father. After finally locating his father's home, the young man was talking to his beautiful young wife when the older man returned. Not recognizing his son, the father fatally stabbed the young man in a fit of jealousy. Another variation of the legend claimed that a drunkard was killed and buried at *El Tiradito* by members of his own family after he assaulted a young girl.[22] Regardless of these different origin myths, however, one common theme emerges. *El Tiradito* commemorated a murder, one committed by relatives rather than strangers.

With a sense of belief that captured the mystery of Sonoran Catholicism, many Tucsonenses came to *El Tiradito* to pray for help where blood had been spilled and a lost soul had gone forth to confront the unknown. Visitation only increased during the depths of the depression.[23] Those hard years spawned another *Tiradito* as well, one located on South 19th Avenue near West Twenty-Third Street where two people named Conrado Villa and Jesse Morgan had been murdered.[24] As people struggled to survive, desperation bred desperate remedies, and both *Tiraditos* flourished.

Notes

1. *Tucson Daily Citizen*, December 15, 1929.
2. *Arizona Daily Star*, July 22, 1930.
3. *El Mosquito*, October 14, 1922.
4. *El Tucsonense*, November 20, 1918.
5. *El Tucsonense*, January 29, 1921.
6. *El Mosquito*, October 15, 1921.
7. *El Mosquito*, October 14, 1922.
8. *El Mosquito*, November 12, 1921.
9. *El Mosquito*, November 5, 1921.
10. *El Tucsonense*, March 31, 1931.
11. *El Tucsonense*, February 4, 1930.
12. *El Tucsonense*, July 19, 1930.
13. *El Tucsonense*, August 14, 1936.
14. *El Tucsonense*, June 23, 1931.
15. Henry García, "Mi joventude en Tucson," *Nuestra Voz* 2(4):12–13, 1984.
16. Interview with Teresa García Coronado, November 1982, conducted by Belén Ramírez and Joseph Noriega, Mexican Heritage Project, Arizona Historical Society.
17. Ibid.
18. *El Tucsonense*, March 15, 1930.

19. *El Tucsonense*, August 2, 1930.

20. *El Tucsonense*, December 20, 1930; December 23, 1930.

21. *El Tucsonense*, January 13, 1931.

22. Interview with Eloisa López Ybarra, June 10, 1982, conducted by Belén Ramírez, Joseph Noriega, and Thomas Sheridan, MHP, AHS.

23. *El Tucsonense*, November 13, 1930.

24. Ibid.

24 Selden C. Menefee ◆ Mexican Migratory Workers in South Texas: Crystal City, 1938

During the Great Depression, large numbers of impoverished Mexican Americans residing in towns in South Texas had to engage in migratory farm labor in order to make ends meet. Crystal City, a prime agricultural center, provides a good example of this phenomenon. The following excerpt from a report compiled by the Work Projects Administration describes the dismal conditions that prevailed in this Texas community during the late 1930s.

The Mexicans of Crystal City

Crystal City is an excellent example of a town which has become a winter concentration point for Mexican migratory workers. It differs from other South Texas agricultural centers only in that its population is relatively stable, the great majority of its Mexican families having returned each winter for many years to work in the spinach fields.

The growth of Crystal City as a migratory labor reservoir has been comparatively recent. More than three-fourths of the heads of families interviewed in connection with the present survey came to Crystal City after 1920.[1] Most of these—almost 60 percent—arrived there during the period from 1923 through 1931, when spinach growing was still expanding. Over 80 percent of the Mexicans came to Crystal City to find work, 44 percent of them specifically to work in spinach.

Crystal City was apparently a secondary migration point. Only a fifth of the family heads came directly from Mexico; 77 percent had lived in some other part of Texas before they moved to the spinach center.[2] About 85 percent said that their families had originally come from one of the states of northeastern Mexico; 60 percent of all families had originated in Coahuila, the nearest border state, which is less than 50 miles away from Crystal City. About seven-eighths of the heads of families gave unskilled labor as their usual occupation prior to taking up spinach work. Nearly all of these had been agricultural workers.

Large families were the rule in Crystal City; the average[3] family included 5.5 persons at the end of 1938. More than four-fifths of all families were of the "normal" type, with husband and wife, with or without

From *Mexican Migratory Workers of South Texas* (Washington, DC: Work Projects Administration, Government Printing Office, 1941), 10–11, 41–45.

children.[4] More than seven-eighths of the families had one or more members who were citizens; most of the children were American-born.

The families studied had an average of 3.1 workers each.[5] The number of workers increased in striking progression with size of family. Families of nine persons or more averaged more than five workers; the largest family, with eighteen persons, had twelve workers.

These are the Mexicans who work in the spinach industry of Crystal City and the Winter Garden Area. They consider this South Texas town their permanent home. Year after year they return to cut, haul, ice, and load spinach for the winter market. In the last few years their earnings in spinach work have dropped because of low wages and decreased production round Crystal City, and a few have moved to other places. But most of them have continued to spend their winters in Zavala County in order to get what work they can. They depend mainly on their work in summer crops for their livelihood and draw on their beet and cotton earnings in order to live while they are working the spinach crop during the winter. . . .

Social Conditions among the Mexicans

The Mexican quarter of Crystal City is divided into two main parts, covering roughly a square mile. The larger section, called "Mexico Grande," is located north of the business section; the smaller section, "Mexico Chico," extends to the south and east of the center of the town. There is also a smaller settlement at River Spur, a little more than a mile from the town. These areas are crowded with the houses and shacks of the Mexicans in spite of the abundance of open land near by. They have no modern improvements; sewers and street lights are lacking. The unpaved streets are dusty in summer and muddy in winter.

Within this Mexican section are found the social maladjustments that usually accompany poverty. The ramshackle houses are overcrowded, health conditions are bad and medical care is inadequate, school attendance is poor and unenforced, relief is not available to many of those who are unemployed, and the social life of the Mexicans is hedged about with economic and racial restrictions.

Housing

The houses of the Crystal City Mexicans are mostly unpainted one- or two-room frame shacks with single walls, the cracks being covered on the outside with narrow strips of lumber. A few are adobe huts, a cheap and durable type of sun-baked brick construction used widely in Mexico.

The majority have dirt floors; only comparatively prosperous families possess houses with wooden floors. Tin roofs predominate, often with no ceilings below, so that in sunny weather the insides of the shacks become very hot. Most of the houses have one or two glass windows, but some have only cheese cloth or flour sacks over the window openings to keep the insects out. Flies, attracted to the Mexican quarter by the open toilets and the lack of any system of refuse disposal, find their way into the houses in spite of such safeguards.

The poorer houses are patched together from scraps of lumber, old signboards, tar paper, and flattened oil cans. They usually have one room, with a lean-to kitchen in some cases. Some of the occupants do not have stoves, but cook outside over open fires in warm weather and in open washtubs inside when the weather is cool. Many of these shacks were built by squatters on public land or on land rented for 50 cents per month.

Less than a tenth of the three hundred dwellings visited had electric lights, and still fewer had indoor plumbing. The usual procedure in obtaining water was for several families to share a single outdoor water faucet, each paying 50 cents to $1 per month water rent for this privilege. About one family in ten used wells, cisterns, or river water.

Most of the Mexicans' houses were filled to overflowing, there being an average of 2.6 persons to the room.[6] As size of family increased, the number of rooms per house failed to keep pace: two-person families averaged about one person to the room, while families of ten persons or more had an average of more than four persons to the room. Fifteen families of ten persons or more lived in one- or two-room houses. . . .

Health

Because of low incomes, poor housing, unsanitary conditions, and inadequate medical care, sickness and disease are common among the Mexicans of Crystal City and the Winter Garden Area. According to a relief official in a neighboring town, the tuberculosis rate is extremely high in the Winter Garden because the Mexicans have been undernourished over a long period of years. Enteritis, tuberculosis, and other diseases are widespread in the Crystal City area.

From April to July of 1939 there was an epidemic of diarrhea in Zavala County. At least two thousand persons became ill. When one member of a family contracted the disease, almost invariably all other members would catch it. Several infants died before a doctor could reach them. By the end of June, sixteen persons, fifteen of whom were Mexicans, had died of diarrhea in the county. All of these but one were babies less than a year old. This epidemic was directly traceable to poor sanitation in the Mexican communities.[7]

Many cases of tuberculosis were reported among the three hundred families studied. In the first ten months of 1939, twenty-five persons died of tuberculosis in Zavala County; this is equivalent to about 290 tuberculosis deaths per 100,000 population per year.[8] The Mexicans reported great difficulty in gaining admittance to a state institution for the treatment of tuberculosis because beds were not available except for the most advanced cases.

Illness was very common among small children, partly because of the hardships accompanying extended periods of migration to the beet and cotton fields. Not only the long trips but also the unsanitary housing and living conditions prevalent in agricultural work had especially deleterious effects on the health of the children.

Many of the families complained that they could not afford the $2 fee charged for each visit by private physicians and that the public health services available to them were inadequate.

Education

Almost 22 percent of Zavala County's population was illiterate in 1930.[9] Nearly all illiteracy was among the Mexicans. The older generation is limited by its background of recent immigration and low economic status; and the younger generation is further handicapped by inability to attend school regularly when following migratory agricultural work.

Only about 17 percent of the children aged 7 to 10 years and about 40 percent of those from 11 to 13 years attended school for the full year in 1938.[10] Of the remainder almost half were in school during part of the year; many attended only during the spinach season, from November or December through March. The rest did not go to school at all in spite of a legal requirement that all Texas children 7 to 16 years of age must attend school for at least 120 days each year.[11]

The schooling offered in Crystal City consists of a grammar-school course and four years of high school. Most of the Mexican children go to a grade school on the edge of the town. There is an implicit understanding that the Mexicans shall attend this school, partly because of their language difficulties and their peculiar attendance problems.

Few Mexican children go beyond the third or fourth grade. The usual reason for dropping out is the necessity of migrating with their families. The Crystal City high school is open to Mexican students but few attend. Only the children of the most prosperous families are apt to go beyond grade school, and these are likely to be excluded from most of the high school's social activities.

The years of school completed by Crystal City Mexican youth by 1938 increased progressively from an average of 1.3 years for 8-year olds to 3.0 years for 14-year olds. Among 18-year-old youth, who had had time at least to enter high school, the average number of school grades completed was only 2.6. One in five had never completed the first grade and one in seven had completed five grades or more.[12]

Because of their poverty and inadequate schooling, American-born Mexican youth have scant opportunity to find employment except in the migratory agricultural work followed by their parents.

Notes

1. Only 38 percent of the San Antonio Mexicans came to that city after 1920.

2. In San Antonio 41 percent had come directly from Mexico.

3. The term "average" means median hereafter in this report unless otherwise specified.

4. Among the San Antonio Mexicans families averaged only 4.6 persons. Only 57 percent of the families there were of the normal type; 31 percent were "broken" families.

5. This compares with an average of 2.0 workers among the San Antonio pecan shellers.

6. The Mexicans of San Antonio averaged 2.2 persons to the room. The maximum number compatible with health and decency is usually estimated to be 1 person per room.

7. Data from Earle T. Norman, Director, Uvalde-Zavala County Health Unit, Uvalde, Tex.

8. By way of comparison, the tuberculosis death rate in the city of San Antonio was 129 per 100,000 population in 1928, and that of the San Antonio Mexicans alone was about 247 per 100,000.

9. Bureau of the Census, *Fifteenth Census of the United States: 1930*, Population Vol. III, Part 2, U.S. Department of Commerce, Washington, DC, 1932, p. 1010. In San Antonio the percent of illiteracy was 7.7.

10. The San Antonio children of migratory families had a much better record of school attendance, half of all those aged 7 to 10 and 62 percent of those aged 11 to 13 having attended full time in 1938.

11. *General Laws of Texas, 1939*, 46th Legis., ch. 4, p. 227. Earlier legislation included similar provisions.

12. In San Antonio 18-year-old youth averaged 5.2 school grades completed; only 5 percent had not completed the first grade.

VI Interdependence: Blessings and Curses

Since World War II transnational interdependence in the U.S.-Mexican borderlands has increased dramatically, converting twin-city complexes, such as Juárez-El Paso and Tijuana-San Diego, into highly integrated communities. Trade, tourism, migration, commuter workers, *maquiladoras* (foreign-owned assembly plants), and smuggling amply illustrate the dynamic relationship that binds the two sides of the border. This situation has proved beneficial to both nations. Working- and middle-class Mexicans have contributed significantly to the U.S. economy by providing abundant labor and by consuming American goods on a massive scale, whereas affluent Mexicans have made hefty investments in real estate and commercial establishments in cities throughout the U.S. Southwest. American corporations have channeled significant amounts of capital into the *maquiladoras* and other sectors of the expanding Mexican economy, and tourists from the United States have flocked to the border and to destinations in the Mexican interior in ever-increasing numbers.

Interdependence has institutionalized a climate of amiability and cooperation on the border, but the usual stability also has been interrupted repeatedly by frictions emanating from the sheer intensity of the cross-border interaction. Issues that have loomed large in border controversies include competition for space and resources, undocumented migration, ethnic tensions, drug trafficking, pollution, crime, and the exploitation of labor. With the enactment of the North American Free Trade Agreement in 1994, it is likely that issues that trouble the region will command more attention from Washington and Mexico City and that more resources will flow into those communities most affected by the extraordinary growth experienced in recent decades. That would be a welcome development for borderlanders, who have long had to confront on their own the myriad problems created by international forces far beyond their control.

A variety of issues that illustrate binational interdependence are discussed in this section's essays (Selections 25 and 26), including commuter workers, international migration, urban symbiosis, economic growth, environmental problems, and drug trafficking. Themes addressed in the documents include the *maquiladora* program (Selection 27), the world of undocumented Mexican maids (Selection 28), and the sense of isolation and neglect often felt by border people (Selection 29).

25 Lawrence A. Herzog ◆ Border Commuter Workers and Transfrontier Metropolitan Structure along the U.S.-Mexico Border

Mexicans began crossing the border on a daily basis to jobs in the United States in the latter part of the nineteenth century, when cities such as El Paso, Texas, then in the midst of rapid expansion, began recruiting foreign workers. By the midtwentieth century, all U.S. border cities relied on workers from the Mexican side to meet a large portion of their labor needs. Today, the Mexican worker commuter population is estimated at 160,000. Lawrence A. Herzog, a geographer intimately familiar with contemporary patterns of interdependence in the transfrontier metropolitan areas, offers an informative and insightful overview of the commuting system.

Commuter workers, Mexican citizens who travel across the border each day from residential locations on the Mexican side to employment on the U.S. side, are an important layer of the modern borderlands social system. The continuing movement of population, over the last three decades, into the U.S.-Mexico border corridor has created a unique human settlement configuration, one in which U.S. and Mexican urban centers straddle an international boundary and are economically and socially united within a single functional living space. We might call this space the "transfrontier metropolis" (Herzog 1990). Within the transfrontier metropolis, one finds intricate networks of communication and interaction. The frontier worker moving within this transborder space emerges as a unique phenomenon, requiring an understanding of not only the social, economic, and political elements of labor movement, but also of the geographic context, the transfrontier metropolis, within which that movement occurs. In this article, the analysis of origin-destination survey data for commuter workers in the Tijuana-San Diego region serves to illustrate the nature of transfrontier social structure in border metropolitan areas. . . .

The Transfrontier Metropolis on the U.S.-Mexico Border

The period 1950–1980 marked a time of profound demographic transformation for the U.S.-Mexico border region. In the decade of the 1970s,

From the *Journal of Borderlands Studies* 5, no. 2 (Fall 1990): 1–20, tables omitted. © 1990 *Journal of Borderlands Studies*. Reprinted by permission of the *Journal of Borderlands Studies* and the author.

seven U.S. metropolitan areas along the border experienced growth rates between three and five times the national rate of 11 percent, while in Mexico, border city population grew at rates of between 67 percent and 96 percent, far exceeding the national average for Mexico of 37 percent (Hansen 1984:140–141). This pattern continued in the 1980s, though at lower rates. These changes were fueled by escalating patterns of labor migration out of central Mexico toward the border. A steady migration stream fed the population of northern Mexican border cities, and, over time, several generations of Mexican Americans were created north of the border. Thus evolved a unique regional social system (Alvarez 1984) where family structures, culture, social interaction, and factors of production were fused across the boundary. Its most important byproduct has been the bicultural, transfrontier metropolises that have evolved along the border.

The existence of a regional need for Mexican labor in the United States, and thus the promise of temporary employment south of the border, led to urban development on the Mexican side of the international boundary. These settlements could house Mexican citizens who periodically migrated into the U.S. to engage in temporary employment, thereby supplying a source of income vital to their well being in their permanent residences in Mexican border cities. As the U.S. Southwest matured into a dynamic economic region, Mexican border cities evolved into important interim destinations for migrant workers. Later, during periods of mass deportations out of the U.S., they served as points of return and temporary residence for expelled workers seeking to sneak back into the U.S. Martínez has referred to these two important functions as "springboard/receptacle" functions (Martínez 1977).

The growth of paired urban centers, or "twin cities," at the U.S.-Mexico border is an outcome of the century old social system that evolved in the borderlands. The cross-border interconnections between pairs of settlements were recognized early in the evolutionary history of the modern border zone (McWilliams 1968). Increasingly, studies of border cities have emphasized the transborder nature of their social formation. Among these have been analyses of Ciudad Juárez (Martínez 1978), El Paso (Garcia 1981), and Tijuana (Price 1973, Pinera 1985). More intriguing, however, has been the question of symbiosis associated with these paired urban places. Researchers studying such border city complexes as Brownsville-Matamoros (Gildersleeve 1978), Laredo-Nuevo Laredo (Sloan and West 1976, 1977), El Paso-Ciudad Juárez (D'Antonio and Form 1965, McConville 1965), and San Diego-Tijuana (Duemling 1981, Herzog 1985, 1990) have identified a pattern of transborder interdependence that is cultural, economic, and even spatial (Dillman 1983). Price's study of

Tijuana (Price 1973) spoke of "international symbiosis," or the interdependence of two or more cultural systems.

The U.S.-Mexico transfrontier metropolis is an urbanized area enclosing a single functional spatial domain that transcends the international border. This zone of transnational settlement space is functionally unified by common daily activity systems (work, shopping, school, and social trips), shared natural resources and environmental features (air, water, flora, fauna, etc.), and product and labor markets that overlap the political boundary. The international border line sharply cuts across this social landscape, dividing the two culturally defined cities. These cities retain the elements of their nationally derived ecological structure in terms of density, social geography, road configurations, centrality, etc. The transfrontier metropolis thus embraces two opposing forces: the traditional cities, as defined by national culture, and the integrated metropolis, defined by evolving social, cultural, and economic processes that connect the U.S. and Mexico across the border on a daily basis.

The Evolution of Commuter Workers along the U.S.-Mexico Border

Commuter workers represent a unique layer in the process of immigration into the United States, a geographically concentrated system of daily or weekly movement north and south of the boundary. There is, of course, a large literature on the more general subject of Mexican immigration to the U.S.; however, until recently (Aramburo 1988, Acuña González 1988), little has been written about commuter workers to the U.S.

The Mexican commuter worker essentially was born in the period following the 1924 Immigration Act in the U.S. The early quota system organized in 1924 established that the number of immigrants from a given country permitted to enter the U.S. in any year could only be equivalent to three percent of the total number of foreigners resident in the U.S. from that country in 1910. The law immediately had an impact on legal immigration into the U.S. Total legal immigration decreased from 707,000 in 1924 to only 294,000 a year later (Calavita 1981:363).

The quotas created by these laws did not apply to immigrants from the Western Hemisphere, thus Mexican, Canadian, or other alien immigrants entering from Mexico or Canada could cross the border into the U.S. by obtaining a visa which classified them as temporary visitors. This created an enormous loophole by which foreign workers from quota-bound countries could enter the U.S. for employment (La Brucherie 1969). In 1927, under pressure from the American Federation of Labor, the U.S. Bureau of Immigration (now the Immigration and Naturalization Service [INS]) passed General Order 86, which redefined temporary visitors, so that quota-country aliens who entered daily as border crossers would be subject to, at their first entry, quota limitations applicable to their native countries. Once those quotas were filled, no more temporary visitors could cross the border. This order did not affect nonquota countries like Mexico and Canada, but it did institutionalize the creation of a class of commuter workers who had no intention of living in the U.S., but who were granted the same legal status as alien immigrants residing in the U.S. (La Brucherie 1969:1753). This order was challenged, but unanimously upheld by the Supreme Court in 1929. The 1929 case established that commuter workers would legally be defined as immigrants who had been granted permanent residence in the U.S. Each time they crossed the border to work in the U.S., the immigrants were considered to be returning from a temporary visit abroad. Since the commuter worker did not actually live in the U.S., under existing law he or she might lose immigration privileges if no domicile was established, but apparently the rules for commuters stretched the intent of the law, and allowed that the commuter's job in the U.S. could be a substitute for domicile (La Brucherie 1969:1754).

During the 1930s, restrictions were placed on the entry of Mexican workers into the United States because of the depressed American economy. But the infrastructure that had created the commuter worker phenomenon did not wither away. Indeed, the bracero program, established in the 1940s to bring Mexican labor into the U.S. to work in food production and other labor-intensive areas created by World War II, resurrected the cross-border legal flows of Mexican labor. After World War II, the Immigration and Nationality Act of 1952 continued the policy of regarding Mexican commuters as returning immigrants. Various court cases in the 1960s tested the legality of Mexican commuters' immigration status. In one, the 1963 *Texas State AFL-CIO v. Kennedy*, 1964, the INS reexamined the legal question of whether commuters needed to establish a residence in the U.S., and decided that they did not; "lawful admission for permanent residence" was a status gained by having been accorded the privilege of residing in the U.S. Whether that privilege was realized did not matter, concluded the INS. In general, the INS continues to operate under this philosophy today. The main legal restriction on commuter workers is that they are not permitted to cross into the U.S. as strikebreakers. They also must not be out of work for more than six months, although this rule is rarely enforced (North 1970).

In the 1960s, a new quota system was conceived in which the quantity of aliens permitted into the U.S. was calculated on the basis of skills, class, and education. In 1965, the U.S. Congress attached an amendment to the Immigration and Nationality Act of 1952. The new amendment imposed a ceiling on immmigration from the Western Hemisphere of

120,000. This went into effect on July 1, 1968. At about the same time, there were forces in the United States seeking to eliminate the Mexican commuter workers' status. Organized labor and certain Mexican-American groups wanted tighter border controls. In 1967, Massachusetts Senator Edward M. Kennedy introduced an amendment to the 1965 Immigration Act that would only allow commuter workers to enter the U.S. every six months upon certification of a need for their labor. This amendment was defeated. In 1968, the Select Commission on Western Hemisphere Immigration recommended termination of the commuter status of green card holders and creating a new form of border crossing authorization for noncitizens residing outside the U.S. The White House did not act upon these recommendations despite the fact that several studies suggested that border commuters may reduce wages on the U.S. side of the border and create unemployment for U.S. laborers (Jones 1969, North 1970). This has led observers to believe that U.S. policy serves the interests of employers, while skirting the letter of the law (Greene 1972).

It seems clear that the commuter workers continue to be an important part of the transborder social system, and recent social science research reports corroborate this (Aramburo 1987, Acuña González 1988). Mexican commuters appear to be permanently embedded in the social structure of the border region. The most recent immigration legislation, the 1986 Immigration Reform and Control Act (IRCA), does nothing to diminish the commuter phenomenon (U.S. House of Representatives 1986). In fact, it may have increased the flow of border crossers by creating two new legal forms of border workers: Special Agricultural Workers (SAW) and Replenishment Agricultural Workers (RAW). The SAW program offered legal immigrant status to any alien who could establish that he worked in agriculture in the U.S. for more than ninety days between May 1985 and May 1986. Over five hundred thousand Mexican workers may have qualified. The RAW program will annually import Mexican citizens to work for three years in agriculture; they can then apply for permanent resident status (Calavita 1989:163). While these programs are theoretically available to all foreigners, they will primarily affect Mexican nationals (North and Portz 1988).

Mexican Commuters and the Transboundary Metropolis

In the nine largest metropolitan areas along the U.S.-Mexico border, nearly 160,000 Mexican workers, according to one estimate (Aramburo 1988), commute to jobs on the U.S. side of the border each day. They form part of an intricate network of emerging transborder linkages between settlements on each side of the border. Such linkages demonstrate the extent to which the boundary has become more permeable to increased interactions between residents, businesses and institutions in the U.S. and Mexico.

Cross-border interactions do not occur randomly. They are part of a logical urban order: the transborder metropolis. In urbanized areas, human interaction around the boundary has become more consistent and predictable over time. Interaction can be studied within a variety of spheres: cross-border family ties, consumer travel linkages, labor market and business ties. The most significant sphere is economic: consumer and labor markets. Consumers find comparative advantages for goods and services on either side of the line. Workers migrate to jobs north of the border. The labor market connection may be the most important of all along the border.

More than one million Mexican border residents possess a border crossing card which allows them to enter and stay for up to seventy-two hours in a zone of not more than twenty-five miles from the border. The border crossing card does not permit the user to work in the United States. Yet, since there is no control on the use of these cards, it is probable that a large number of these border crossers work in the U.S.

Until recently, little was known about travel between U.S. and Mexican border cities such as San Diego and Tijuana. Ironically, although San Diego-Tijuana represents the most heavily traveled boundary zone in the world, the only regional data available on border crossings and international commuters has been collected by the Immigration and Naturalization Service, and estimates of monthly flows are considered to be rather crude (see U.S. Immigration and Naturalization Service 1983).

Given the extensive flow of daily labor between Mexican and U.S. border cities, primary data on Mexican commuters offers an opportunity to better understand the transfrontier social structure of border metropolitan areas. One source of such data comes from a study in which the author supervised direct field surveys of Mexicans commuting to U.S. jobs in the Tijuana-San Diego region. During two different weeks in the month of June 1983, a team of trained Mexican field researchers interviewed 436 Mexican commuters traveling north. The surveys were executed at the San Ysidro border gate, either in the vehicle inspection area or in the pedestrian entry zone. The sampling procedure was stratified by time of day, day of the week, and mode of transport at the border crossing. Only commuters were interviewed. Two thirds of the sample was selected from commuters crossing by automobile, while one third came from pedestrian commuters (this represented an approximation of the expected proportions from each transport type based on background research). The survey team randomly selected interviewees during stratified time periods (designed to intercept travelers during peak journey-to-work periods). All days of the week were covered. The survey included questions involving the origin and destination of commuters, frequency of travel, purpose of trip, typical modes of transport used in trips, and immigrant status.[1]

The survey revealed that commuters work in a variety of jobs, but are especially drawn to unskilled and semiskilled employment in services (45.1 percent of sample population), manufacturing (24.5 percent) and construction (13.3 percent). The transfrontier dimensions of these worker flows can be illustrated by geographically tracking the worker origin points in Tijuana and matching these with worker destination points in San Diego.[2] The origin data indicate that commuter workers in Tijuana tend to come from more established neighborhoods, clustered around the Mexican border city's central business district (Zona Centro, La Mesa, Independencia) or along the international boundary (Libertad).

This pattern is clearly tied to the logic of Tijuana's spatial organization. The structure of Tijuana is such that, in general, its population is highly concentrated in an urbanized core surrounding the less populated central business district. San Diego, by contrast, is a spatially decentralized metropolitan area with an extensive freeway system, public buses, and mass transit lines allowing considerable mobility. In Tijuana limited transport technology and cultural preference for the central city have led to residential location preferences being clustered closer to the center of town. The result is that most middle- and upper-class inhabitants traditionally live near the downtown core, while migrants from the interior of Mexico are usually forced to occupy squatter housing on the edge of the city, or in remote canyons isolated from the downtown (Griffin and Ford 1980).

Tijuana's physical structure thus offers an explanation for patterns of commuter worker origins in Mexico. Most commuter workers are residents who have lived in Tijuana for longer periods of time, allowing them to make arrangements to be able to legally commute to jobs in the U.S. These residents, as the data suggest, live in the middle-upper income districts of central Tijuana. There is thus a distance decay pattern with respect to the origin areas of commuter workers, but it may be that distance from the border is less important than distance from downtown (which happens to be near the border). Poorer residents live further from downtown (and the border in many cases), and tend to cross the border less regularly. The urban poor, and more recent migrants to the city, are less likely to possess border crossing cards which would allow them to participate in the legal flow of commuters between the two cities.

Although no single zone of Tijuana provides a majority of commuters coming to San Diego, the neighborhood displaying the highest levels of daily commuter migration to San Diego deserves attention. This area, known as Colonia Libertad, contributed nearly 13 percent of all commuters surveyed in the 1983 data, the highest proportion for any single neighborhood in Tijuana. Several explanations for its importance as a source area of commuters can be offered. First, Colonia Libertad is the oldest neighborhood in Tijuana, having first been subdivided in the early twentieth century when Mexicans in California were being deported south of the border (Hernandez 1983, Bustamante 1985). Residents of Colonia Libertad have lived near the border since the 1920s and, in some ways, are more Americanized than other Mexicans in Tijuana. They demonstrate a long history of transboundary travel, and have developed a bicultural heritage of language and work skills. Over time, many have obtained legal residence in the U.S., and the skills and knowledge to find employment north of the border.

A second reason for Colonia Libertad's large contribututionto the commuter labor force is that it lies strategically adjacent to the port of entry into San Diego. Residents are able to walk across the border and find passage directly to their work locations, speeding up their overall journey-to-work trip. This strengthens the already strong pull force of the U.S. minimum wage on Tijuana's civilian labor force. Equally important, although Colonia Libertad is an old, established neighborhood, there is still considerable poverty among long-established residents. Thus, economic need imposes a push force upon residents of this area, which, over time, has translated into the emergence of a commuter work force within the neighborhood.

The international journey to work, from Tijuana to San Diego, is possible only because workers have extensive networks of information about employment in San Diego. Information systems don't only extend to employment possibilities, they often involve *access* to job sites, as well. For example, clandestine private automobiles (*raiteros*) that link Mexican workers with places of employment have been developed to facilitate the journey to work. Personal friendships are also helpful in this process. Within Tijuana, there appears to be extensive shared knowledge among neighborhood residents about who works in the U.S. and their degree of success there.

Legal transportation connections between Tijuana and San Diego are highly accessible and extensively used by Mexicans. Workers both drive across the boundary as well as walk across. Those who walk can continue their work trip by connecting into the local public bus system, using the Greyhound bus, or by riding the light rail trolley system, all of which give adequate service from the border at San Ysidro to the City of San Diego, twenty miles north. Approximately 65 percent of the 1983 commuters surveyed who walked across the border utilized mass transit to arrive at their jobs; the others relied on private automobiles.

Workers who walk across the border, according to informal interviews carried out in the field, are the main users of the private automobiles available to take workers to specific job sites. Commercial parking lots near the border provide waiting areas for pedestrian crossers, ready to commute to their jobs. Separate rider systems exist for sweatshop manufacturing, restaurant and hotel locations, household service workers, and agricultural and landscaping workers. A substantial number of commuters are legal U.S. citizens, and thus can cross the border to work without difficulty. Many others, however, as mentioned above, do not possess green cards and may be crossing illegally to work.

Work destination locations for Mexican commuters display a greater degree of dispersion than do points of origin. Tijuana commuters work all over San Diego County, from the southern portions of the county (San Ysidro, 14 percent of total; Chula Vista, 27.9 percent of total) to the east (El Cajon, 4.0 percent) and north county (5.2 percent). While 75 percent of the commuter workers from Tijuana came from within six miles of the border port of entry, over three fourths of the destination sites were located within a zone extending fifteen miles from the international boundary. Employment patterns are highly specialized, and can be disaggregated by type of employment. The result is that specialized clusters of work trips are identified in the data, showing knowledge by Mexican workers of labor markets in San Diego. Specialized labor markets that are filled by Mexican commuter workers can be identified from the survey data in sectors such as automobile repair, hotel services, agriculture and landscaping, construction, and manufacturing.

Automobile repair worker jobs (10.8 percent of the sample commuter population), which included mechanical and upholstery repair, as well as painting, tended to cluster in Chula Vista, National City, and south San Diego. This labor market spills across the border from Tijuana, where automobile repair and recycling began as a necessity for residents driving used cars purchased in Southern California, and evolved into an important cross-border service industry. While Tijuana provides automobile repair services at low rates to Americans, San Diego's south bay area (including Chula Vista and National City) provides a similar set of inexpensive services to the San Diego metropolitan areas.

A second labor submarket is the hotel service sector (9.8 percent of commuter sample). San Diego is one of the leading U.S. cities for convention promotion, as well as a major tourism destination for U.S. and international visitors. The hotel industry (and tourism more generally) is an important part of the urban economic base, and Mexican commuter workers are crucial to the labor force in this sector. Female Mexican workers are especially important to the servicing of the city's approximately 30,000 hotel rooms. Geographically, two zones were heavily represented in the data: San Diego/Mission Bay and Mission Valley.

Agriculture and landscaping (18.3 percent of commuter sample) represented another category of workers displaying a distinct spatial pattern. San Diego County, with its four thousand square miles of terrain, usually ranks among the nation's ten most productive counties in terms of the aggregate economic value of agricultural products. Workers are mainly clustered in south San Diego County (San Ysidro and Imperial Beach), an area in which truck farming of commercial crops (mainly vegetables) remains vital, although these activities are gradually giving way to urban development. Interestingly, a much smaller proportion of commuter workers in the data set ventured into northern San Diego County, a larger agricultural production area than south San Diego. One might attribute this pattern to the distance-decay effect, yet a better explanation is tied to the recognition that this area employs a substantial number of undocumented Mexican workers in the production of avocados, flowers, and citrus fruits (Nalven and Frederickson 1982). Aside from farming cash crops, Mexican commuters also work as landscapers, principally in the north county area, the zone in which the largest number of new housing tracts are located.

Mexican commuters also worked in the construction (13.3 percent of commuter sample) and manufacturing (24.5 percent of sample) sectors. Construction jobs tend to be scattered throughout the urban area, but were especially noticeable on the urban fringe, the area where the largest proportion of new urban growth is taking place. In this sector, Mexicans tend to perform the lower-paying jobs, such as building foundations and laying concrete. Mexican commuters often work at minimum wage, and are not union members. The more sophisticated construction jobs, such as heavy grading, electrical finishing, plumbing, and framing, are typically filled by unionized Anglos.

Similar to the plight of construction employees, Mexican commuter workers in the manufacturing sector find themselves at the bottom end of the worker hierarchy. Work environments where the Mexican commuters dominate tend to be the least desirable of the manufacturing sector, and involve exposure to noise, dirt, danger, and other unhealthy conditions. Work locations for San Diego were concentrated in the south bay region (Chula Vista and National City) and the adjacent CBD [Central Business District], two of the principal industrial zones in the metropolitan area. Typical jobs filled by Mexican commuters included clothes manufacturing, manual assembly, cannery work, and laundry work. The area houses such industries as food and fish processing, shipbuilding, kelp processing, and chemical production.

Conclusions

Urbanization along the U.S.-Mexico boundary has produced a unique prototype of the human use of space: highly integrated, transfrontier metropolitan areas. The linking of U.S. and Mexican settlements along the border is clearly illustrated by commuter worker movement patterns. The Mexican commuter survey offers evidence of the dimensions of cross-border integration in the border metropolis of Tijuana-San Diego. The border crossers' international journey to work appears on the surface to be a simple case of intra-urban movement across an international border; in essence, it is a more complex phenomenon revealing how labor is exchanged when a city from a world industrial power shares a border area with a city from a Third World developing nation.

The international commuter data shows that in Tijuana-San Diego, commuters have become well entrenched in the region; they demonstrate considerable knowledge about labor markets on the U.S. side of the boundary. At least one neighborhood of origin (Colonia Libertad) owes much of its formation to daily commuters. In some ways, we might label this neighborhood a Mexican bedroom community for jobs in the U.S., since so many commuters reside here.

International commuters utilize formal transport infrastructure. In other cases, clandestine private automobile systems have been set up to help commuters reach specialized work destinations, and even to recruit temporary labor. Information is exchanged through these networks, allowing regular employment for those with commuting experience. Over time, linkages between origin zones and specialized job site destinations have evolved.

What the commuter worker patterns confirm is the notion that the international boundary tends to fade in highly urbanized areas, giving way to broader transfrontier domains where U.S. and Mexican cities are joined within a single transnational living space. The implications of emerging transfrontier metropolises continue to require further research. What will the demand for services near the boundary line be like in the future? Is binational coordination between the two nations possible for the planning of such infrastructure as sewer systems, energy plants, and health facilities? How will environmental problems that spill across the border in either direction be managed? What will be done to regulate the transboundary impacts of land uses near the border? These questions represent perhaps the greatest challenge facing border area policymakers, and it remains for scholars, writers, consultants, and others to begin to tackle these most difficult issues.

Notes

1. It should be noted that this kind of survey is limited by the logistics of the research environment. Automobile passengers and pedestrians waiting to cross the boundary are typically in a hurry to get to their destinations in the U.S., and therefore reluctant to participate in surveys. Some commuters feared that being interviewed might affect their crossing status even though the interviewers identified themselves as university researchers.

2. The author was assisted by Professor Frederick Stutz (San Diego State University) in the tabulation and mapping of the original commuter worker data.

References

Acuña González, Beatriz. 1988. "Transmigración legal en la frontera México-Estados Unidos." *Revista Mexicana de Sociología* (4):277–322.

Alvarez, Robert. 1984. "The Border as Social System: The California Case." *New Scholar* 9(1 and 2):119–133.

Aramburo, Guillermo. 1987. "Commuters en la frontera México-Estados Unidos." *Estudios Fronterizos* 5(12–13):81–93.

———. 1988. *Encuesta sobre transmigración en la frontera norte.* IIS-UABC, Mexicali.

Bustamante, Jorge. 1985. "Surgimiento de la Colonia Libertad," pp. 316–331, in David Pinera, ed., *Historia de Tijuana.* Tijuana: Centro de Investigaciones UNAM-UABC.

Calavita, Kitty. 1981. "United States Immigration Law and the Control of American Labor." *Contemporary Crisis* 5:342–468.

———. 1989. "The Immigration Policy Debate: Critical Analysis and Future Options," pp. 151–177, in Wayne A. Cornelius and Jorge Bustamante, eds., *Mexican Migration to the United States.* La Jolla: Center for U.S.-Mexican Studies, UCSD.

D'Antonio, William V., and William H. Form. 1965. *Influentials in Two Border Cities.* Notre Dame: University of Notre Dame Press.

Dillman, C. Daniel. 1983. "Border Urbanization," pp. 237–244, in Ellwyn Stoddard, Richard Nostrand, and Jonathan P. West, eds., *Borderlands Sourcebook: A Guide to the Literature on Northern Mexico and the American Southwest.* Norman: University of Oklahoma Press.

Duemling, Robert. 1981. "San Diego and Tijuana: Conflict and Cooperation between Two Border Communities." *Executive Seminar in National and International Affairs.* Washington, DC: U.S. Department of State.

Garcia, Mario T. 1981. *Desert Immigrants: The Mexicans of El Paso, 1880–1920.* New Haven: Yale University Press.

Gildersleeve, Charles. 1978. "The International Border City: Urban Spatial Organization in a Context of Two Cultures along the U.S.-Mexico Boundary." Ph.D. dissertation, Department of Geography, University of Nebraska.

Greene, Sheldon. 1972. "Public Agency Distortion of Congressional Will: Federal Policy toward Non-resident Alien Labor." *George Washington Law Review* 40(3):440–463.

Griffin, Ernst, and Larry Ford. 1980. "A Model of Latin American City Structure." *Geographical Review* 70(4):397–422.

Hansen, Niles. 1984. "Regional Transboundary Cooperation Efforts in Centralist States: Conflicts and Responses in France and Mexico." *Publius* 14:137–152.

Hernandez, Alberto H. 1983. "Historia de los asentamientos humanos fronterizos: El caso de la colonia libertad." Paper presented at the meeting of the Society for Applied Anthropology, San Diego, California.

Herzog, Lawrence A. 1985. "The Cross-Cultural Dimensions of Urban Land Use Policy on the U.S.-Mexico Border: A San Diego-Tijuana Case Study." *The Social Science Journal* 22(3):29–46.

————. 1990. *Where North Meets South: Cities, Space, and Politics on the U.S.-Mexico Border*. Austin: CMAS/University of Texas Press.

Hirschman, Albert. 1958. *The Strategy of Economic Development*. New Haven: Yale University Press.

Jones, Lamar. 1969. "Alien Commuters in United States Labor Markets." *The International Migration Review* 55(3):65–87.

La Brucherie, Roger. 1969. "Aliens in the Fields: The 'Green Card Commuter' under the Immigration and Naturalization Laws." *Stanford Law Review* 21(6):1750–1776.

Martínez, Oscar J. 1977. "Chicanos and the Border Cities: An Interpretive Essay." *Pacific Historical Review* 46:85–106.

————. 1978. *Border Boom Town*. Austin: University of Texas Press.

McConville, James L. 1965. "El Paso-Ciudad Juárez: A Focus on Inter-American Culture." *New Mexico Historical Review* 40:233–247.

McWilliams, Carey. 1968. *North from Mexico: The Spanish Speaking People of the United States*. New York: Greenwood Press.

Nalven, Joseph, and Craig Frederickson. 1982. *The Employers' View: Is There a Need for a Guest Worker Program?* San Diego: Community Research Associates.

North, David. 1970. *The Border Crossers*. Washington, DC: Transcentury Corporation.

————, and Mary Portz. 1988. *Through the Maze: An Interim Report on the Alien Legalization Program*. Washington, DC: Transcentury Development Associates.

Petras, Elizabeth. 1980. "The Role of National Boundaries in a Cross-National Labor Market." *International Journal of Urban and Regional Research* 4:157–195.

Pinera, David. 1985. *Historia de Tijuana*. Tijuana: Centro de Investigaciones Historicas UNAM-UABC.

Price, John. 1973. *Tijuana: Urbanization in a Border Culture*. Notre Dame: University of Notre Dame Press.

Ricq, Charles. 1982. "Frontier Workers in Europe." *West European Politics* 5(4):98–108.

Sassen Koob, Saskia. 1988. *The Mobility of Labor and Capital*. Cambridge: Cambridge University Press.

Sloan, John W., and Jonathan P. West. 1976. "Community Integration and Border Politics among Elites in Two Border Cities." *Journal of Inter-American Studies and World Affairs* 18 (November):451–474.

———. 1977. "The Role of Informal Policy Making in U.S.-Mexico Border Cities." *Social Science Quarterly* 58 (September):270–82.

Texas State AFL-CIO v. Robert F. Kennedy, 1964. 330 F. 2d. 217 (D.C. Cir.), Cert. denied, 379 U.S. 826.

United States House of Representatives, Committee on the Judiciary, 1986. *The Immigration Reform and Control Act of 1986*. P.L. 99–603. Washington, DC: U.S. Government Printing Office.

United States Immigration and Naturalization Service. 1983. Report of Permanent Resident Alien Commuters and Seasonal Workers. Washington, DC.

26 Bill Lenderking ◆ The U.S.-Mexican Border and NAFTA: Problem or Paradigm?

The enactment of the North American Free Trade Agreement (NAFTA) in 1994 dramatically affirmed the determination of the United States and its neighbors to pursue multinational integration. As the debate leading to NAFTA's passage pointed out, however, free trade entails both benefits and liabilities. NAFTA produced impressive trade growth and job expansion in both the United States and Mexico during its first year of operation, but, by the beginning of 1995, Mexico had plunged into an economic crisis that threatened to reverse these gains. In response, the U.S. government felt compelled to guarantee new loans needed by Mexico to rescue its sinking currency.

A long-standing concern connected with free trade on the border has been the inevitable environmental and social pressures that accompany rapid economic and population growth. In this essay, Bill Lenderking, a retired U.S. Foreign Service officer currently a free-lance writer based in Washington, DC, reflects on the meaning of NAFTA in the context of the many challenges that confront borderlanders. Lenderking calls for greater understanding of such problems as migration, population growth, job competition, poverty, drug trafficking, and pollution, and he urges increased cooperation between the United States and Mexico in solving these problems.

Introduction: The Tortilla Curtain

There is a ten-foot high, fourteen-mile stretch of welded steel fence along the U.S.-Mexican border not far from Tijuana known locally as the "tortilla curtain." Even though the fence is formidable, it is easy for nimble young Mexicans to climb over it and slip into the United States, often in full view of U.S. Border Patrol guards. During the day, there is a steady trickle of "undocumented aliens" entering the United States at this and scores of other places along the two-thousand-mile border. At night, the trickle becomes a stream.

On the U.S. side of the border, Interstate Highway 5 extends north from the Tijuana crossing point past San Diego and on up the California coast. It is a typical American highway, engineered for fast multilane driving, except for one unique feature: near the border, there are yellow high-

From *North-South Focus* (Miami: North-South Center, University of Miami) 2, no. 3 (1993): 1–6. Reprinted by permission of the North-South Center.

way signs with black silhouette figures of a woman running, clutching two children by their hands, bedraggled hair flying. The message is stark: watch out for crossing aliens. Since 1987 more than 150 people have been killed by high-speed autos.

The U.S. Border Patrol catches over one million of these illegal entrants every year and turns most of them back into Mexico. But for every person turned back, nearly two enter—to shop, find day work, commit crimes, or disappear into the massive illegal work force that is seemingly a permanent, some would say essential, presence in towns and cities all over America. On any given day, the number of undocumented aliens in the United States ranges between two and four million. According to the Immigration and Naturalization Service, 96 percent of all illegal aliens apprehended in the United States in 1992 were Mexicans.

This massive south to north migration is fodder for the increasingly polemical debate about the North American Free Trade Agreement (NAFTA) in the United States. Politicians and special interest advocates utter apocalyptic fears about being inundated by illegal aliens or warn of massive job losses and environmental degradation. Although these fears are not entirely without foundation, a more balanced assessment suggests that there are good reasons why they may not be realized.

A look at the dynamic but troubled U.S.-Mexican border region is instructive. It comprises a huge regional, highly integrated economy. Although beset with problems, border communities have worked out a pattern of pragmatic problem solving that provides a foundation for future economic growth and conflict resolution. What the border suggests is that complex international problems can be dealt with constructively if the people and institutions at the local level cooperate instead of recriminate. Certainly, the resolution of international problems cannot be left entirely to local populations. But the experience of the U.S.-Mexican border points toward the idea that, in many cases, solutions must be community-based and built on the expertise and concerns of the people on the scene. However, for NAFTA to work, more than good will and pragmatism will be required, because there are dauntingly complex problems to be faced, such as illegal migration, growth and developmental sprawl, drugs, job gain and loss, and protecting the environment. What insights does the border provide on these issues?

Undocumented Aliens

Although the influx of undocumented aliens is only one aspect of the web of interrelated border problems, it is the one that arouses the deepest emotions. Current U.S. policy is that "only documented people should enter the country," but no one denies that fences and other barriers are only a partial deterrent. Nevertheless, some politicians and citizens' groups want to build even bigger fences and fortify them with searchlights and armed troops. Such extreme views do not yet have many advocates, but if problems associated with illegal aliens continue to grow, this update of the "fortress America" mentality will grow with them.

Many people realize that undocumented aliens bring benefits as well as problems. They provide a pool of cheap, indispensable labor and generally do not take jobs from Americans, although their effects on the labor market are complex. They send money home to their families, and their ability to find work in the United States has been an enormous safety valve, shielding both Mexico and the United States from the social explosion that might be caused by millions of Mexicans living in poverty south of the border with no hope of finding work.

However, illegal aliens from Mexico also put a huge burden on U.S. social services, especially health and education. For example, a woman giving birth and requiring intensive care could cost a hard-pressed municipal health service thousands of dollars a day. Public health problems have worsened in several large border cities. In El Paso, tuberculosis has increased; 60 percent of those with the disease are foreign born. Harried health workers stress that, although Mexico has made great strides in public health, the potential for a major health disaster has also grown larger.

Schools also feel the pressure. Under U.S. law, school-age children must be educated, whether illegal or not. In some communities, already overburdened schools are unable to cope with the extra load. A controversial study at San Diego State University estimates the cost to California of taking children of undocumented aliens into the school system as $60.6 million per year.

In August 1993, California Governor Pete Wilson complained that illegal immigrants cost the state $2.3 billion per year and urged the federal government to deny citizenship to American-born children of illegal immigrants, a proposal that would require amending the Constitution. Senator Dianne Feinstein of California revived a proposal for border crossing fees to raise money for additional border patrol guards and other immigration-related costs, but El Paso Mayor Larry Francis criticized the move saying, "Any attempt to reduce the flow of people . . . will initiate another economic downturn, another peso devaluation, and ultimately a new massive illegal immigration north."

According to Paul Ganster, director of the Institute for Regional Studies of the Californias at San Diego State University, undocumented aliens account for 15 percent of felony arrests in the San Diego area. He also notes a change in the composition of those entering illegally: "Some years ago, most people coming in were rural workers. But starting in the 1980s there was an increase in urban thugs and troublemakers." Car-jacking, smuggling, and similar crimes are major concerns. A study by the State of California calculated the cost of confining undocumented criminals as $.5 billion per year.

What impact will NAFTA have on the ebb and flow across the border? No one can say with certainty, but common sense and historical experience have established a simple rule of thumb: if the economy in Mexico is good, migration slows. If it is bad, people will find a way to get to the United States and get a job. One of the principal intended effects of NAFTA is to increase greatly the amount of investment and new jobs in Mexico.

Some border experts say that a more important factor than NAFTA in determining whether migration increases is the change in Mexico's traditional ejido, or land tenure system. For the first time, Mexican farmers can sell their lands. Many individual plots are being bought by large companies that use modern technologies, thereby radically changing labor-intensive, traditional methods of agriculture. The inevitable result, already being felt, is to reduce greatly the number of farmers on the land. Further, if Mexico's relatively inefficient and labor-intensive agriculture is exposed to competition from the United States and Canada, many Mexican farm workers are likely to be displaced. Without new investment in rural areas and new jobs, the expectation is that they will head for the border and on into the United States. This could swell the tide of undocumented aliens by hundreds of thousands.

The Border: Long Neglected, Now a "Living Laboratory"

The total population of the U.S. and Mexican border states is projected to increase to 72 million people by the year 2000 and will include some of the richest and some of the poorest people in the Western Hemisphere. In general, though, the border cities and their populations are perceived as relatively poor, overwhelmed with unsavory problems and long neglected by state and national governments. Although there is some residual truth to this stereotype, the situation is changing rapidly.

The border region, which links two profoundly different economies and cultures, is already highly integrated, and cross-border ties will increase regardless of NAFTA. The economies of border cities are growing rapidly, although, for example, rapid population growth has resulted in a net decline in per capita income in Tijuana. Nevertheless, despite enormous problems, there has been discernible progress in recent years. Takeshi Nishii, vice president of the modern Sanyo plant in Tijuana, contrasts the city today with conditions ten years ago, when he first arrived. Then, there were few paved roads, many parts of the city had no running water or electricity, and setting up a modern industrial plant seemed an impossible task. Today, nearly 70 percent of the roads are paved, and water and electricity flow reliably to the main parts of the city. The middle class in Tijuana and other Mexican border cities has grown and prospered, and the cities on both sides of the border witness countless transnational economic and social interactions every day.

For this reason, the border is an ideal place—a "living laboratory"— to observe what many describe as the most complex bilateral relationship in the world. It is not by chance that trade is the aspect of that relationship presently receiving the greatest attention. Two-way trade between the United States and Mexico is now at $75 billion per year, and Mexico recently passed Japan as the second-largest importer of U.S. manufactured goods, with Canada still first.

Not all the bilateral linkages are positive. Every Mexican border city dumps hazardous wastes into its contiguous waters, and many American cities do so as well. Uncontrolled burning on both sides of the border fuels air pollution. A copper plant in El Paso pollutes the air not only locally, but also across the border in Juárez. Clouds of dust and exhaust fumes produced by thousands of vehicles in Mexico driving on unpaved roads and using leaded gas pollute the air over El Paso, which has been in violation of federal clean air standards for years. The two cities have established an environmental border commission, which has found no easy solutions at hand, but has initiated a process of consultation and consensus building.

The *Maquiladoras*

Central to any discussion of NAFTA and border problems are the *maquiladoras*—production and assembly plants set up on the Mexican side of the border that import components duty-free and whose processed goods are subject only to import duties on value added in Mexico. Taking advantage of Mexico's low wages, there are now approximately two thousand *maquiladoras*, employing a total of nearly six hundred thousand people. They range from small shops with a few workers to the large state-of-the-art assembly line factories of such multinational firms as General Electric, General Motors, Sanyo, Sony, and Hewlett Packard, some of which employ as many as five thousand workers. Most of the *maquiladoras* are U.S.-owned, and the American labor movement has been upset for some time about the loss of jobs they represent.

Working conditions in the factories run the safety and environmental gamut. Some *maquiladoras* are "clean," but in others the workers do not wear protective clothing or equipment when working with dangerous or toxic substances, nor do they dispose of toxic wastes properly. In most factories, a large majority of the workers are women, and the wages are low, even with the numerous bonuses and benefits required by Mexican law. For example, a large multinational *maquiladora* might pay its assembly line workers a base of 50 to 60 cents per hour, but with benefits, which include bonuses, social security, and health care, the total package rises to $1.50. Critics charge that unless *maquiladora* wages rise substantially, the low-wage factories will constitute unfair competition and attract large numbers of U.S. companies with a resultant massive loss of jobs in the United States.

Assessments of the impact of the *maquiladoras* must not only consider such factors as jobs lost when American companies set up on the Mexican border, but jobs saved when companies continue to operate profitably, buttressed by the benefits accrued from *maquiladora* operations. NAFTA supporters also point out that increased investments and exports create jobs, using the commonly accepted yardstick of twenty thousand new jobs created for every billion dollars of merchandise exported. A number of smaller American company owners state that they would have failed without the lower costs they achieved by moving to the border. There is also a difference if a company relocates to the Mexican border or to a place such as Malaysia or Taiwan. Companies on the border tend to obtain supplies and spare parts from the United States rather than from suppliers in East Asia.

El Paso businessman William Tilney, former mayor of the city, sees advantages for his city in providing warehousing and supply facilities for the large *maquiladoras* in Juárez just across the border. Since roads and infrastructure are better on the U.S. side and land and warehouse space are cheaper, Tilney believes that El Paso has a competitive advantage.

In Harlingen, at the eastern end of the Rio Grande near the twin cities of Matamoros and Brownsville, local entrepreneurs are beginning to discover the potential of providing supplies and services to the *maquiladoras*, rather than conceding the business to traditional sources outside Texas. For example, Sonny and Dora Ybarra have a growing business providing eighty *maquiladoras* with machine calibration services. The Rio Grande Valley area has generally been slower than other border regions to capitalize on business opportunities provided by the *maquiladoras*, mainly because of a history of business failures in the area, but NAFTA could well change that. Dr. Michael Patrick, director of the Center for Entrepreneurship and Economic Development at the University of Texas-Pan American, says NAFTA offers the Valley a choice between becoming "a truck stop, a super-truck stop, or maybe a full-fledged player in this game."

Measuring jobs saved or lost and estimating future prospects are not the only ways to assess the economic impact of the *maquiladoras*. Workers in the factories spend part of their wages in the United States or buying American products. They send money back to their families, possibly helping to alleviate pressures to migrate. Other factors include such things as the cost of cleaning up or protecting the environment as a result of *maquiladora* operations, and the actual price tag for that can only be roughly estimated. . . .

While numbers of jobs to be lost or gained is a subject of emotional debate, it is highly likely that the nature of the *maquiladoras* themselves will change under NAFTA, and this has not been sufficiently analyzed. The emphasis will shift from companies that are attracted by cheap Mexican labor to assemble products for sale in the United States, to plants that are capable of producing for a greatly expanded market of Mexican consumers. New plants would not necessarily relocate on the border. If more of them were to set up in Mexico's interior, the migratory pull of the border would lessen.

Growth without Development?

The Mexican government has staked its prestige and a bold program of economic and social reform on the enactment of a free trade agreement. But concerns about NAFTA and the border linger in Mexico, too. Although northern Mexico is less traditional and more entrepreneurial than other parts of the country, skeptics fear that economic growth will mean only that cities get bigger and more unmanageable, that basic services will be increasingly overwhelmed, and that there simply will not be sufficient resources to cope with all the problems associated with rapid development.

For example, Tijuana expands by about six acres per day. In the central parts of the city, there are sewage, electricity, running water, and a basic transportation system, but in outlying areas these function poorly or not at all. There is no realistic scenario under which Tijuana can bring basic urban services to its rapidly expanding population and outlying areas with present or projected resources. Despite increased efficiency and greater expenditures, city officials are straining merely to keep up with the tide of new arrivals. They fear that the city is expanding so rapidly that the growth of the middle class or any gains in services are quickly overwhelmed and that the net effect is growth without development.

Similarly, the population of Juárez has tripled in size in twenty years. With its twin city of El Paso across the Rio Grande, this cross-border area comprises a highly integrated urban mass of about four million people.

Signs of middle-class prosperity and dynamism on the Mexican side of the border are readily apparent; yet dirt, poverty, disease, and the social problems that accompany underdevelopment are also visible on every street corner.

Despite these difficulties, it is evident that Mexican border cities have come a long way in a short time. There have been unmistakable improvements in the expansion of the middle class, urban services, and business opportunities, but the problems remain formidable.

Narcotics: A Greater Challenge

One of the few things on which everyone seems to agree is that NAFTA will increase the difficulty of interdicting the already huge volume of narcotics that crosses the border every day. A Drug Enforcement Agency official says that 20 percent of the heroin and 48 percent of the marijuana consumed in the United States comes from Mexico. Cocaine entering from Mexico was not much of a problem until the late 1980s, but successful interdiction of shipments coming through the Southern Hemisphere and the Caribbean shifted the traffic to Mexico. According to *The Financial Times*, between 50 and 70 percent of United States-bound cocaine now comes through Mexico. Air patrolling has cut deeply into the amount of drugs entering by air, but the traffickers employ ever more sophisticated means of getting massive amounts of drugs in overland, especially by truck. Greater scrutiny of vehicles crossing the border adds significantly to traffic delays and costs businesses money. Hundreds of idling motors also add clouds of exhaust to the pollution levels hovering over border crossing points.

It is clear that even with the rising number of drug busts and successful interdictions, the huge volume of traffic will require both countries to find more effective countermeasures to deal with the drug trade and its social consequences. U.S. officials cite improvements in cooperation and overall effectiveness of their Mexican counterparts but add that every gain in enforcement is seemingly matched by greater volume and sophistication on the part of the traffickers. Nevertheless, NAFTA is likely to result in an acceleration of cross-border cooperation on drug interdiction.

The Environment: Prevention and Cleanup

Environmental opposition to NAFTA has tended to focus on the pollution caused by the *maquiladoras*, but that is by no means the only, or even perhaps the most serious, cause of environmental concern. Serious environmental problems are visible all along the border, whether in the viscous sludge of the streams in most border communities, the filth in the Rio Grande, Rio Bravo, and New Rivers, the pollution of Mission Bay, or the dirt-laden air over the border caused by auto traffic and factory emissions. Less visible but more disturbing is the high incidence of anencephalitic babies—babies without brains—born in certain neighborhoods near large *maquiladoras* in Matamoros, just across the border from Brownsville, Texas.

While scientists and advocates try to pinpoint a definite cause for this last phenomenon—an excruciatingly slow process—at least the consciousness of the general population has been raised dramatically. But even when the causes for a given environmental problem are known, border communities and states lack the resources to enforce environmental laws, check up on polluters, or repair damage already done. Even though Mexico's environmental laws are comparable to those in the United States, corruption and insufficient funds and trained personnel make it difficult to insure that laws are obeyed and enforced. Adding to the problem is the rapid spread of sprawling, unplanned border communities lacking in basic services, including wastewater treatment, public transportation, and disposal of solid waste.

Fear of potential environmental damage also plays a part. The sale to private investors of the huge $1.6 billion Carbon II thermoelectric plant in northern Mexico has been placed in doubt by concerns over possible emissions drifting over the border and polluting the air, especially in Big Bend National Park, 130 miles away. The U.S. Environmental Protection Agency (EPA) wants the nearly completed plant refitted with emission control equipment that would meet higher environmental standards but might cost as much as $300 million—a sum that no one connected with the project is prepared to spend.

Mexican officials point out that raising environmental standards to new levels is not so simple, at least until Mexico's economy further improves. The dispute illustrates the complexity of border relationships when developmental and environmental priorities collide, and attempts to harmonize them take place in the context of the ongoing NAFTA debate.

However, some progress is being made. A recent breakthrough is the agreement by Mexico and the United States to clean up an abandoned lead recycling plant in the dusty hills outside Tijuana. The landmark case calls for a U.S. company that had improperly transported lead wastes from Los Angeles to Mexico to pay $2 million for cleanup of the site, which contains lead ash and slag. The company will also donate funds to a foundation that provides medical care for border residents. Additional funds generated from recoverable lead at the site will be used to pay back wages to workers at the plant, which closed in 1991. Observers say that without cooperation between the U.S. and Mexican governments, neither the cleanup nor the benefits to be provided for border residents could have been negotiated. The Los Angeles environmental prosecutor who pursued the case, David Eng—who reportedly once felt that NAFTA would bring an increase in environmental crimes—now feels that the treaty will improve prospects for binational enforcement of environmental laws.

The lead recycling plant case features a rare instance of a company pleading nolo contendere and making restitution. For the most part, company officials of the *maquiladoras* and their supporters insist that they have been getting a bad rap from environmentalists. They assert that offenders tend to be the smaller firms that are less likely to attract the attention of inspectors. Mexican law requires all waste from the factories to be reexported; some undoubtedly is trucked back over the border into the United States for legal disposal, but nobody knows how much of the waste is disposed of properly. There is no system to monitor the production of waste material, nor to track it to its place of disposal. No one disputes that much of it is taken out and dumped illegally. *Maquiladora* spokesmen explain that they contract with outside firms to dispose of the waste, and after it has left their premises, it is no longer their problem.

Environmentalists complain of being stonewalled in their attempts to collect factory samples or monitor disposal procedures, of employer intimidation of workers who might provide information about health hazards, and of the refusal of factory managers to cooperate with community concerns about the environment. Clearly, this is one area where consensus building and cooperation have not yet replaced confrontation. From small beginnings, however, the environmental movement has grown so that now activists operate in the main cities along the border, albeit often with feelings of pessimism and being overwhelmed. But they have established working ties with city and state officials, academic environmental researchers, journalists, politicians, and city officials, both within their communities and with cross-border counterparts. As environmental consciousness grows, the influence of environmental groups should also increase.

For example, environmentalists and local residents in Las Playas, Mexico, recently succeeded in persuading Mexican President Carlos Salinas de Gortari to revoke a permit for the construction of a large hazardous waste incinerator. Despite the victory of the "NIMBY" ("not in my backyard") activists, the larger problem remains: how and where to dispose of highly toxic hazardous wastes?

Although environmental issues often pit activists against the *maquiladoras*, in general the environmentalists are not seeking to cripple the *maquiladoras*, recognizing them as crucial elements in the economic development of the region. Rather, they are working for enforcement of environmental laws already on the books, accountability, reversal of environmental degradation, heightened awareness, and more resources for safeguarding the environment and eliminating health and safety hazards.

U.S. and Mexican federal government support for environmental protection of the border areas has increased. The EPA budget for fiscal year 1993 earmarks $241 million for border environmental projects, up from $103 million in 1992. The government of Mexico's total antipollution budget for 1993 is $460 million, with increases over 1992 both in total funds and those earmarked for the border. The number of environmental inspectors assigned to the Mexican side of the border has been increased to 200—still not enough, but a significant increase. The United States has helped with training and equipment.

Some environmentalists fear that NAFTA will worsen environmental problems by increasing trade without a corresponding improvement in environmental safeguards. But Terry Anderson, professor of economics at Montana State University, asserts, "Environmental arguments tug at the heartstrings of the American public while raising trade barriers in the name of environmental quality." He says that NAFTA can be a positive force for environmental quality, using such imaginative approaches as tradable pollution permits, water marketing, performance standards, emission fees, debt for nature swaps, and other promising measures. What is clear is that NAFTA by itself need not worsen the environment. Legitimate environmental concerns must be dealt with by both governments but not used to provide political cover for protectionists.

"Think Small"

It is ironic that the region, so long neglected, is beginning to be recognized in this era of globalization as one of the world's most dynamic and fully integrated international regional economies. What has been learned through this experience may be useful to communities and governments elsewhere. Universalist solutions imposed by central governments in national capitals will not work. Policymakers must take into account local characteristics and concerns and solicit grass-roots involvement in decision making. Progress is likely to come about gradually, based on local compromises, rather than in any kind of quick fix, which is a mirage many Americans still tend to chase after. As Mexican border scholar Gustavo del Castillo of the Colegio de la Frontera Norte in Tijuana puts it, the key is to "think small." That means choosing smaller but important, measurable problems to tackle where patterns of cooperation can be established and working outward. The methodology is already established in some border situations and offers a practical blueprint for future cooperation.

An example of the kind of local initiative that shows great promise for the future is the United States-Mexico Border Progress Foundation, established in 1992 to assist local agencies, nongovernmental organizations, and volunteers in carrying out community health, education, and environmental programs. Funded by local governments, foundations, border businesses, and individual contributions, the foundation operates on the premise that local expertise and commitment are often superior to that available from outsiders. While it is too soon to evaluate the effectiveness of such cross-border efforts, the concept is imaginative and may offer a model for other interdependent and binational regions.

The Border and Beyond

The upbeat attitudes that have accompanied economic development in certain border areas and that strongly favor NAFTA must also be balanced by the sober agenda facing the region—the fearsome problems of poverty and illegal migration, crime, the rampant drug traffic, massive environmental damage, exploitation of labor, and the degradation of cities. Border communities are acutely aware of these problems and are engaging in an impressive array of activities to cope with them. But the communities and region alone cannot solve their problems without help. More pragmatic and targeted assistance is needed from state and national governments, international financial institutions, private foundations, and specialized agencies of the United Nations. Their help should allow sufficient latitude for local initiatives and community-based problem solving. An encouraging recent example of such assistance is a $50 million World Bank loan to the Mexican government to address border environmental problems.

While mutual hostility was frequently the most salient characteristic of past Mexican-American relations, new developments present opportunities to usher in an era of dramatic economic growth, to forge a more cooperative binational political relationship, and to expand social and cultural ties that can erode old prejudices and benefit both countries. Mexico has changed course dramatically, but it lacks the resources to do the job entirely by itself and will need assistance from the United States, especially in improving its environmental performance, checking drug traffic, and making good on economic and political reforms.

The U.S. government needs to help defray the socioeconomic costs for those citizens who lose their jobs and border communities whose health and education infrastructures are overburdened. The commitment to address socioeconomic costs has not yet been made, eclipsed by the political need to downplay the possible negative effects of NAFTA. But the way to secure the fullest advantages from NAFTA is not only to push ahead with economic and political reforms and increased investment and trade, but to face squarely the agenda of daunting problems and their political, economic, and social costs. . . .

NAFTA presents a rare historical opportunity. It will stimulate the enormous economic potential of the world's largest market, with 360 million consumers and a total yearly output of more than $6 trillion. It will expand trade opportunities, lower prices, increase competition, and improve the ability of North American firms to exploit economies of scale. It offers the best chance for rapid economic development and political reform in Mexico, a country that is inextricably linked with the United States and whose future prosperity is clearly in the United States' interest. How the drama plays out will test whether the players can transcend ideology, nationalistic grudges, and unilateral concerns to make NAFTA work.

Skeptics need look no farther than the long-neglected border to see that regional integration is irreversible and that pragmatic cooperation can best maximize the benefits and minimize the social costs of a challenging new prospect.

27 Sandy Tolan ◆ *La Frontera*: Land of Opportunity or Place of Broken Dreams?

Mexico's decision in the early 1960s to promote foreign-owned assembly industries on its northern frontier brought profound changes to the border communities. By the early 1990s, two thousand maquiladoras *(assembly plants), employing more than one-half million workers, had become the dominant sector of the Mexican border economy. Unquestionably, the program has brought benefits to the region, but from its beginning there has been considerable controversy.* Maquiladoras *thrive on the low wages and labor surpluses that prevail on the border; many companies have also been accused of degrading the environment. In this thoughtful and sensitive article, Sandy Tolan, a frequent contributor to National Public Radio and the* New York Times, *probes the different perspectives of* maquiladora *supporters, including company officials, and of line workers, many of whom live in wretched slums adjacent to the factories.*

On winter mornings before the Nogales dawn, in the hundreds of shacks perched on bare hills two miles from the United States, the cold drifts in like fog.

Frost clings to the glass of the darkened oil lamps. Ice forms in the plastic wash basins. The chill surrounds the steel kitchen tables, the metal folding chairs, the Coleman camping stoves, the fifty-five-gallon drums of water that once held toxic chemicals.

It settles into the clothes in the small wooden dressers, the hard earth floors of the bedrooms, the crucifixes nailed to cardboard walls, the framed pictures of children reluctantly sent south for the winter.

At five o'clock on this Monday morning in December, in a two-room shack ringed by modern American factories, the cold rests on the faces of seven young Mexicans, asleep for the moment under mounds of covers. One by one, these brothers and sisters have come north from the small farming town of Navojoa, Sonora. Work in the Navojoa fields has dwindled. The pull of the factories on the border, eight hours to the north, is strong.

Juanita Rodriguez, 24 years old, crawls from her blankets in the family's pitch-black *casita de carton*, dresses quickly and prepares for another day at the garage door opener factory.

From the *Tucson Weekly*, October 18–24, 1989, pp. 4–6, 18, 29. © 1989 Sandy Tolan. Reprinted by permission of the author.

Her brothers and sisters sleep: Rosalinda, home from the night shift at the sewing factory; José, soon to begin another day at the carburetor factory; Pancho, looking for work at the vegetable packing houses on the other side of the line; his wife Leticia, pregnant, recently a laborer at the sunglasses assembly plant. Juanita leaves them all to their dreams.

Outside, the $7 million factory looms like a concrete fortress. Floodlights bathe the building's eastern face, spill over the hillside, and cast a harsh glow onto the tiny shacks clustered in the gully below.

The factory belongs to Juanita's employer, the Chamberlain Group of Chicago. They built it last year with profits from their seventeen years of making garage door openers in Mexico and shipping them to Sears stores in the U.S. The plant's immensity indicates the company plans to stay in Mexico for a while.

The shack belongs to the Rodriguezes. Juanita and her brothers built it with their own hands from materials discarded by the factory.

Wooden pallets became the frame and roof. Cardboard boxes, once used to ship garage door opener parts into Mexico, are now the family's interior walls. The Rodriguezes fastened the cardboard to the frame by driving nails through bottle caps. Juanita bought some glass for a window, found a door, made a picket fence of pallets.

She hangs her laundry there on Sundays.

"Poorly made," Juanita says with a shrug, "but here we are."

Mexicans like Juanita, unable to find work in the *campo* and unwilling to clean houses for strangers, have come north to survive.

U.S. companies like Chamberlain, struggling to compete in the hard-nosed world of international manufacturing, have come south in their own fight for survival.

My journey has brought me to this hill on the northern edge of Mexico to watch these two migrations come face to face as they forge a new industrial revolution on the border.

Every day, thousands of garage door openers come off the assembly line in Nogales, bound for Sears stores north of the line. The $149 retail price is equal to a day's wage for twenty of the company's fifteen hundred assembly line workers.

Chamberlain saves millions of dollars a year in labor costs and has captured the market at home.

"We are the cost leader in our industry," says Chamberlain Vice President Ray McMinn. "And we believe our location in Mexico has enabled us to achieve that status."

Juanita, who arrived at Chamberlain's factory door six years ago, now makes one of the top factory wages in town: the peso equivalent of

$7.50 a day, plus two meals. That comes to $38 a week for forty-eight hours of work.

When Juanita came north on the bus from Navojoa at age 18, she hoped the factory work would be a stepping-stone to college and a career as a nurse. But heading for work on this cold morning in December, Juanita is no closer to her dream than she was in 1983.

"Our salaries are only enough to buy food, clothes, and shoes," Juanita says matter-of-factly. Her hard plastic shoes crunch along the dirt street, cutting the dark silence. "Sometimes we make enough to make ends meet; sometimes we don't."

They call the border the new Hong Kong. At thirteen hundred U.S.-owned factories, nearly four hundred thousand workers churn out jeans, hospital gowns, saxophones, radar detectors, file folders, chain saws, and false teeth. In less than a decade, Nogales, Sonora, has become a center of international commerce, a base for ITT, IBM, Rockwell, United Technologies, Kodak, Memorex, and Kimberly-Clark.

These companies have been lured south by the free fall of the Mexican peso. In 1981, 25 pesos would get you a dollar. Now it takes twenty-five hundred. With that slide went the Mexican minimum wage—from the equivalent of $1.59 an hour eight years ago to barely 50 cents today. American manufacturers looking for cheap labor markets suddenly had a nearby option.

"There's no real magic about it," says Dick Campbell, Jr., who has brought three dozen companies to his Parque Industrial in Nogales. "The cost of labor here is cheaper than almost anyplace in the world."

Mexico now competes with Asia and Indonesia for low-wage manufacturing jobs hired out by the biggest companies in the world. The Mexican *maquiladora* program is part of the new global economy. Increasingly, manufacturing is being done in stages by workers in different countries. The process is called "production sharing."

In the *maquiladora* program, parts and raw materials are shipped to Mexico from the U.S., assembled at low cost, and sent back under special tariff provisions for purchase in the United States.

"The *maquiladora* program has been the cornerstone of bringing our two countries together economically," Rep. Jim Kolbe, R-Ariz., told industry executives gathered at Loew's Ventana Canyon [Hotel] in June. Kolbe, a leading supporter of the industry in Congress, argues the industry can help build a "golden age" along the border.

Under the *maquila* arrangement, everyone is supposed to come out ahead. Manufacturers keep costs down, maximize profits, and fight off foreign competitors. Mexico gains a key source of foreign exchange to help pay off its crushing $108 billion debt. (*Maquilas* are now Mexico's second largest generator of foreign exchange, second only to oil and now ahead of tourism.) Thousands of unemployed Mexicans find work and a means of survival. Even the U.S. workers making the raw goods, whose jobs would be lost if the manufacturing process were moved to the Pacific Rim, stay employed.

But this shining vision does not incorporate the cardboard shacks that crowd the factory gates. It doesn't account for the hundreds of toxic chemical drums discarded by the factories and reused for drinking water by families who can't read warnings printed in English. It ignores the twenty-six partial amputations of fingers in Nogales *maquilas* last year, the raw sewage flowing across the border from cardboard squatter camps, the thick trails of smoke made by people who burn tires to keep warm, the 13-year-old children who forsake school for ten hours a day on the assembly line, the mothers who must send their children south in the winter when they contract bronchitis and pneumonia, the workers who are warehoused 140 to a room in cramped Nogales barracks run by the factories.

John P. Sommers remembers the shacks. It's been a long time, and right now he's two thousand miles away, at the other end of a telephone line in Villa Park, a suburb of Chicago. But the former president of Chamberlain recalls the day seventeen years ago, his mind full of questions on whether to bring his company to Mexico, when he crossed into Nogales for the first time.

"All those shacks," he says, his distant voice cradling the memory. "Driving down the road, and looking up and seeing all those shacks. It's really heartrending to try to figure out what to do."

A year later, with garage door openers gliding off assembly lines in Nogales, Chamberlain executives set up a cafeteria. Sommers figured the least his company could do was feed its workers. Practically, it kept the workers from thinking about food while on the assembly line. Also, says Sommers, "By doing that, you get the feeling you're at least doing something. It'll be about the only two good meals they'll get all day."

The cafeteria now feeds fifteen hundred workers in five different shifts. They file in one group at a time, while the others keep the garage door openers churning down the lines.

On the floor, steel baskets carry parts from one worker to the next. "It's quite a sophisticated network of conveyors," says Bill Rojan. Chamberlain's manufacturing manager, as he and other company executives take me on a tour of the plant.

I stop behind a young woman sitting in a long row of workers. She stares down at the conveyor as a shiny black chassis slides into place. She grasps an electric air gun, presses a switch, and spins a tiny metal bolt into place. She repeats this operation every nine seconds. At this rate, she will spin 3,480 bolts by the end of the day.

Across the shiny gray floor, on the other side of the factory, I spot Juanita and her sister Magdalena. They smile broadly. Juanita laughs, flashes a peace sign, whispers to her coworkers. I smile back, but worry the Chamberlain executives will note the recognition. Will the sisters get in trouble for talking to a reporter? I move on without waving back and head off to talk with the executives.

In a back conference room set off the factory floor, the squeak of conveyors and the drone of muffled air guns are barely audible through the closed doors.

"This company is guided by a feeling that there is a responsibility to the people that work for it," says Ray McMinn, the company vice president. McMinn's dark business suit is offset by a white mustache and a thick crop of white hair combed back with precision. "We believe the best business can be made by making sure that we're doing the right thing," he says. "We care about our people as employees."

McMinn notes the company vacation benefits, the cafeteria service, and the day care center going in at the new plant.

But McMinn and his fellow executives make it clear there is a limit to what the company is willing or able to do in Mexico. "We are part of a world economy," McMinn says. "We can't solve all of their problems. Certainly we're here because the labor costs are less expensive than they are in the United States. If we weren't here, and if the other *maquiladoras* were not here, the conditions in Mexico would certainly be much worse than they are."

In a global economy, businessmen worry about their own fight for survival. They cannot be preoccupied with trying to raise the standard of living for floods of immigrants newly arrived on the border from southern Mexico. Or who've flocked to Seoul or Taipei or Bangkok or Rio de Janeiro. The idea is to keep costs down, stay in business, and maximize profits. That means finding the cheapest labor possible among the many countries competing desperately for low-wage manufacturing jobs.

"I don't see the role of corporate America as being philanthropists throughout the world," says Dick Campbell of the Parque Industrial. I don't think the companies came down here to benefit Mexico. They came down here to benefit themselves, and secondarily to benefit Mexico through these jobs."

"If it wasn't for the *maquiladora* industry, where would these Mexicans be?" asks Rudy Piña, who promotes the industry for Collectron of

Arizona. "They'd be in Los Angeles. They'd be in New York. They'd be in San Francisco. They'd turn to crime. (Here) they're working."

In the north, the Rodriguezes make a lot more than they ever could in Navojoa. Juanita left right after high school when she saw her options: sporadic work in the fields or a dead-end job cleaning houses. Her brother Pancho was already long gone. Determined to find work, he snuck into the United States eleven years ago and found work in the fields near Phoenix. At the time, he was 12 years old. Now he has a green card.

Their older sister, Rosalinda, stayed in Navojoa until last year, working long hours as a waitress for the minimum wage. Finally she had enough. Armed with visions of a good job, night school, and a future as a kindergarten teacher, Rosalinda brought her two children north to Juanita's house. She found a job making electrical outlet strips for a small New Jersey company on the border.

Then came winter. The cold air in the unheated shack gave Rosalinda's children asthma attacks. They developed bronchitis, so she sent them to live with her parents in Navojoa.

At the factory, Rosalinda recalls, the manager shouted for more production. His words slammed into Rosalinda's ears. She'd come home tense and worn out at two in the morning, crawl into bed, and think about her kids down south.

"It's hard having them so far away," she says. "I feel terrible wondering how they're doing. I call all the time to see how they're doing."

Sometimes Navojoa didn't seem so bad. Rosalinda began to see why turnover at the *maquilas* was so high—somewhere between 180 and 240 percent per year.

"People come with the illusion of making money," she says. "Not to become rich, but to make some money. But they can't live on their salary. And there's no house for them to live in. You see that a lot of people get disillusioned and leave."

One cold afternoon on the hill at Los Tapiros, I stop by to visit the Rodriguezes. Juanita isn't back from Chamberlain yet, but Leticia and her cousin Pedro are home, sitting in kitchen chairs in their winter coats, listening to *norteño* music on the radio.

Leticia makes coffee on a small camping stove. Eighteen and pregnant with her second child, Leticia has just quit work at the Foster Grant factory in the Parque Industrial. Her husband Pancho has temporary work at a discount retailer in Nogales, Arizona. Rosalinda has just left for the night shift at Kimberly-Clark.

"You suffer a lot here to earn a little more," Leticia says, pulling her old down jacket tightly around her. Back home she picked vegetables for a while in the fields of Sinaloa. The pay was worse, but most things were less expensive than on the border.

Here, the family does most of its shopping at the Safeway on the U.S. side. A lot of items—chicken, milk, even beans—are cheaper over there. Still, to buy a chicken, Leticia must work half a day. Two hours of work on the assembly line will buy a toothbrush. Even a pound of beans is equal to an hour's work in a *maquila*. An extra pair of shoes, a magazine, a soda, a ticket to the movies—these are luxuries.

"We came with the idea that things would be better," Leticia says. "But I don't see anything better here. *Nothing*."

A hard wind rattles the cardboard and sends a small gust under the door. The doors of all the shacks are closed against the wind.

Pedro holds a Raleigh between finger and thumb. He flicks the ash, takes a drag, paces the tiny room.

"Most of us earn the minimum wage. It is very little to survive on. In reality, it's not enough. We make these cardboard homes because we don't have enough to pay rent for good houses—to live better. There in the United States, most people have their nice cars, their nice homes. And what do we have? Shacks. Cardboard shacks."

For a long moment, you can hear the wind.

Leticia unrolls her curlers, combs out her long, black hair, looks into a pocket mirror, applies some eyeliner. She stops, squints, looks at me with a question in her eyes.

"Is it sad like this on the other side, too?"

Marian Elena Gallego eases her jet-blue Saab Turbo down the steep Nogales hill, past the children playing in the dirt, through the deep ruts in the unpaved street.

Gallego, herself a *mexicana* living on the U.S. side, works for Sonitronics, a U.S.-owned company which operates two dozen factories and nine *dormitorios* for the factory workers. The industry likes to call them dormitories. Barracks would be more precise.

"Just like in the Marines," Gallego jokes as we move through spotless, tiny rooms packed with bunk beds in the women's dorm. These are the first shift rooms. It's four in the afternoon; the workers will be coming home soon.

"They have the TVs, they have a little gym area, a little cafeteria area, their own bed, 24-hour guard service. And we change their sheets twice a week," Gallego says cheerfully.

Back in the Saab, I ask if these conditions—from cardboard huts to toxic barrels to workers warehoused in her company's own barracks—ever gnaw away at Maria Elena Gallego. "It's better than being homeless in Tucson," she shoots back. She taps her long fingers on the steering wheel, matching the soft beat of an FM rock station on the other side of the line.

"It doesn't really get to me because I'm Mexican. I understand that it's just the way it has been. You gotta remember, Mexico's another culture. It would bother me more, all I see, the conditions in Mexico, all this poverty. But you look at the people, and they're a happy people. It's more of an acceptance. Mexican people are survivors. They're not after success. They don't work in a company to get a gold watch. Or be driving a new car. Do you understand what I'm saying?"

The U.S.-Mexican border is one of the only places in the world where the First World meets the Third. For that reason, the contrast between the life-styles of the workers and that of the bosses is all the more apparent.

A man awakens in his Spanish-tiled home in Rio Rico, Arizona, eases his Cadillac past putting greens and fairways, then past cardboard cities made of factory refuse, finally pulling up at his reserved parking spot at the Nogales plant gate.

Mexico is only one player in the game of hardball played by international business. *Maquiladoras*, like assembly plants in Asia, Indonesia, Africa and other parts of Latin America, are part of a constant search by manufacturers to lower labor costs.

"If they do not reduce costs," says Rudy Piña, "more than likely they'll go out of business."

Low cost labor is at the heart of the new global economy. Higher wages could bite into the competitive edge that brought manufacturers to Mexico in the first place. Manufacturers believe that, even though they are saving up to $25,000 per worker per year, they cannot afford to provide their workers with enough to live decently.

And living decently means a roof and four walls, says Catalina Denman, a researcher at the Colegio de Sonora in Hermosillo. "It means public utilities, enough for food, health care, and clothing. Your salary should cover this. For the *maquiladora* worker, the salary doesn't cover this."

It's not likely the nonunionized work force or the pro-*maquila* Mexican government will pressure *maquila* operators to raise wages any time soon. If they're ever forced to pay more in Mexico, many say they'll just start looking somewhere else. And there are plenty of places to look.

In Bolivia, the minimum wage stands at 24 cents an hour. In other countries, it's less. Dick Campbell tells the story of the fishhook company working out of the Philippines. They'd managed to totally eliminate overhead.

"They were operating out in the jungle, without a roof," Campbell told a visiting class from the Thunderbird School of International Management in Phoenix. "The people were wearing grass skirts. They (the company) were paying 18 cents an hour. We can't compete with that here in Nogales."

Something's happened to the old idea of the social contract between worker and management. International competition has forced companies to pay as little as possible, provide as few benefits as necessary, and look for a new place when things get bad. They provide what's required— a paid vacation, medical benefits, a housing tax to the government—but not a lot more.

Henry Ford had the revolutionary idea that a worker should be paid enough to afford the product he made. This wasn't pure altruism; Ford wanted to broaden the market for his product.

Imagine Juanita having any use for a garage door opener.

A few labor experts argue the idea of the social contract should be revived—this time on an international scale.

"What we need is a global New Deal," says Walter Russell Mead, a senior fellow at the World Policy Institute in New York.

"Roosevelt understood that the standard of living of the average working person is the real key to national prosperity in a modern economy. Today that's true on an international scale.

"It's the living standard of the average citizen of the world that is going to determine whether we all prosper together or we all go down together, in economic terms."

To Jim Kolbe, that sounds like soft-headed liberalism.

Mandating higher wages, he argues on a warm Sunday morning at his cabin in Sonoita, would create massive inflation and even greater chaos on the border.

"There's no economic rationale for a legislative minimum wage," he says, emphasizing each word like a pianist on a staccato riff. We sit and drink lemonade in the tiled living room, twenty minutes north of the Rodriguezes.

"If that's the answer," he says, smacking his forehead with an open palm, "then great! Why in hell should we stop at $4.55? Why not just raise the minimum wage to $20 an hour?"

Free market economics will bring prosperity to Mexico, Kolbe argues, just as it did to Taiwan, Japan, Korea, and Singapore. Eventually, wages will rise in Mexico as the industrial base takes hold, Kolbe says. "I firmly believe a rising tide raises all boats."

Kolbe's view has plenty of company: A few days later, in his sixteenth-floor office in Phoenix, former Arizona Gov. Bruce Babbitt says *maquilas* will help bring prosperity to Mexico. "It's inevitable that as a country industrializes, wage scales go up. Wages will begin to rise in Mexico."

But raising wages by government decree, Babbitt says, is not the answer. "Frankly," he says, "the notion that we should be in a position of saying the Mexican laborers are being inadequately paid is absurd. We don't measure their standard of living by our wage scales."

But real wages in Mexico have plummeted in the last eight years. Juanita Rodriguez must work fifteen to twenty additional hours per week to match the standard of living she had when she arrived on the border six years ago.

And so on this Sunday morning at Kolbe's cabin, I press the issue. If you can't justify better wages, I say, is there no limit to how low they'll go? If it's as low as 18 cents an hour in the Philippines, how much lower can it go? Three cents an hour? A penny? If this is the new industrial revolution, do we have Dickens' London on the border?

"I don't know whether it's Dickens' London in Nogales," Kolbe says quietly after a long pause. "I do believe that in the long run, you will raise the standard of living.

"It is, I think, an inevitable phase of development—that you have tremendous disruption and change in the lives of people."

In the spring, the harsh chill of the Nogales evenings fades. Rosalinda finds a good job caring for a rich elderly woman and a *casita de carton* of her own across the dirt lane from Juanita's place.

She hangs a horseshoe over the doorway. On the cardboard wall above the green gas stove, she places a picture of the Last Supper. Then she sends for her children in Navojoa.

Leticia had her baby in early April. Jeovita, they called her. She weighed less than five pounds at birth. Pancho and Leticia moved into their own place, too, right across from Juanita's, four houses up from Rosalinda. They brushed white paint onto the cardboard walls.

Juanita lives by herself now. Every morning at five, she still gets up and goes to the Chamberlain factory up on the hill. But she's learning how to cut hair. Maybe someday she'll open a little beauty shop. And there's still the idea of nursing school. Lord knows there'll be enough people to care for. They keep coming north all the time.

"When we first got here," Juanita recalls, "there were very few people in Nogales. Now there are so many people you have to step down off the sidewalk and walk in the street. And day by day, more and more people are coming. You have to wonder—if we live here, where are *they* going to live?"

28 Michael Quintanilla and Peter Copeland ◆ Mexican Maids: El Paso's Worst-kept Secret

Mexican maids constitute one of the largest sectors of the low-wage popu-
lation on the border. From Matamoros to Tijuana, tens of thousands of
undocumented women commute across the boundary on a daily or weekly
basis to their domestic jobs in middle- and upper-class neighborhoods in
U.S. cities. They are a highly vulnerable work force, as journalists Michael
Quintanilla and Peter Copeland point out in this newspaper article.

Even though they risk being overworked, swindled, and even sexually
abused, they come to El Paso by the thousands, taking off their shoes,
rolling up their pants, and wading the Rio Grande in the early morning
hours.

They come, says one official, "like a ghost battalion," working behind the closed doors of Country Club Road mansions and tract homes in
East El Paso. Some stay just a day, others for a week, others for months.

They come to take care of El Pasoans—to rear their children, cook
their meals, and scrub their floors.

They are Mexican maids—in El Paso legally and illegally, working
in an underground economy offering meager wages. There is little vacation. There is no workman's compensation. There is no retirement
pension.

Still they come because, as one maid put it, "It's the dollar I want,
not pesos. I need to buy food and shoes for my children."

The maids are El Paso's worst-kept secret. Their easy, low-cost availability is well known but seldom discussed publicly. They are part of the
good life in the city. El Pasoans keep it that way by keeping quiet.

To tell the story of the maids, the *Herald-Post* worked on both sides
of the border, interviewing dozens of maids, housewives, government
officials, academic experts, and social workers. The investigation found
that:

• While no figures are available on how many maids work in El Paso,
there may well be more maids per home in the city than anywhere else in
the nation. The reason is the low wages and shortage of jobs in Juárez. At
$40 plus room and board a week, many El Pasoans can afford them, not
just the rich.

From the *El Paso Herald-Post*, Special Report on the Border, Summer 1983,
pp. 83–86. Reprinted by permission of the *El Paso Herald-Post*.

• Evidence of the large numbers of maids is provided by the city bus system. Even though many maids are given rides by their employers, bus officials say so many use buses that the system would be in trouble if Border Patrol agents stopped every maid from crossing.

• But the Border Patrol is not able to stop the women from crossing the Rio Grande to work in El Paso homes, nor does it concentrate on stopping them. "Maids are a low-level priority," said James Smith, chief of investigations for the El Paso sector of the Immigration and Naturalization Service.

• Many middle- to upper-income homes in El Paso have "maid's quarters," but those who conceal illegal maids are guilty of harboring illegal aliens, the INS says.

• While many El Paso maids say they are treated well and appreciate the opportunity to make far more money than they could in Juárez, some are swindled. Others have breakage fees deducted from their pay. Some work and are never paid. Many are overworked. On the other side, there are occasional reports of maids committing thefts, and some housewives complain the maids aren't dependable.

• Social Security Administration officials say employers are illegally avoiding taxes on wages, and that maids are denied benefits they are entitled to. Some maids work their whole lives cleaning homes but are left with nothing when they retire. Although most maids, even illegals, are entitled to the U.S. minimum wage of $3.35 per hour, few receive it.

• Maids who live in El Paso homes must often leave their own children in Juárez to be taken care of by relatives. The maids might get home only once a month. One maid said she never married because she has had to work all her life as a maid to help support her family.

"Yet everybody has one because the maids need the jobs," said Smith, the INS investigator.

"Even though they are working cheap here, they are making more money than they would in Juárez," he said. The minimum wage in Juárez, where unemployment is 25 percent to 40 percent, is about $4 a day. The average daily salary for a weekly live-in maid in El Paso is $15. A weekly live-in maid earns anywhere from $25 to $40 plus her meals and room. Some live-in maids go home to Juárez on the weekends. Others return to Mexico rarely.

"I wouldn't be surprised if at one time or another every working El Pasoan has hired a maid or thought about hiring one because they work cheap," Smith said. He too once hired a maid—a "legal one."

City Planner Nestor Valencia said, "It's an industry that is part of the fiber of the community."

The maid industry is a unique mixing of people from a powerful, industrial country and those from a developing country. Often, the maid and the housewife do not even speak the same language.

The story of the maids is a story about people—people from El Paso and Juárez, some benefiting, others exploited.

"If I didn't have a maid, it would be impossible for me to work," said a wife and mother who also is pursuing a career.

"My paycheck would be drastically lowered if I had to pay a day care center to babysit my two children. If I didn't have a maid I'd be working just to pay day care and end up with 50 bucks in my pocket."

The woman, who pays her maid $30 a week, asked not to be identified.

When asked if she paid taxes and Social Security on her maid's salary, the woman said she did not. She was surprised to learn she was breaking the law. Social Security must be paid when an employer pays a salary of $50 or more during a three-month period.

"I didn't know that. I pay her in cash because that's how she wants it. I imagine she would have problems cashing a check here, and, it's easier for me. I feel like I'm giving her a job and a room to stay in. I'm nice to her. She likes it here."

But not every maid in El Paso likes her job.

Anna, a former live-in maid for a Westside family, said she was raped by her employer on a junked sofa in the garage.

The man said he wanted her to clean something outside, but then attacked her.

If she complained or told the man's wife, Anna recalled, the man said he would have her deported.

"I was scared. I was very scared. After the second time it happened I told a friend who was a maid at another house. She helped me find another job and I left without telling anybody. I never went back. I was so happy to leave I left before I got paid that week."

"It's human nature—the abuse and exploitation. If it happens they can quit you, like this girl did, and go somewhere else," the INS's Smith said.

"And," he said, "you'll have those employers who will say, 'Do it my way or I'll call Immigration.' They fill the maid—usually a young girl— with horror stories about what they are capable of doing to them. So the girl usually runs away as soon as she can find another job or will run back to Juárez."

While some maids complained about physical and mental abuse, Smith said most are just plain overworked and underpaid.

One maid said she not only cleans the house but also cars.

While her employer's friends are playing bridge in the house, the maid is told to wash all of their cars.

"I don't argue because I don't want to lose my job," said the maid, in her early 40s.

Another maid told how her boss makes her peel onions by the bushel. The onions, she said, come from her boss's neighbors who were told to bring their onions over every Wednesday when the maid is there.

"I do it because she pays me $20 a day," she said.

And, another maid said she is also a part-time gardener for her employer every spring and summer. She spent a recent afternoon shoveling dirt over a backyard lawn.

Usually the maids who endure the abuse are the illegal ones, Smith said, because they can be threatened.

But, legal maids such as Isabel Garcia-Medina will have no part of it.

"One time a Mexican-American lady wanted me to clean her house and iron two big plastic bags full of clothes—do everything for $5. And, she kept telling me to wash my hands. She must have thought I was dirty or had a sickness. She made me feel degraded.

"When I told her I wouldn't iron for that price she said she would call Immigration and have me picked up."

That's when Miss Garcia-Medina proudly pulled out her resident alien card which entitled her to work in El Paso legally and told the woman to call whoever she wanted. The cards are hard to come by.

"I walked out the front door and went home. I was so upset I cried. That's why today I only work for gringo ladies. They treat me nicer," she said.

The maids are all ages. Some have been doing it all their lives. Others are young women hoping to make it big in the United States.

"I make more money here," said Isela, a live-in maid for three years. "It's the dollar I want, not pesos. I need the money to buy food and shoes for my children."

Many of the maids have children in Juárez or other parts of Mexico. They usually are not abandoned, however, explained Gay Young, a professor of sociology at UT [University of Texas] El Paso who specializes on women in the workforce.

"It's not like what we think of when a woman leaves her family. She's not leaving the children alone because of a very strong network of female kin."

The children often are watched by relatives, she said. Others, however, are left at homes for children such as Ciudad del Niño in Juárez where the children are watched by nuns.

Someone else is watching their mothers. One day recently, Louisa Jimenez and four other maids scampered across the river where the Rio Grande parallels Paisano Drive across from ASARCO [American Smelting and Refining Company].

Crossing was no problem, she said. "It's waiting for the bus that makes me nervous," she said while hiding behind junked cars some thirty yards away from a bus stop. The women on that day arrived at their bus stop hiding place shortly after 6 A.M., clutching their purses and wrapped in worn-out sweaters. They waited intently, keeping a watchful eye for what would come first—a pale green Border Patrol van or a city bus.

The bus beat the van.

As it came into eyesight, barreling down Paisano, the women ran to the bus stop. One woman made the sign of the cross over her chest as she boarded.

Next stop was the San Jacinto Plaza where more maids plunked down their fare and greeted other maids on the same route. They chatted among themselves about work, home, the news in *El Diario*, a Juárez newspaper, and about a maid nicknamed *la chiquita*, the little one.

Apparently *la chiquita* missed her bus, one maid said to another.

A half-hour later, the bus wound its way on Country Club Road. Each woman sounded the bus chime, departing the bus block after block.

"*Que Dios le ayude*," one maid told another as she walked off the bus. Translation: "May God help you."

The INS's Smith said if an illegal maid is apprehended by Border Patrol agents the woman can voluntarily return to the bridge or request a deportation hearing.

"They always just go back to Juárez. We can't hold them [or] incarcerate them. And they don't want that either. We drive them back to the bridge," he said.

Norma Pacheco, an illegal maid, said she has been picked up by Immigration and driven to a border bridge with other Mexican aliens. But, she said, the bridge was not the familiar Santa Fe Street Bridge.

"They drove us to Fabens—the bridge there," she said.

"They [Immigration] think they're so smart by taking me so far away from here. But all I have to do is this," she said, cranking her thumb in the air like a hitchhiker.

Immigration officials are aware that a large number of illegal aliens work as maids, but still their resources are stretched thinly and it is more effective to concentrate on illegal aliens working in high-paying jobs.

"The government is telling me to go after the drug pushers, the criminals, the smugglers, the aliens who have jobs that are well-paying, jobs they are taking from U.S. citizens," said Smith.

"We know thousands of illegal maids are coming across, but they're not hurting anybody and they're not taking jobs away.

"When you're working for the U.S. government you have to prioritize your work and maids are a low-level priority.

"If the government told me to go after every illegal maid in El Paso, I would go at it," Smith said. "But, we don't go door to door looking for maids."

"In some cases maids will tell on each other to get their jobs. Those complaints come from maids I call *bochincheras*—sort of slang for tattletale," Smith said laughing.

Although it is not illegal to hire an illegal alien, legislation pending in Congress could change that.

It is illegal to harbor an illegal alien, however, which means hiding a person from immigration authorities. Many of the maids are violating U.S. law by working without proper documents.

"The given lady in Juárez that wants to work [legally] in El Paso, flatly, can't," said Mike Trominski, deputy district director of the INS.

"If you have a maid from Juárez, unless she is what we call a commuter, then it's likely you have an illegal alien." A commuter is a person who legally could live in the United States but chooses to live in Mexico—the so-called "green card" holders.

A person with only a temporary crossing card—*pasaporte local*—is not allowed to work.

Many maids are among the hundreds of people arrested each day by the Border Patrol, but no one knows how many get through.

"No statistics are known on wetback maids," Smith said. "It's like asking me how many illegal aliens are in El Paso at this moment. We don't know. They are a ghost battalion."

The ghost image is a good one because the women disappear into El Paso homes where records also disappear.

It is difficult to count the troops in the ghost battalion.

The 1980 census reported that 1,063 private household workers lived in El Paso. That figure is ridiculously low because it does not include the Juárez commuters or many of the illegal aliens.

"Of all the undocumented workers, finding the maids is the hardest. They are the most unfindable," says Leo Chavez, a University of California professor who is studying illegal immigrants.

The maids work in what El Paso economist Tom Lee calls the "underground economy," where few records are kept, wages are in cash, and taxes and Social Security rarely are paid.

Valencia of the City Planning Department said that if only 10 percent of El Paso's households had maids, that would be more than 13,400 maids and a "significant employment sector."

Maids are more common in the border area because women from Mexico are willing to work cheap, Valencia said.

"The maids are not only for the well-to-do. A single lady trying to run a house will have one," Valencia said. "Low and moderate income breadwinners hire maids full-time. It touches all sectors."

Smith reported a case where an illegal alien living in El Paso and working as a seamstress at a factory had an illegal maid working for her.

One group of El Pasoans convinced there are a lot of maids in El Paso is city bus drivers.

A dozen bus drivers polled recently by a SCAT official estimated that nearly 50 percent of El Paso bus riders are maids. SCAT riders take about 28,300 trips a day.

"If they ever cracked down on domestic help, especially illegals, we would lose our ridership," SCAT spokesman Manny Escontrias said.

Because the maids remain uncounted and undocumented, many will be left with nothing when they retire, said Frances Whited of the Social Security office.

Most of them, if they receive citizenship documentation, are entitled to Social Security benefits when they retire or become disabled. Few receive those benefits, however, because they and their employers don't pay Social Security taxes.

Some maids know about the program but prefer to have all their pay up front.

And for most maids that pay should be the U.S. minimum wage of $3.35 per hour, according to the U.S. Department of Labor. Few maids say they receive that much, however.

But the maids aren't the only group with complaints.

Some women say their maids are unreliable.

A Westside woman lamented about her maid who did not show up for work.

"She flew the coop. I'm looking for another one," said the woman. Her maid, a 17-year-old girl from Torreon, worked for $15 a day.

"You can't find a dependable maid in some of these young girls. They come from the ranch and don't know how to use electrical appliances, dishwashers, and washing machines. Once you get them trained, they decide not to come back."

Other housewives complained that maids steal from the houses.

However, most of the thievery reported included small, inexpensive items such as soap, toilet paper, and cereal. One housewife said the thefts weren't noticeable until the items were needed. She said she would have gladly given them to her maid if asked.

When major thefts by maids are reported to police and INS officials, they jokingly are referred to as "Maria-has-struck" cases.

"The maids are usually maids for a day and left alone in the house to clean. The maid's boyfriend will come over with a pickup truck and in half-an-hour clean out a house. When we ask what the maid's name was, it's always 'Maria,' " Smith said.

El Paso Police Department records, however, show that thefts by maids are not reported often.

Burglary Sgt. Robert Rivas theorized residents are scared to report maid-related thefts for fear of revealing themselves as maid employers to law-enforcement authorities.

"The calls we usually get deal with maids who have ripped off their employer" and then left town, Rivas said.

In the past two months the burglary unit has handled two calls believed to have been the work of a "Maria," he said.

"One housewife reported her maid took expensive jewelry. We tried to find her but got nowhere. The woman didn't have an address, phone number, nothing on her maid," Rivas said.

"Sometimes the people who hire maids take them into their confidence and then this happens. I'm sure more of it goes on. It's like shoplifting. It's happening but it's hard to retrieve the stolen goods unless you're caught in the act," he said.

However, there's another side to the same story.

Homemaker Sony Malletta is $350 richer because of her maid who found the cash—three $100 bills and a $50 bill stashed away in a book.

While the maid, Ramona, dusted the bookshelf and the books, the money was found.

"Ramona could have kept the money. I would have never known about it. I remember my husband gave me the money to take to the bank but I probably put it in the book for safekeeping and forgot.

"When I got home Ramona was angry with me. She took me to the book and the money and said, 'Señora, Señora, no, no, no," Mrs. Malletta said.

Housewives, officials, and maids describe the system of locating maids as word-of-mouth. El Paso housewives did organize in 1953, however, under the banner of the Association for Legalized Domestics. They urged Washington to make it easier for Mexican maids to work in El Paso, and were shocked when their proposal was turned down by the Department of Justice.

Maid smuggling also has been big business.

A Westside housewife, who has employed both live-ins and once-a-week maids for nearly a decade, said her friend used to run a maid racket.

For a fee beginning at $300, the woman would find maids for takers throughout Texas and fly them to their new homes in Houston, Dallas, Fort Worth—wherever. The fee would depend on the cost of a plane ticket.

"It's all underground. It's both legal and illegal maids getting paid under the table," Smith said.

"It's people hiring them, violating laws, and we at the INS catch the heat. And, at the bottom of it all, those deriving the greatest benefits are employers."

Economist Lee summed it up this way. "There is something hypocritical about the maids. We complain about illegal aliens, yet we have an illegal maid or a yardman. I suspect you would find the same people who complain about illegal aliens are the ones who have an illegal maid."

A Washington lobbyist for tougher immigration laws had a harsher view. "We tried slave labor once before, and it didn't work," he said.

29 Bob Duke ◆ Border Ignored:
Congressmen Fight Nationwide Indifference

As frontiers on the edge of nation-states, borderlands are often isolated from heartland areas and experience a sense of separateness. Borderlanders feel ignored and neglected by federal authorities. For example, U.S. border leaders have long complained that Washington cares little for the area's needs. Reporter Bob Duke captures the spirit of this phenomenon in this article on El Paso.

Former El Paso Rep. Richard White remembers it as one of the worst experiences during his eighteen years in the House.

He was speaking to the House Armed Services Committee about the needs of El Paso's Fort Bliss when a committee member stopped him.

The question hurt. "Is El Paso in the United States or Mexico?" the congressman wanted to know.

"The ignorance of most congressmen about border problems is terrible," White said. "As far as they're concerned we [border areas] might as well be on the moon."

White's successor, Democratic Rep. Ron Coleman, periodically rises to his feet in the giant House chamber and harangues the House about the unique problems facing El Paso and other Southwest border cities. Congressmen yawn. Some use the time to answer nature's call. Few listen.

Although the response is frustrating, Coleman refuses to give up.

"We (the Congressional Border Caucus) have an educational program going in the House, and I am optimistic that it will eventually succeed," said Coleman, the caucus chairman.

The indifference of most House members to border concerns is nothing new. It's always been present and probably will continue to be unless something dramatic happens to shatter it—such as Mexico facing a serious Marxist threat.

Since congressmen from other areas have their own local ills to help solve, they see no reason to become closely involved in efforts to ease problems in border districts.

One border congressman, Rep. Kika de la Garza, D-Texas, chairman of the House Agriculture Committee, has been trying unsuccessfully for years to educate House members on border problems.

From the *El Paso Herald-Post*, Special Report on the Border, Summer 1983, pp. 8–9. Reprinted by permission of the *El Paso Herald-Post*.

"You keep trying even though you know they're not really interested," he said. "Someday perhaps they will realize the importance of our area."

Until then, de la Garza said, border lawmakers will have to trade votes with other congressmen to get the assistance they need.

Congress' apathy to border matters is mirrored to a lesser extent in the executive branch of the government, although a U.S. State Department official denies it.

"It is not true that we are indifferent to problems along the U.S.-Mexico border," he said. "We are well aware of the importance of the Southern border area and its intimate relationship with Mexico, and we have bilateral programs reflecting our interest."

He was speaking for the State Department that has an interest in promoting good relations with other nations, and not specifically for the Reagan administration.

Attempts by the *Herald-Post* to contact an expert on U.S.-Mexican border issues at the White House failed. Apparently President [Ronald] Reagan has no one there who would be considered an authentic expert—which means his border initiatives are based primarily on his own instincts, presidential task forces, and the State Department's Mexican Desk.

Reagan, of course, isn't the only president to take this approach. Former presidents Jimmy Carter, Gerald Ford, and Richard M. Nixon did the same.

Thus, some congressmen say, the executive branch must bear a major share of the blame for the lukewarm federal attempts to ease border problems. If it had constantly briefed and cajoled Congress over the years on the plight of the border cities, border congressmen wouldn't be having such a difficult time selling their colleagues on the need for special assistance and programs, it is argued.

If one issue clearly demonstrates the executive branch's ignorance of border woes, it is the Environmental Protection Agency's recent threat to cut off certain federal aid to El Paso and other border cities that had failed to meet U.S. clean air standards.

EPA made the threat despite the fact that much of the pollution covering El Paso and San Diego comes from across the Mexican border. In El Paso's case, the pollution wafts in from Juárez.

Finally, after pleas and pressures from the cities affected and border congressmen, EPA agreed to extend the "comment period" and review the proposed sanctions.

There also are flagrant instances in which both the executive branch and Congress have refused to remedy a border problem resulting from federal inaction.

For example, there is the funding crisis in border public schools caused by the influx of legal and illegal alien children.

Neither Congress nor the U.S. Department of Education has shown any inclination to provide financial assistance for a problem stemming partly from the federal government's failure to enforce immigration laws.

Sen. John Tower, R-Texas, has a bill pending that would appropriate up to $68 million a year for three years to help local school systems which have at least 500 alien children. It would authorize $1,000 per alien student.

Sen. Lloyd Bentsen, D-Texas, tried to get a similar measure through Congress in recent years, but failed. Consequently, there is no assurance Tower will succeed where Bentsen didn't.

Phyllis Armijo, president of the Ysleta Independent School District, testified about the extent of the problem before a Senate subcommittee on July 25.

She quoted a 1976 study that showed the Ysleta district had 3,184 Mexican immigrant students (7.8 percent of the enrollment). She said it probably has more now.

Mrs. Armijo said a statewide study this year revealed the largest increases in undocumented alien students had occurred in border-area school districts and in Texas' major urban centers.

"Ysleta Independent School District meets both of those criteria," she said. "Thus, it seems very likely that the figure of 7.8 percent is a minimum estimate of the percentage of Mexican immigrants."

El Paso is confronted with other problems Congress and the executive branch have refused or neglected to remedy.

Among them are a shortage of Immigration and Naturalization Service [INS] officers needed to control illegal immigration along the border, an absence of sufficient lanes on international bridges spanning the Rio Grande, and the lack of a stabilizing U.S.-Mexico money exchange system for converting pesos into dollars during a peso-devaluation crisis in Mexico.

Border congressmen believe the Reagan administration is making a tragic mistake in reducing rather than increasing the number of INS patrolmen on the Southwest border. If the border were adequately protected, they maintain, then there wouldn't be any pressure for immigration reforms.

The paucity of lanes on Rio Grande bridges is serious. Resulting traffic snarls affect sales and trade in both El Paso and Juárez, merchants say.

The backed-up traffic and idling cars and trucks also add to the air pollution.

In spite of a State Department official's assertion that the Reagan administration has given priority to the problem, there is no evidence this is so.

So far, the most the administration has done is ask the International Boundary and Water Commission, a joint U.S.-Mexico group, to consider expanding the Zaragosa Bridge. The State Department official said the administration would like to see the span expanded now, but hasn't been able to obtain Mexico's cooperation.

"That project is complicated by the fact that half of the bridge is owned by the United States and the other half by Mexico," he said. "The project has not been approved by Mexico, and it's doubtful that they will approve it unless, and until, they conclude it's in their interest."

Mexico is aware that El Paso wants traffic lanes expanded and increased in order to lure more Mexicans to El Paso shops and stores, the official said. For the Zaragosa project to be endorsed by Mexico, he said, Mexican authorities would have to believe that it would draw more American consumers to their side of the border.

The official admitted the administration had not pressured the Mexicans on the issue, fearing such tactics might anger Mexico. Yet, he emphasized, the administration had discussed traffic problems on El Paso's three international bridges with Mexico six times between early 1982 and June 1983.

"Another problem is that there are more projects than Mexico is willing to approve at this time," he said.

Concerning air pollution, the State Department official said Mexico had disputed El Paso's contention that much of its pollution originates in Juárez.

"The Mexicans claim that the ASARCO [American Smelting and Refining Company] plant in El Paso is primarily responsible," he said. "And they claim it's still emitting lead despite claims by ASARCO that it isn't."

The official said there are numerous bilateral agreements between the United States and Mexico, including pacts relating to water, housing, health and safety, and law enforcement.

"For example, U.S. and Mexican customs officials meet periodically and try to solve their mutual problems," he said. "There are channels and means of communicating."

Although he concedes the peso crisis is a serious problem for Southwest border merchants, the State Department official doesn't see any need for the special peso-dollar exchange mechanism proposed by de la Garza and Coleman.

In lieu of their "costly" proposal, he recommended the United States do everything possible to help Mexico improve its economy.

"There was a lot of inflation in Mexico," the official said. "In the midst of it the peso was being held up artificially at the rate of 22.5 pesos to the dollar. The Mexicans finally had to let it float, or devaluate to a rational figure [currently about 149 pesos to the dollar]."

He said several U.S.-help programs for Mexico are in progress, including a $1 billion advance payment for Mexican oil, roughly $1 billion in Commodity Credit Corp. credits, and Agriculture Department loans at low interest rates.

Although the State Department official defended the administration well, it would be a mistake to assume that the administration has a crash campaign for solving border problems. Like previous administrations, it focuses strictly on the most basic problems, such as health, safety, and narcotics traffic, leaving other pressing matters to some future chief executive.

Understandably, Coleman and the other border congressmen aren't depending on the Reagan administration to expand its border problem-solving endeavor voluntarily.

Instead, they plan to keep lobbying Congress for understanding and assistance.

VII A World Apart

There is widespread agreement among Americans and Mexicans that the borderlands are fundamentally different from the heartlands of both countries. Such uniqueness is rooted in various factors, including location on the periphery of the two nation-states, pronounced transnational interdependence, acute internationality, and vast ethnic, cultural, and linguistic mixture. Of necessity, borderlanders have developed their own way of life and their own institutions. A sense of "otherness" and "separateness" is clearly detectable among people who live in the binational urban centers from Brownsville-Matamoros to San Diego-Tijuana. On the border, deviation from the national norm is taken for granted; away from the border, such divergence breeds curiosity and fascination.

The Taco Bell television commercial inviting hungry Americans who yearn for Mexican food to "make a run for the border" cleverly capitalizes on the romantic, even mythical, perceptions and images that pervade U.S. society about Mexico and its northern frontier. Crossing the border means leaving behind the predictable and mundane world in the United States. For pleasure seekers, it means escaping from restrictions that govern daily behavior back home, or venturing into a mysterious and exotic land where fantasies can come true. For entrepreneurs, shady or otherwise, it means greater freedom and opportunity to make quick money.

Like Americans, Mexicans are at once repelled and attracted by the borderlands. They are critical of American cultural influences and controls over the region, yet they do not hesitate to put aside nationalistic sentiments when pursuing personal interests. For example, affluent Mexicans regularly "make runs for the border" on shopping sprees and vacations in U.S. cities, and the poor jump the boundary with impunity in search of jobs and the American dream.

As a land where the unorthodox and the unusual stand out, *la frontera* has no equal. It is a compelling place of great contrasts, contradictions, and paradoxes. That is what makes it interesting and why it demands our attention. The essays in this section depict the border as a haven for unusual business practices and as a unique tourist destination (Selections 30 and 31). Document Selections 32 and 33 explore the special nature of the border's human environment, including cultural anomalies and contrasting world views. The section—and volume—closes with the poem, *"La Frontera"* (Selection 34).

30 Tom Miller ◆ The Borderblasters

*Shady entrepreneurs who feel constrained by laws or customs in their
own countries frequently move abroad to carry on their business activities as they see fit. In the twentieth century, Mexico's border cities have
served as havens for a variety of flamboyant hucksters, including U.S.
radio personalities who, without much interference from Mexican authorities, have broadcast controversial messages and peddled bizarre wares
to vast international audiences. Tom Miller, a writer from Tucson, illustrates this phenomenon with case studies from the recent past.*

John R. Brinkley was not a popular man with America's medical establishment. In the late 1920s, Brinkley diagnosed medical problems over
his radio station, KFKB, in Milford, Kansas, often prescribing remedies
available at one of his own drugstores. His most ambitious medical activity was a "rejuvenation operation" for men. Feeling tired and run-down?
he asked listeners. Not as active as you once were? Come to my clinic.

The minor surgery "Doctor" Brinkley sold on the radio consisted of
opening a man's scrotum and implanting goat glands in the center of the
testicles. Brinkley claimed the results would make patients more active
and healthier, lower their blood pressure, and, not incidentally, make them
better lovers. "We make old men execute young ideas," Brinkley crowed.

Brinkley earned the ire of the Kansas City *Star*, which vilified him
from its front page. The American Medical Association—which he called
the Amateur Meatcutters Association—brought him to court, alleging his
credentials false and his operations useless.

Some of Brinkley's former patients were his best defense witnesses.
From hill-country farmers to Texas oil millionaires, they journeyed to
Kansas proclaiming the wonders of goat-gland surgery. Other former patients were among the best prosecution witnesses, charging that they had
been duped. By the trial's end, Brinkley was professionally discredited.

Brinkley used his one asset, KFKB ("Kansas First, Kansas Best"),
for revenge against the state's establishment. A gubernatorial race was
scheduled soon, and Brinkley campaigned over the airwaves as a write-in
candidate. Despite his lack of political experience and late entry into the
race, one-third of the electorate wrote in his name. Shortly after Brinkley's
defeat the Kansas State Medical Board revoked his license to practice,

From *On the Border: Portraits of America's Southwestern Frontier* (New
York: Harper and Row, 1981), 76–86. © 1981 Tom Miller. Reprinted by permission of the author.

and the Federal Radio Commission, forerunner of the Federal Communications Commission, shut down his station. Brinkley decided to relocate his business.

Communities throughout the United States wrote the ersatz doctor, each urging that he move his enterprise to their town. A letter from the Del Rio, Texas, Chamber of Commerce was especially intriguing: Why not make Del Rio your headquarters, but broadcast from across the Rio Grande in Villa Acuña, Coahuila?

The idea appealed to the forty-six-year-old goat-gland doctor, and in 1931, John R. Brinkley—who listed himself as M.D., Ph.D., M.C., LL.D., Sc.D., and Lieut. U.S.N.R.—founded Mexican radio station XER with a power of seventy-five thousand watts. As Brinkley said, "Radio waves pay no attention to lines on a map." An era of broadcasting history had begun.

"This is X-E-R," Brinkley's friendly voice told listeners throughout North America, "the sunshine station between the nations." Brinkley solicited listeners' letters, which started arriving from all forty-eight states and fifteen foreign countries. One week in January 1932 more than twenty-seven thousand pieces of mail came in.

Brinkley's goat-gland clinic took over the top floor of the Roswell Hotel in Del Rio. Between Brinkley's three hundred employees and the many townspeople who catered to the steady stream of patients arriving daily by train, Del Rio thrived during the depths of the depression. Brinkley's Del Rio estate became a shrine to which listeners made pilgrimages. Electric lights spelled out his name in front of his mansion. Flamingos, tortoises, and penguins graced the elaborate grounds. Sunday mornings he would play organ music over the air from his living room. John-Boy, his son, became a national celebrity sitting on his pappy's knee.

Brinkley's folksy delivery was the source of his appeal. He'd tell the gang back in Mule Gulch, Tennessee, that Charlie from down at the general store had arrived safely, was at the clinic that day, sends his love, and will be home by next weekend.

Business was brisk until the Mexican government threatened to close down XER in 1933. Brinkley dispatched Charles Curtis, vice-president under Herbert Hoover, to intercede, but the final Mexican demand— 350,000 pesos (about $175,000)—was too exorbitant. *Federales* shut down the station.

Brinkley rebounded quickly by advertising his Del Rio clinic on U.S. stations and by taking over station XEAW in Reynosa. And he established a second clinic at nearby San Juan, Texas—this one to treat problems of the rectum. "Remember," Brinkley cheerfully advertised, "San Juan for rectal trouble, and Del Rio for the old prostate!"

The election of Lázaro Cárdenas as president of Mexico in 1934 gave Brinkley a new opportunity to reestablish a station at Villa Acuña. Using a Mexican *prestanombre*, or front man, Brinkley was soon back on the air with XERA, pitching his potency operations with renewed fervor. Prices ranged from "The Poor Man's Special" at $125—good for one examination and a prostate treatment—to the $1,000 "Businessman's Treatment," which came with a lifetime guarantee. Those complaining about high prices were reminded that "Doctor Brinkley will use the money for the betterment of mankind." In fact, only a fraction of his income was spent in the interest of others—new uniforms for the Villa Acuña police and a library for Del Rio. The rest of his wealth was spent on ranches, farms, mines, a plane, three yachts, and countless automobiles.

Brinkley's success inspired other entrepreneurs to start borderblasters. The nearest was XEPN at Piedras Negras, with one hundred thousand watts, opposite Eagle Pass about fifty miles downriver. XEPN listeners were invited to write in questions—accompanied by a dollar per query— to astrologers and psychics who replied to them on the air. A lady would write that her ring was lost, and "the spooks" would tell her that a plumber would find it while working on her sink.

Aside from goat glands and spooks, the biggest influence early border stations had on American culture was in the field of country music. Reaching parts of rural America that city stations could not, the borderblasters provided for many the only nighttime entertainment available. Hillbilly singers performed on the air, then plugged their records and songbooks. Best-known of the hillbilly groups on XERA was the Carter Family from Appalachia, who made Del Rio their home from 1938 until 1941, when they relocated in San Antonio to prepare weekly shows for another Mexican station in Monterrey. The Carters—A. P., Sara, Maybelle, Janette, Anita, Helen, and June—would crowd into a studio, a Pentecostal preacher named Brother Bill Guild would introduce them, and they'd light into their theme song, "Keep on the Sunny Side." Between songs Brother Bill promoted Carter Family records and products such as Colorback ("Just comb it through your hair and you'll get your color back!"). Each week tapes of the sessions were shipped from San Antonio to Monterrey.

In 1941 the new administration of President Avila Camacho shut down XERA. Devastated by the loss, outquacked by rival stations, sued by dissatisfied patients, and harassed by authorities in two countries, Brinkley quickly went bankrupt. He died a broken man the following year.

A few years later a third station was started in Villa Acuña—XERF, whose main office, like its predecessors, was in Del Rio. While the Mexican ownership of XERF has remained a mystery, control of the station has always rested with whoever maintained the U.S. advertising accounts. The key to border stations was always American business acumen and technology. The announcing was in English; the audience was almost entirely American; the programs and commercials were usually recorded on the U.S. side; advertising time was sold in the United States to American companies; and the station's mailing address was invariably north of the border. Mexico supplied land for the studios and broadcast towers, some technicians, and the call letters.

On-the-air entertainment at XERF was provided by cowboy singers and evangelists, both of whom found the X-stations ideal for their purposes. One of the first preachers to take advantage of the border stations was the Reverend J. C. Bishop, who paid $100,000 for forty years of fifteen minutes of airtime nightly. During his peak years—1956 to 1962—Bishop, who operates out of Dallas, received four hundred letters a day.

The most colorful of the preachers, Dallas Turner, started on the air in the 1940s and has been there ever since. Turner is filled with tales of the X-stations, a subject he dearly loves.

"When I got to my first border station I learned very fast that they didn't hire you to sing, they hired you to sell, sell, *sell*. I was a pitchman. A pitchman's success depended entirely on his ability to pull mail. The greatest announcers in the country would come to the border and they wouldn't last overnight. The best radio pitchmen came off the carnival circuit or from the vaudeville halls. The first and greatest of them was Don Baxter, who called himself Major Kord. He specialized in selling piano lessons by mail, but he did most of the other ads, too. He was a pioneer—a guy who could stand up and fight the microphone. He'd wave his arms and go through all sorts of calisthenics.

"We had one fellow, Billy Truehart, who sold tap-dancing lessons over the air. He'd bring a board to the studio, put a microphone down by his feet, and tap dance and pitch at the same time. He sold thousands of courses that way. We also had Don Howard doing 'Frank the Diamond Man,' or 'Bill the Diamond Man'—he'd change his name on each station. 'Friends,' he'd say, 'I wish there was television at this time because I hold in my hand the most *beau*tiful diamond. . . .' He had a deep melodic voice.

"Every morning I'd just take a jug of cough syrup and start recording. I might record for X-E-R-B at Rosarito, south of Tijuana, in the morning, for X-E-G in the afternoon, and at night for X-E-N-T at Reynosa. All my shows were basically the same, but I had to keep track of which name I used on which station. I'd do one as Nevada Slim the Yodelin' Cowboy,

another as Cowboy Dallas Turner, and a third as Yodelin' Slim Dallas. I
also pitched my songbooks over the air for a dollar; the station would
keep half the take. On a good day I'd get a hundred fifty orders.' "

In 1950, when Acuña was growing from a *villa* to a *ciudad*, Turner
sold advertising time to the preachers for some of the borderblasters.

"One of them, Gerald L. K. Smith, always had two bodyguards with
him. I signed him to a twenty-five-thousand-dollar contract. He was a
very anti-Semitic individual, and because of this they had to throw him
off the air at X-E-L-O. He promised me he wouldn't say anything against
the Jews but we ended up giving him his money back."

By this time Turner had become a heavy drinker. One day in a run-
down Kansas City hotel he was about to shoot himself. As fate would
have it his radio was playing "God Put a Rainbow in the Cloud." Hearing
the song, he laid down his gun, picked up a Gideon Bible, and Jesus walked
in. Turner went into on-the-air evangelism where he has stayed since.

*This is your good buddy, America's cowboy evangelist, Dr. Dallas
Turner,* his nightly spiel begins, *speaking to you from the studios of
X-E-R-F at beautiful Ciudad Acuña on the banks of the silvery Rio Grande
in romantic old Mexico.* Actually Turner is speaking to you from the den
in his house in Reno, Nevada. Station XERF simply plays tapes he ships
to Del Rio. "On a border station you never admit you're pre-recorded,"
Turner explained. "On American stations you have to say if you are. I
wouldn't be half as effective if listeners knew I was really in Nevada."

Paul Kallinger has been on XERF since 1949. Billed as "your good
neighbor along the way," he booms the station ID with the slightest encouragement: *"Coast to coast, border to border, wherever you are, wherever you may be, we're right here at fifteen-seventy on your dial at X-E-R-F
in Ciudad Acuña, Coahuila, Mexico. Our mailing address is Del Rio,
Texas. . . ."*

In the mid-fifties, when country and western music dominated XERF,
Kallinger was among the most popular disc jockeys on American radio.
Most of the developing country-music stars of the day—Johnny Cash,
Faron Young, Porter Waggoner, and others—dropped in to sing on the air.
"Getting exposure on my show was essential for breaking a national hit.
One time Elvis Presley came down here while he was still on the Sun
label. I told him, 'I'm sorry, Elvis. I don't allow any rock 'n' roll on my
show.' He said, 'Well, thank you anyway. I was just passing through Del
Rio and I thought perhaps you'd put me on your program.'

"I pitched 'Sunshine Chicks': *'one hundred number-one, first-grade
baby chicks for two-ninety-eight!'* We sold double-edged, surgical-steel
razor blades, rosebushes, fruit trees, d-Con rat poison—we introduced
that. Most of our ads were on a P.I.—per inquiry—basis. The advertiser

didn't pay for air time, but he did split the money with the station once the mail orders came in. So it was in the station's interest to draw the biggest response. I've even been accused of selling autographed pictures of Jesus Christ! We'd never do that on X-E-R-F. I think they did it on X-E-G."

The legendary $2.98 autographed pictures of Jesus Christ are part of borderland mythology. Whomever I spoke with at one station insisted the ad was on another. Although no one has actually seen one, everyone readily concedes the autographed pictures do exist. (Would you settle for a Lord's Last Supper tablecloth?)

Bob Smith had just finished a stint as "Big Smith with the Records!" on a Shreveport, Louisiana, station in the late 1950s when he and a friend figured that big money was waiting for them in border radio. Smith thought XERF was the greatest stage in the world and he wanted to be front and center on that stage. After driving the 550 miles to Del Rio, Smith walked into the middle of a management-labor dispute. Station employees were disenchanted with their bosses and were willing to go with the highest bidder. In effect, the station was up for grabs. Bob Smith was the first to flash some cash.

Within a day the station was under his control. Smith altered the programming, took over the advertising accounts, changed his name, and started a genuine underground cult throughout teenage America. At the center of the cult lay rhythm and blues and gritty rock 'n' roll. The cult's mysterious guru was Bob Smith's better-known alter ego, Wolfman Jack.

Smith captured teenage imaginations with his crazed style as Wolfman Jack. His on-the-air growl, his manic chatter, and his savvy record selection combined to make the most of XERF's powerful range, then at 250,000 watts. *"Dis is de WOLFMAN talkin' atcha!"* he'd bark. He urged listeners to get naked, vote for him for president, "blow the evil weed," wiggle their toes, kiss their teachers. The mystique of the border enhanced his image. His was an unknown quantity with a most bizarre quality. To hear him tell the XERF story is alternately illuminating and frustrating. He is the master of shuck and jive.

"The ole Wolfman come on from midnight till four in the morning pitching all kinds of mail-order deals: gain weight, lose weight, buy records, roach clips, songbooks, everything. I tried selling something called Florex which we advertised as sex pills. The Federal Trade Commission made me stop. They got a sample and discovered we were selling sugar pills.

"X-E-R-F had thirty employees along with facilities for them to eat and sleep. We grew our own food—we had sheep and ugly goats and the works. Twice a month we threw a big party for the *federales*, the cops, who came on horseback. We'd hire either a country band or some *mariachis*. The women from town would all show up and we'd cook the goats and drink wine and get totally blitzed while the Reverend J. Charles Jessup was on the air screaming about God. We were the hot item in Acuña. You'd go down to Boys Town, to the red-light district, and you'd hear the station in all the bars, especially when I was on. They were very proud that the station was in their town.

"People who came to Acuña looking for the studio would have to pay a cabdriver fifty bucks to get him to take them out there. A few of the preachers wanted to visit the facilities but I always told them their lives would be in danger if they came. It was tough enough to keep the bad dudes—the ones who wanted to gain control of the station—away from the door. We had to stay armed all the time and keep sandbags around the station. I always traveled with bodyguards. We tried to act as bad as we looked."

The greatest controversy about XERF during Wolfman's tenure revolves around a shoot-out over control of the station. Early one morning while Wolfman was at home in Del Rio listening to some preacher on the station, a kid's voice interrupted: "*¡Pistoleros! ¡Pistoleros!*"

Wolfman headed out across the river to the station.

"A rival faction had come back and tried to scare us out of there. They were like Indians circling the fort. They rode on bicycles, motor scooters, motorcycles, horseback—all those rinky-dink Mexican things. It was comical to see them trying to shoot at us. The scene was like an amusement-park shooting gallery: you'd watch a guy riding, someone shoots at him, and *kchiiiing!*, he falls off his bicycle. We finally chased them all away. Nobody got hurt bad on our team, just a couple of wounded. Two guys on their team got killed.

"We kept the peace by giving them money and kisses at the same time we showed them force. We paid *mordida* to the *federales*, *mordida* to the union bosses, and *mordida* to the troublemakers. If we didn't come up with the green, nothing would get done," Bob Smith, a.k.a. Wolfman Jack, became a pirate king. Station XERF was his kingdom.

"We kept the business operation very hush-hush because there was *so* much money. To pitch 'The Lucky Forty,' an oldies album package, I'd cut one seven-minute spot where you play a little bitty portion of each song, and run it on Monday night. Wednesday, when the mail came in, I'd get four to five thousand orders for that one record. The major broadcast executives in America were trying to get their hands on that station because they knew what a gold mine it was. We had the most powerful signal in North America. Birds dropped dead when they flew too close to the tower. A car driving from New York to L.A. would never lose the station. I had listeners in New Zealand! I made funny remarks about Khrushchev and they jammed X-E-R-F in Moscow!

"Hundreds of people tried to reach me with payola but I never talked with any of them. I knew the one time I'd step out of line I'd have the U.S. boys on my rear end. Record companies would send me tons of new releases without me even soliciting. I threw half the stuff away—gave it to the kids in Acuña."

Stories about American children who sneaked their transistor radios under the sheets at night to listen to the Wolfman's deranged babble are legion. He brought an outlaw spirit to the airwaves, turning on an entire generation of white youngsters to greasy rhythm and blues. In the last years of the Eisenhower administration when Percy Faith, Connie Francis, and Paul Anka were topping the charts, XERF played Wilbert Harrison, Joe Turner, Jerry Butler, and Lloyd Price nightly.

"All my listeners assumed I was black. Most of my orders came from the white population though, 'cause they wanted to be hip, to get into what's happening. I didn't realize I was influencing people that much until many years later when songs were written about me. At the time, I was more into, 'How many pieces of mail did we pull for the record package we pitched last Tuesday?' That's all I was concerned with."

The hellfire and brimstone preachers remained on the air, despite the new direction in which Smith took the station. "The station was their life's blood—they'd bring the Lord down Himself to stay on the air. X-E-R-F made millionaires out of a number of preachers."

After a few years Bob Smith left Del Rio. The station—or rather the advertising accounts—reverted to Arturo Gonzales, the local lawyer who had handled XERF's U.S. dealings prior to Smith's arrival. Wolfman moved to another border station on the West Coast. Listening to XERF, however, you'd have thought the Wolfman was still in the studio screaming away. Every night for another two years he continued to growl his way through more mail-order madness and rhythm and blues. Station XERF was simply playing tapes he sent every week. Wolfman Jack's new West Coast home was the setting for his scenes in *American Graffiti*, the 1973 movie in which he portrayed a frenzied and compassionate border-station deejay—the way he likes to be remembered on the X-stations.

31 Daniel D. Arreola and James R. Curtis ◆ Tourist Landscapes

Geographers Daniel D. Arreola and James R. Curtis have done consider-able research on the use of space in the Mexican border cities. In this essay they use the concept of "other-directed places" to interpret the nature of tourist districts. Their analysis is significant because "border-style" tourism has left an indelible impression of the region on millions of visitors, especially Americans.

It is probably fair to suggest that most North Americans consider the tourist districts in Mexican border cities to *be* the border cities. They are the only places that most tourists traditionally visit, and they are the places often depicted in the mass media about the border. The landscapes of these districts are among the most colorful, if contrived, of all those found in the Mexican urban scene. In its appearance as well as in its goods and services, the tourist district typically combines elements of a 1920s Hollywood version of "romantic old Mexico" with a kind of raunchy, military-oriented, honky-tonk drag associated with the 1940s and 1950s. It is an illusionary, anachronistic place where merchants cater to tourists' expectations by marketing a vision of Mexico that is a product of history, myth, reality, and fantasy. To cite an example that has become a cliché, one still sees tourists having their pictures taken with serapes thrown over their shoulders and wearing big sombreros with terms like BORRACHO (drunk) and JUST DIVORCED emblazed across them while perched atop wooden-wheeled carts with burros dyed to resemble zebras. Yet, while these tourist areas are caricatures of both the border town and the country and could be criticized for perpetuating distorted images, in their own way they vividly express cultural and economic dynamics operating along the frontier. Although relatively small in size, tourist districts have played an important role in the economy, culture, and landscape of border towns.

There is a paradox to tourism in the Mexican border cities. On one hand, they are among the most popular tourist destinations within Mexico, attracting several times over the estimated six million tourists who visit the country's interior each year. Indeed, Tijuana claims to be the most-visited city in the world. By one account, in 1986, it attracted nineteen

From *The Mexican Border Cities: Landscape Anatomy and Place Personal-ity* (Tucson: University of Arizona Press, 1993), 77–79, 90–96, figures and tables omitted. © 1993 University of Arizona Press. Reprinted by permission of the University of Arizona Press.

million tourists who contributed over $700 million to the local economy (Griffin and Crowley, 1989: 334). Tourism has been and continues to be big business along the border. On the other hand, these cities are widely and often vehemently scorned as places to visit. To appreciate this contention, one need only consider how they have been depicted in tourist guidebooks. Characteristic of the genre, one travel writer summarily dismissed Nuevo Laredo as "a typical border town, with nothing of interest to see," while another cautioned that it "should not be viewed as representative of the Great Republic to the south" (Bashford 1954: 38; Terry 1935: 3). Coupled with the terms "dusty" and "nondescript," these observations have been applied countless times to nearly all of the border towns, if they have generated comment at all. Most of the border towns have been ignored altogether in popular literature about Mexico travel and tourism. Moreover, even when tourist "attractions" are identified, they typically are treated in an exaggerated and pejorative fashion; the focus is on stereotypical elements associated with the near-legendary reputation of these places as swinging "sin cities." Consider the comments of a travel writer who in the 1920s declared that "Tia Juana [*sic*] is a 'wide open' town, exclusively devoted to racing, gambling, and drinking" (Carpenter 1927: 12). Such sweeping, condescending statements about the border towns continue to be aired, as evidenced by a recent guide that concluded that "Juarez has so many bars that just counting them can make you tipsy. Most of them are rather unsavory, and even the savory ones can be dangerous" (Slater 1989: 525). It is paradoxical, then, that although Mexican border towns have a questionable popular image and historically have been derided as tourist destinations, they nonetheless have their appeal. This is confirmed by the millions of tourists who cross the border each year to visit border cities, or to phrase it more accurately, cross the border to visit *parts* of them—the tourist districts. . . .

On the windows and exterior facades of commercial structures in almost all of the tourist districts are signs, tile mosaics, pictures, and other renderings that depict certain recurring themes. These symbols may provide important clues about the meaning of the tourist districts. The most common images seen are pottery, serapes, sombreros, and mounted bull horns, and the most common scenes portrayed are bullfights, mission-style churches, likenesses of Emiliano Zapata and Francisco "Pancho" Villa, and desert landscapes that include giant saguaro cacti and peasant men and boys (campesinos) wearing sandals and the traditional baggy, white cotton garb. The single most widespread image is probably of a campesino reclining against a saguaro with his knees drawn up to his chest and his sombrero tilted over his face while he takes a siesta. When a woman is portrayed, she typically has a high lady-of-Spain hairstyle and is wearing a frilly, low-cut, off-shoulder dress. Her head is thrown back gaily, and yes, she has dark "flashing" eyes and a rose in her mouth. These romanticized, stereotypical images perhaps symbolize a distinctive American way of thinking about Mexico, and as such may reflect the deep-seated cultural and historical forces that have shaped the landscapes associated with these districts as well as shed light on the attraction they hold for the average North American tourist. Indeed, one could argue that the cultural landscapes of these districts and the goods and services found there play on the preconceived images of what most North American tourists think Mexico *ought* to look like and what it *ought* to offer them for sale. In this sense, it has little to do with the Mexican people or culture and much to do with pleasing outsiders, especially American tourist-consumers.

Because of this external orientation, the tourist districts may be classified as "other-directed places" (Curtis and Arreola 1989). This term was coined by J. B. Jackson, one of the preeminent American landscape scholars, in a mid-1950s article that appeared originally in *Landscape* magazine. The article was entitled "Other-directed Houses," and it was concerned with the then-emerging roadside architecture (Jackson 1970: 55–72). In the article, Jackson defines other-directed architecture as characterized by "conspicuous facades, exotic decoration and landscaping, a lavish use of lights and colors and signs" and meant for pleasure and popular mass entertainment (Jackson 1970: 68). Another scholar who has recently expanded upon the concept notes that "the total effect of such architecture is the creation of other-directed places which . . . declare themselves unequivocally to be 'Vacationland' or 'Consumerland' " (Relph 1976: 93). Some criticize these touristscapes as being synthetic or even absurd and having a forced atmosphere of gaiety. However, Jackson writes, "Go in when you are looking for a good time and for an escape from the everyday, and at once the place seems steeped in magic" (Jackson 1970: 63). Viewed that way, the superficiality of these places does not in itself diminish the tourist experience and may even enhance it.

A great deal of research has suggested that most tourists enjoy, or at least are not put off by, contrived or unauthentic attractions, especially if they conform to preconceived notions (Cohen 1979; Curtis 1981; Curtis 1985; Eckbo 1969; Jackson 1962; MacCannell 1976; Pearce 1982). One distinguished scholar has gone so far as to conclude that tourists seldom like the authentic, preferring instead caricature that validates their own "provincial expectations" (Boorstin 1961: 100). There is evidently a certain ineffable satisfaction or wish-fulfillment that comes when a place lives up to preexisting images, even if it does so through contrivance. Although critics may assail such tourism, one important purpose served is that "contrived attractions also protect a locality from its visitors by focusing touristic activities temporally and geographically" (Jakle 1985: 23). These themes help explain not only the nature of tourist-district landscapes in border cities but also the characteristics and motivations of tourists who visit them.

In all likelihood, few tourists come to these cities for sight-seeing purposes, although "negative sight-seeing," or viewing disturbing scenes such as begging or poverty-ridden living conditions, may be a motivation for some. Rather, we contend, most tourists want to eat, drink, and purchase selective goods and services in an idealized "Mexicoland" that is somewhat insulated from the real world and danger but that evokes at least a veiled sense of excitement and foreign adventure. The romanticized imagery of pretty señoritas with roses in their mouths and peasant men taking a siesta in the desert sun and the associated iconography seems to support this position.

So, too, does the tawdry reputation of the honky-tonk border town, which continues to lure and fascinate. This might explain why the old Tijuana jail was remodeled and converted to a tourist attraction in the early 1970s. The Tijuana Convention and Tourist Bureau put up $60,000 of the cost, and the rest came from city funds (*San Diego Union* 1972). Through such renovation and clean-up efforts, the tourist districts have in many ways parodied themselves as they have offered an increasingly sanitized version of what they were, but not so sanitized a version that they have deflated tourists' expectations. To be successful, they must contain all that is usual and expected.

This desire for a mildly stimulating time in a "faraway" exotic land where tangible and mental souvenirs can be collected is not unlike the motivations that draw tourists by the millions to theme parks or even to Third World countries, especially those in the tropical realm (Britton 1979; Lea 1988; Matthews 1977). In essence, it represents a form of escape or "diversionary tourism." Some theorists have argued that such "escapes to fantasyland" are quests for individual survival and identity (Cohen and Taylor 1976), while others have suggested that they are a means of ego-enhancement (Dann 1977). A philosophy professor, Ruben Vizcaino, at the Autonomous University of Baja California, shares these views. He has been quoted as saying that tourists come to Tijuana "looking for *their* identity. They see themselves as supermen, leaders of the Free World, technological gods. They see Third World poverty—the skinny dogs, the people begging, the *indigenas* (Indians) kneeling before them—and they prove to themselves that *they* are great" (quoted in Martínez 1989: 20).

Regardless of whether or not one accepts this somewhat radical critique, the tourism-as-escape theme conforms to the compensatory leisure-

behavior theory, which argues that people seek the opposite kinds of stimu-
lation in their leisure environments to what they have at work (Pearce
1982: 20). This provides a context for interpreting the tourist-district landscapes as well as tourist motivations.

Since at least the Prohibition era (1918–1933), when large numbers
of Americans first headed "down Mexico way," the vast majority of tourists have been "day visitors," or as they have been formally classified,
"excursionists," who stay less than twenty-four hours. Although tourism
statistics for these cities are notoriously unreliable, if available at all,
conventional wisdom for the state of Baja California has it that only 15 to
20 percent of the tourists stay three or more nights. The figure is probably
less in other Mexican border states (San Diego Union 1987). In fact, by
all reports, the average tourist stay in the border cities ranges from about
six to eight hours in Ciudad Juárez and Tijuana to less than four hours in
most of the other cities.

Based on available data, it appears that most tourists from the United
States arrive from states immediately adjacent to the respective border
cities. A 1985 study conducted by the Ministry of Tourism in Baja California found that 84 percent of foreign tourists in Baja were residents of
California, 12 percent came from other U.S. states, 2 percent came from
Europe, 1 percent came from Canada, and 1 percent came from elsewhere
(Luis Valles 1985: 6; San Diego Union 1987). Although it cannot be substantiated, it appears unlikely that those who arrive from more distant
locations come to the border towns as their primary destinations. In the
case of Tijuana, it is probably visited by non-California residents as a
"side trip" from the tourist mecca of Southern California—Disneyland,
which is less than three hours away. San Diego's principal attractions, the
zoo and Sea World, are only half an hour from the port of entry at San
Ysidro.

Complementing the short stay, the average tourist expenditure is relatively low and concentrated on only a few selected categories of goods
and services. By most accounts, a tourist spends an average of twenty to
thirty-five dollars per visit, depending on location. In Tijuana, per-capita
spending of tourists reportedly increased from twenty-four dollars in 1986
to thirty-four dollars in 1987 (Luis Valles 1988: 8). [In] Baja California
in the mid-1980s, 62 percent of these expenditures were in four categories: restaurants, bars, curios, and liquor. Lodging, which is normally a
high tourist cost, accounts for only 9 percent. It is followed by gasoline,
breads [bakery goods], auto services, entertainment, and other miscella-
neous expenditures.

In Tijuana, at least, there seems to be a significant difference in the
pattern of expenditures between day and night. Reportedly, during the

day about 70 percent of the tourist dollar is spent on curios, whereas during the evening about 90 percent is spent in bars and restaurants (Matthews 1987: 14). Elsewhere in the border cities, studies have documented that the most frequent service expenditures by U.S. tourists include entertainment, medical, dental, selected car repairs, and haircuts, while the most frequently purchased retail goods include liquor, food staples, prescription drugs, and "tourist items" (House 1982: 202).

It is interesting that although families and businessmen reportedly account for an increasingly larger percentage of the tourist trade, attempts to expand the range of tourist activities have apparently met with little success. The Centro Cultural (Cultural Center) in Tijuana provides a good example. Completed in 1983, the impressive and unusual complex is called La Bola because of its round shape. It is located within walking distance of the border in the fashionable Zona del Río district across the street from the new Plaza Río Tijuana shopping center. Designed by renowned architect Pedro Ramírez Vásquez, who also was responsible for the design of Mexico City's National Museum of Anthropology, the Cultural Center contains an anthropological museum, an omnitheater with a curving 180-degree screen, a performing arts center, an outdoor courtyard, gift shops, galleries, and a good restaurant and bar. It now draws over one million visitors annually. In the late 1980s, it hosted international jazz festivals and staged performances by such groups as the Bolshoi Ballet. Yet, less than 15 percent of its visitors come from the United States (*San Diego Tribune* 1987). Likewise, the new U.S.-style shopping centers have failed to generate much interest among foreigners. What tourists want, one might conclude, is what always has motivated them to visit the border: a chance to frolic for a few hours in an "old" Mexico of their fancy. The lure is still escape to an imagined place.

This clearly seems to be the case for the fastest-growing group of tourists—young people aged eighteen to twenty-one. Especially since Texas raised its legal drinking age from eighteen to twenty-one in 1986, tourists in this age group have flocked to the border cities where the drinking age is eighteen, the liquor is relatively cheap, and the atmosphere is generally permissive (*Austin American-Statesman* 1989). In California, where the drinking age is also twenty-one and the bars must close by 2:00 A.M., city officials in nearby Tijuana estimate that as many as twelve thousand youths from north of the border, especially San Diego, visit on a typical weekend night (*San Diego Tribune* 1986). This prompted one newspaper to report that Avenida Revolución "has evolved in recent years from a bastion of sleaze for U.S. servicemen and other pleasure-seekers to a kind of teeny-bopper fantasy-land" (*Los Angeles Times* 1988). The young people are drawn at night primarily to trendy high-tech dance bars, which often have cover charges and even dress codes. One of the latest reported crazes is to drink Tequila Poppers. These are usually served complete with bibs by whistle-blowing barmen, some dressed like firemen or doctors, who pour the liquor and juice into the customer's mouth until they cannot drink any more (*San Diego Union* 1988).

One could argue that the tourist district has come full circle: the more it changes, the more it remains the same. That, of course, is a cliché, but Mexican border cities have long been places of clichés and illusions. Consider again the burros painted with stripes. One of the photographers on Revolución in Tijuana once commented: "People believe they're striped to make them look like zebras, but it's because most of the burros are white, and depending on the light, they don't come out that well on the film" (*San Diego Tribune* 1982: B1).

References

Austin American-Statesman: September 10, 1989, A1.

Bashford, G. M. 1954. *Tourist Guide to Mexico*. New York: McGraw-Hill.

Boorstin, Daniel J. 1961. *The Image: A Guide to Pseudo-Events in America*. New York: Harper and Row.

Britton, Robert A. 1979. "The Image of the Third World in Tourism Marketing." *Annals of Tourism Research* 11: 318–329.

Carpenter, Frank G. 1927. *Mexico*. Garden City, NY: Doubleday, Page and Company.

Cohen, Erik. 1979. "Rethinking the Sociology of Tourism." *Annals of Tourism Research* 11: 18–35.

Cohen, S., and L. Taylor. 1976. *Escape Attempts*. Harmondsworth: Penguin.

Curtis, James R. 1981. "The Boutiquing of Cannery Row." *Landscape* 25: 44–48.

————. 1985. "The Most Famous Fence in the World: Fact and Fiction in Mark Twain's Hannibal." *Landscape* 28: 8–14.

Curtis, James R., and Daniel D. Arreola. 1989. "Through Gringo Eyes: Tourist Districts in the Mexican Border Cities as Other-directed Places." *North American Culture* 5(2): 19–32.

Dann, Graham M. S. 1977. "Anomie, Ego-Enhancement, and Tourism." *Annals of Tourism Research* 4: 184–194.

Eckbo, Garrett. 1969. "The Landscape of Tourism." *Landscape* 18: 29–31.

Griffin, Ernst C., and William K. Crowley. 1989. "The People and Economy of Modern Mexico." In Robert C. West and John P. Augelli (eds.), *Middle America: Its Lands and Peoples*, 3d ed., 284–338. Englewood Cliffs, NJ: Prentice Hall.

House, John W. 1982. *Frontier on the Rio Grande: A Political Geography of Development and Social Deprivation.* Oxford: Clarendon Press.

Jackson, J. B. 1970. "Other-directed Houses." In Ervin H. Zube (ed.), *Landscapes: Selected Writings of J. B. Jackson*, 55–72. Amherst: University of Massachusetts Press.

Jackson, John B. 1962. "We Are Taken for a Ride." *Landscape* 11: 20–22.

Jakle, John A. 1985. *The Tourist: Travel in Twentieth-Century America.* Lincoln: University of Nebraska Press.

Lea, John. 1988. *Tourism and Development in the Third World.* London: Routledge.

Los Angeles Times (San Diego County Edition): October 28, 1988, J2.

Luis Valles, Ron. 1985. "New Plans for Baja Tourism Launched." *The Forum* (November): 6.

———. 1988. "Bustamante Promotes Tijuana through Bureau." *The Forum* (March): 8.

MacCannell, Dean. 1976. *The Tourist: A New Theory of the Leisure Class.* New York: Schocken Books.

Martínez, Ruben. 1989. "Tijuana: Notes from Mexico's New Bohemia." *L.A. Weekly* (July 7–13): 18.

Matthews, Harry G. 1977. "Radicals and Third World Tourism: A Caribbean Focus." *Annals of Tourism Research* 10: 20–29.

Matthews, Neal. 1987. "Gringo Street." *San Diego Reader* (April 23): 14.

Pearce, Philip L. 1982. *The Social Psychology of Tourist Behavior.* Oxford: Pergamon Press.

Relph, Edward. 1976. *Place and Placelessness.* London: Pion.

San Diego Tribune: August 12, 1982, B1; April 22, 1986, E1; January 5, 1987, B1.

San Diego Union: August 6, 1972, B1; January 26, 1987, 12; November 7, 1988, C1.

Slater, Glenn E. (ed.). 1989. *Let's Go: The Budget Guide to Mexico, 1989.* New York: St. Martin's Press.

Terry, T. Phillip. 1935. *Terry's Guide to Mexico.* Boston: Houghton Mifflin Company.

32 Peter Copeland ◆ Border *Ambiente*

On the border, one finds a wide spectrum of cultural orientations, rang-
ing from uniculturalism to multiculturalism. A significant portion of the
population, especially among Chicanos, manifests a hybrid lifestyle, that
is, a lifestyle that combines elements of both Mexican and American cul-
tures. Journalist Peter Copeland probes the implications for borderlanders
of mixing these two ways of life.

The heels of his cowboy boots clicked down the sidewalk in time with
a *ranchera* blasting from a small café, advertising the *comida corrida*
for $2.

A friend stopped to say hello, and the two men, one fair skinned and
the other dark but both wearing *guayaberas*, embraced.

Standing in the shade of a sign that read, "*Aceptamos sus pesos,*"
they chatted for a minute.

They shook hands before parting, saying at once, "*Hay te watcho,*"
Mexican-American slang for "see you later."

Two men met on the sidewalk, but also two cultures, even two
nations.

Scenes such as this fictional one, where cultures mix, take place thousands of times a day in El Paso, the largest U.S. city directly on the Mexican border. And it is one of the few places where people take it for granted.

Ask people what is unique about El Paso, and most answer "the
border."

But what is the culture of the border, what is the *ambiente* or flavor
of life here? That is where the disagreement starts.

One thing newcomers and long time El Pasoans agree on is that here
is something special.

"You assume El Paso is a part of Texas and a part of the United States.
That is a mistake," said Ellwyn Stoddard, a UT [University of Texas] El
Paso professor and dean of the border scholars.

"We are more a part of the border culture than we are American or
Mexican. We are a hybrid of Mexican and American cultures and we belong to neither one.

"We have been taught that there is a legal and political boundary and
that two countries line up and touch it," Stoddard said. "Only after
25 years as a border specialist could I get rid of that idea."

From the *El Paso Herald-Post*, Special Report on the Border, Summer 1983,
pp. 12–13. Reprinted by permission of the *El Paso Herald-Post*.

El Paso is intertwined economically, culturally and socially with the northern frontier of Mexico. And El Paso has its own blend of cultures.

Armenians, Syrians, Koreans, Greeks, and Germans are represented. Native Americans lived here four thousand years ago. Blacks, many who served at Fort Bliss, have come here and stayed.

The two major groups, however, are the people of Mexican descent and the so-called Anglos, who, by most definitions, are whites who are not of Hispanic descent. Nearly 63 percent of El Pasoans are of "Spanish origin," according to the 1980 census.

Within each group there are so many differences it often is hard to generalize. Some people argue that El Paso has developed a unique culture.

Others say there are two El Pasos—one for Mexican Americans and one for Anglos.

Some different views on El Paso's culture:

• "At this point, El Paso is more of a meeting point for two cultures than a melting pot. There is some melting, but it's not like a stew. It's more like a salad. There are little bits and pieces, all very tasty."

—Cesar Caballero, president of El Concilio de El Paso, a coalition of Mexican-American groups.

• "It's a symphony. Each note stays unique but combines to form something beautiful."

—John Haddox, UTEP professor of philosophy.

• "I think it is difficult to say there are two completely separate cultures. I think the cultures are different but they intertwine. They create a nice tapestry with threads of different colors giving the whole border that border culture that is unique in itself."

—El Paso Bishop Raymundo J. Pena.

The Rio Grande has been the official U.S.-Mexico border for only 135 years, although people lived here thousands of years ago.

After a U.S. war with Mexico, the border was plopped down in 1848 on top of a culture that already existed.

A unique border culture developed that can be seen in the food we eat, the music we listen to, the way we celebrate weddings and feasts, and even the clothes we wear.

The way we speak ranges from Spanish to English and a border *calo* that is something in between. Many people switch effortlessly from English to Spanish, sometimes in the same sentence.

And culturally we switch back and forth, taking from Mexico, the border, and the rest of the United States.

Haddox recalled watching his 11-year-old son step up to bat at a baseball game.

"He blessed himself like a little Mexican boy, but his name is Richie Haddox. It tickled me."

Born in Boston to English and Scottish parents, Don Pearson says the border attracted him to El Paso.

Today he is the news director for Spanish-language Radio ZOL.

"I have managed to internalize so much of the Mexican-American culture that I am not perceived as an outsider," Pearson, 37, said.

"I don't have an identity problem. I identify very strongly with Chicanos or Mexican Americans.

"I haven't lost my Anglo orientation, but I have developed a new orientation.

"Knowing someone's name in El Paso is not a way to know someone's cultural identity," Pearson said.

Among the audience of Radio ZOL, "some people just came from Mexico. Some are second or third generation. The only common denominator is they like what we are playing."

Even within a family, the cultural differences on the border can be sharp.

Juan Rodriguez Oliva was born in Mexico, but joined the U.S. military to become a U.S. citizen.

"I don't want to get away from Mexico. Certain habits, the traditions are deeply rooted in El Paso."

But, he said with an exasperated look, one of his 11-year-old twins "doesn't want to go to Mexico. He says it's too dirty.

"And he doesn't want to speak Spanish. I talk to him in Spanish and he answers in English."

For Juan Sandoval, moving to El Paso from Eugene, Ore., was strange at first.

"For someone who looks more Mexican than a cactus, I had to learn to live in a city where you are not a minority.

"I went back to Oregon at Christmas, and it was strange to see all those pasty faces."

El Pasoans have a "push-pull" relationship with Juárez—it pulls some toward Mexican culture and pushes some away.

The closeness of Juárez provides a steady transfusion of *Mexicanismo*—people and ideas—into El Paso.

"If I lived in some other community, I probably would lose my cultural uniqueness," Caballero said.

But for others, Juárez is poor and dirty and very different. One Mexican-American El Pasoan said, "You know, when I come back from there I have a feeling of relief. We are different. That is why we call ourselves Chicanos."

For some Mexican Americans there is a tension between their roots in Mexico and their lives in the United States.

"I think sometimes you become a schizophrenic," said Rosa Guerrero, a first generation Mexican American who has been teaching traditional Mexican dancing since the 1940s.

"Maybe Saturday and Sunday you are a Chicano, and Monday through Friday you are Anglo, and it's very hard for you. A lot of people say 'You are speaking too much English. You are forgetting about us, you have sold out.'

"I think the Mexican American is getting up the ladder, but many organizations would never have a Latino or Hispano unless he was a *tio taco*. That means he was burned out and sold out to the establishment completely.

"Sometimes all of us have to be sold out and *tio tacos* and Uncle Toms to get accepted because that is the system.

"I just want to stand up and say, 'Wake up, city. Here we are. We also are. We have the dominant people in El Paso in Hispanos, but people don't even care. The Mexican American wants his child to take ballet because that is kosher, man, not to be a Hispano or a Mexicano.'"

Anglos in El Paso also react differently to Mexican culture on the border.

Some have lived here all their lives and have never visited Juárez. They know few Mexican Americans and are filled with prejudices bred by ignorance.

A Chihuahua woman living in El Paso recalled dating an Anglo man: "He said, 'I love Mexicans. My maid is Mexican and so is my gardener.'

"I couldn't believe it. I stopped going out with him."

Other Anglos, such as UTEP economics professor Jeff Brannon, like El Paso because of the Mexican flavor.

"I like the cultural mix," Brannon said. "El Paso really is a fascinating place socially and culturally.

"The [predominantly Anglo] Westside is like Peoria or Indianapolis, Ind.," he joked. "You can't even buy a fresh tortilla on the Westside."

With a twinkle in his eye, El Paso politico George Rodriguez, Jr., says that the Sun City is not so unique.

"We want to say we have a different *ambiente*. I don't think we do. We live in a dream world.

"What about kids who don't speak any Spanish? What makes them any different than a German American?"

Border culture is different from other parts of the United States, he said, but similar things can be seen worldwide.

"What about tortillas? It is just unleavened bread. Go back to biblical times.

"The family traditions are the same as Italians in Chicago," Rodriguez said.

"What is America but a melting pot, and that's what we've got here.

"I don't think the Mexican American has ever wanted to be unique, but it's in vogue now," Rodriguez said.

Stoddard argues that since Mexican Americans are concentrated in lower income groups than Anglos, "we don't have cultural differences as much as we have class differences.

"They call the idea of becoming like us being Anglicized as if to say there is something Anglo. I had to become Anglicized. What they mean is middle class-ized.

"I have always said that if we wanted to get along better, what we need to do is transport an honest to goodness white slum to El Paso. We would suddenly realize that our problems in school are not problems of language but one of class."

Tom Lee, El Paso pollster, agreed: "I'm not going to go as far as saying there are no cultural differences, but we don't find [significant] differences among Anglos and Mexican Americans within the same income level in terms of attitude and opinions."

Ethnicity and class are intertwined, however, and the culture of Mexican Americans, especially the use of Spanish, was suppressed when they lacked political and economic power.

Countless El Pasoans recall being punished for speaking Spanish at school or at work. That has changed, but for some there still is a stigma attached to speaking Spanish.

"I see a lot of Chamber of Commerce people talking about the uniqueness of the area. But say we want a mural, all of a sudden there is no money," Caballero said.

"I don't think the people in power mean bad. They mean well.

"They just haven't discovered to take pride in the whole culture of El Paso," Caballero said.

"They have become, in effect, ethnocentric.

"It happens not only with Anglos but with Chicanos. El Paso needs to look at itself and discover itself."

33 María Puente ◆ So Close, Yet So Far: San Diego, Tijuana Bridging Gap

Although U.S. and Mexican border cities share much in common, vast differences still separate them. One side is economically developed, and its culture is shaped by Anglo-Saxon traditions; the other side is economically underdeveloped, and its culture is shaped by Latin American traditions. For each side, to understand the other has been a continuing challenge. This topic is explored by María Puente, currently a journalist with USA Today, *who focuses on the relationship between San Diego and Tijuana.*

Viewed from a jetliner, the cities of San Diego and Tijuana appear to blend with the nightfall into a carpet of lights tossed at the edge of the continent.

So much for the aerial perspective. The facts on the ground tell a different tale of two cities.

Unlike the eight other communities straddling the two thousand-mile border between the United States and Mexico, San Diego and Tijuana are not and never have been twin cities or even sister cities, notwithstanding the ceremonial rhetoric of politicians over the years.

Instead, the relationship between San Diego and Tijuana for the past century is best described as a long marriage, one that started out with warmth and intimacy in youth, then grew cold and distant with maturity. There have been long periods when they barely spoke to each other, the silences occasionally punctuated by bickering and recrimination over broken plumbing and spilled sewage.

But now, as they face another century together, there are signs of reconciliation between San Diego and Tijuana. Romance, however, has nothing to do with it; pragmatic, bottom-line calculation does.

For instance, the two convention-and-tourism bureaus—aware that each city benefits from the other's tourism—are holding joint meetings and working together on projects for the first time. Even the two city councils, for the first time in memory, have held joint meetings—a meaningless ceremony, perhaps, but the symbolism is important to the Mexicans.

Both San Diego city and county have established binational affairs offices—the first such offices along the entire U.S.-Mexico border—staffed by bicultural and bilingual officials. Public health officials from

From the *San Diego Tribune*, July 11, 1989. Reprinted by permission of the *San Diego Tribune*.

both sides are working on developing common procedures to cope with mutual problems of disease control, public safety and trauma care.

Most important, the two cities are gradually recognizing their inter-dependence—their common economic interests in the tourism and *maquiladora* industries.

Tijuanans have always been aware of their dependence on San Diego. Now more San Diegans are becoming aware of their dependence. Tijuanas spend an estimated $950 million in San Diego every year, about 2 percent, a conservative estimate, of the annual $50 billion gross regional product is generated south of the border, according to economic statistics.

The two cities are increasingly aware that in the macroeconomy of the Pacific Rim, separation could weaken them both—and union could make them an economic powerhouse.

Superficially they are similar. Both are cities of recent immigrants, many of them ignorant of the early, common history of the two towns. Both cities are enjoying booming economies. Both are enjoying the benefits and suffering the problems of uncontrolled growth. Both have serious infrastructure problems. And both are deeply conservative.

But they are more different than alike in their conflicting social and cultural values, in their dissimilar political and government structures and in their distinctive ways of doing business.

"In the U.S., it's know-how; in Mexico, it's know-who," said one bicultural Tijuana businessman.

In the beginning, of course, there was no border. California was part of the vast Spanish colony when the communities that became the two cities first sprouted. Even years after the boundary was drawn following the Mexican War in 1848—when the United States appropriated a huge portion of Mexican territory, including California—the border was as invisible on the ground as it still is from the air.

American and Mexican historians say San Diego and Tijuana both began as a collection of ranches served by the old Franciscan Mission San Diego de Alcalá. The early families—such as the Arguellos, the Estudillos, and the Bandinis—owned land in both communities, and moved back and forth often for fiestas and weddings.

"One member of one of the founding families used to get up at his place in Rosarito at 3 A.M. every Sunday so he could ride his horse along the beach to go to 8 A.M. Mass at the mission," said Ted Proffitt, a historian who has just completed a doctoral dissertation on the history of Tijuana.

After the U.S.-Mexican war in 1848, the community that would become Tijuana was left on the Mexican side of the border, inaccessible from the rest of Mexico and dependent on San Diego for everything from food to spiritual sustenance. It was the beginning of Tijuana's isolation from Mexico and its satellite relationship to San Diego.

"San Diego was Tijuana's reason for existence and it defined itself by its relationship to San Diego," said Larry Herzog, a UCSD [University of California, San Diego] professor of urban studies who has written a book about the two cities and the confrontation of two cultures at the border.

But, like some married couples, communities change and grow apart. After the turn of the century and the construction of the railroads, San Diego grew more rapidly and lost its Hispanic roots in the flood of Anglos from across the United States.

The flood grew even greater after World War I and the arrival of the U.S. Navy in San Diego harbor. New border-crossing restrictions also helped create distance between the two cities. And increasing nationalism came between the two countries, with the inevitable trickle-down effect on the two cities.

Then Prohibition came to the United States in 1920. Practically overnight, Tijuana became the red-light district of San Diego, the favorite port of call for rowdy sailors. American investors in Tijuana promoted it as the place where "the drinks never stop," while the prohibitionists damned it as the "road to hell." Thus was born the "Black Legend of Tijuana," as Tijuanans refer to their city's reputation as a sin capital. Meanwhile, San Diego began priding itself as a clean, all-American town.

Eventually, Prohibition was repealed, the casinos were closed, sexual mores changed in the United States, and even the sailors stayed home. Tijuana made efforts to clean up its image, and began promoting itself as a tourist attraction for families. But its tacky, trashy reputation persisted, even up to the present, according to observers in both cities.

"I saw a recent survey that showed there was an astonishingly high percentage of San Diegans who had never crossed the border and would never think of going to Tijuana, largely because of its image," said Miguel A. Cardenas, a graduate and top administrator at San Diego State University [SDSU] and a former high-ranking Baja California government official who was raised in Tijuana. "The reality of Tijuana has changed, but cultural and social attitudes have not caught up to economic changes."

Tijuanans, painfully aware of their dependency and subordinate position to San Diego, grew more resentful and defensive as their neighbor's indifference—tinged with contempt and condescension—increased from the 1940s through the mid-70s.

Herzog of UCSD sees the symbolism in the location of the two cities' downtowns.

"The center of Tijuana is right at the border because [transborder] trade is crucial to its existence, but San Diego's center is 17 miles to the north, the traditional direction of its growth," Herzog said.

"The heart and soul of San Diego has always been north of Highway 94," he added. "That's where all the major development projects—the stadium, the freeways, the universities—have gone, while South Bay is where all the stuff nobody wants goes. It's not accidental. Mexico represented uncertainty."

Tijuanans accommodated themselves to San Diego, mostly because they had no choice. They learned English; few San Diegans bothered to learn Spanish. They read the San Diego newspapers; few San Diegans even knew the names of the Tijuana newspapers. They crossed the border daily or weekly to go shopping, for dinner and movies, for school or to go to their jobs; few San Diegans did the same.

Some Tijuanans refuse to have anything to do with San Diego, fearing discrimination, while others bristle at perceived condescending attitudes of San Diegans, according to Jorge Bustamante, director of the College of the Northern Border in Tijuana, a government think tank and research institution.

"Culturally speaking, Tijuana is closer to Buenos Aires than San Diego, largely because of language," said Bustamante, a member of one of Tijuana's oldest and wealthiest families.

Although Tijuana has long been an honorary member of the San Diego Association of Governments, no officials have ever attended a meeting—"tangible proof that Tijuana also deserves blame for the distance" between the cities, said Homero Reyes, a Mexican economist and government consultant.

Over the decades, some economic links remained between the two cities. Former Mayor Pete Wilson remembers George Scott, owner of the old Walker Scott department store downtown, telling him in the 1970s that about 20 percent of its charge accounts were held by Tijuanans.

There were other less obvious links as well. Wealthy socialites in both towns occasionally mixed. Service clubs often got together for joint charity projects. In 1972, society women from both sides got together to start the Tijuana Home Tour—still an annual affair attracting up to nine hundred people at $38 apiece—to raise money for charities in both cities.

There have always been families with roots on both sides of the border functioning as social links between the two sides even when there were few other exchanges, according to historian Juan Ortiz Figueroa of the Center for Historical Research in Tijuana.

"I had my first communion on that side and my confirmation on this side," says Elsa Saxod, head of the Office of Binational Affairs for San

Diego, who grew up in both cities in the 1950s and '60s. "Crossing the border was a part of everyday life. We knew all the border guards. We didn't think of it as going to another country."

Many early Tijuanans were born in San Diego—making them U.S. citizens—because there were no hospitals in Tijuana. Most pioneer Tijuanans sent their children to school in San Diego, initially because there were no schools in Tijuana, but later so they could learn proper English, Ortiz explained.

Artists and academics usually have maintained links as well. Organizations of poets, writers and painters meet occasionally, and more Tijuana artists are exhibiting in San Diego galleries. The San Diego Symphony had an auxiliary orchestra in Tijuana. And after the formation of the University of Baja California in the 1960s, SDSU officials worked hard to establish innovative joint programs in education and training.

And when fires broke out in Tijuana or the water mains broke, San Diego was always available to lend a hand.

But by the 1970s, most San Diego government and political officials had grown accustomed to not thinking about Tijuana except when problems arose—flooding, sewage, pollution, illegal immigration, drugs. Few spoke Spanish or even thought it was necessary to learn. Fewer still were familiar with the highly centralized nature of Mexican government, or with the key officials in that government.

Norris Clement, a SDSU economics professor and expert on Mexico, believes that the movers and shakers of San Diego—most of them white, non-Spanish-speaking and unfamiliar with Mexico—remain indifferent to Tijuana. If so, that sort of attitude may be ebbing.

After the first peso devaluation in 1976, Tijuanans sharply reduced their shopping trips to San Diego—and it showed up in lower sales-tax revenues.

"That was an economic jolt that made San Diego wake up," said economist Reyes. "The seeds of awareness sprouted, and now they're blossoming, not necessarily because of friendship, but because of crisis."

Clement points out that media coverage of Tijuana has expanded as a result of the increasing awareness between the two towns. Before 1975, he said, there were about 50 to 75 stories a year about Tijuana in the San Diego press. "Now there are about 50 to 75 a month," he said.

The binational affairs office, the increasing links between public health, tourism and education officials, the connections between musicians and artists, the binational families and the friendships between individuals—even the plans for U.S. and Mexican census officials to work together for the 1990 census—all these show San Diego and Tijuana moving toward each other again.

And the pervasive economic interaction might, over time, affect attitudes and bring closer social and cultural interaction.

"We have come a long way and we still have a long way to go," said Juan Tintos, assistant tourism director for Baja California, who was educated in San Diego. "But the relationship is much warmer and much more understanding and accepting, especially on the U.S. side. I think things are going to improve even more."

But the two cities must interact more in planning for the future. Reyes said it's especially important that the two formulate a cohesive binational industrial policy—covering such issues as zoning, infrastructure and urbanization—to deal with the growing *maquiladora* assembly plants. There are more than four hundred plants in Tijuana already—many with twin plants in San Diego—and more are planned.

"When there are proposals for studies or projects that have transborder impact, more effort should be made to seek the opinions of Tijuana and Baja officials," Reyes said.

Reyes also suggested San Diego officials have more contact with Baja state government authorities who have jurisdiction over mutual problems such as pollution and sewage. Tijuana, on the other hand should become more active in SANDAG [San Diego Association of Governments] activities, he said. Bureaucrats on both sides should meet more often, he said. And more San Diegans should learn Spanish.

The Bilateral Commission on the Future of U.S.-Mexico Relations, in a report issued last year, recommended the two nations establish a joint border authority with the jurisdiction to handle binational infrastructure, environmental and trade issues.

As any glance at a recent newspaper would confirm, Mexico is changing rapidly. Democracy flowered in Baja California when an opposition party won a governorship for the first time in Mexico in sixty years. In June, the new administration of President Carlos Salinas de Gortari announced regulations to allow up to 100 percent foreign investment in Mexico in areas such as tourism. Consequently, increased American interest and investment in Mexico is virtually certain.

Will it be followed by progress or long-intractable problems such as drug trafficking and illegal immigration? Not, Norris Clement warned, if the United States moves to an increasingly militarized border in response to those problems.

Every step San Diego and Tijuana take toward each other could be followed by two steps backward due to matters beyond their control. This year's controversy over the planned U.S. border ditch to stop cars carrying drugs or undocumented immigrants is just one example of the binational squabbles that could interfere with rapprochement between San Diego and Tijuana.

And, after all, there is a border, *la linea*, that separates them. There are differences that can't be talked away. San Diego and Tijuana will never be just like El Paso, Texas, and Juárez or the other border communities, where the Mexican city dominates in size and the American city has more Hispanic flavor in its culture and power structure.

But a successful marriage doesn't require individuals to merge or become exactly alike, only to adapt to each other to minimize discord and conflict. That will be San Diego and Tijuana's task in the next one hundred years.

34 Oscar J. Martínez ◆ *"La Frontera"*

This poem focuses on the dilemma-ridden nature of much of the border experience, a theme reflected in many of this volume's essays and documents. Written especially for this collection, it seems an appropriate conclusion.

It is the best and it is the worst,
la frontera, the borderlands,
a world of acute contradictions,
a place of pungent human drama.

It lifts the spirit and sinks the heart,
for *la frontera* is laced with intense passions.
Devotees feel exuberance, vitality, zest;
detractors see drabness, ugliness, crassness.

On one side dollar power, freeways,
skyscrapers, malls, radiant suburbs.
On the other boom and bust, gaudy tourism,
maquiladora sprawl, shantytowns.

A land of abundant sunshine
that keeps the body warm, the soul aglow.
Yet that same *frontera* sun
turns summer into scorching hell,
an inconvenience for the fortunate,
a life-threat for the destitute.

Generations of poor migrants from the south,
driven by poverty and despair,
have headed to the imagined desert paradise,
enticed by the promise of a better life.

Embraced by those who profit from their labor,
quite dependable, plentiful, and cheap.
Abhorred by those who see social blight,
economic threat, cultural menace, demographic peril.

Affluent and leisure-conscious northerners,
captivated by *la frontera*'s mildness,
its picturesque scenery, its relaxed way of life,
gleefully descend upon its cities, towns, and trailer parks.

These settlers and sojourners revere this land,
its desert beauty, its resplendent sunsets,
and some hold dear the indigenous human landscape,
the Indians, the Spaniards, the Mexicans.

But far too few of the northern newcomers
find enchantment in the native heritage;
indifference and token recognition are more the norm,
and all too often contemptibility and overt hostility.

Los fronterizos: people of one, or more, identities,
mono or multi—national, ethnic, lingual, cultural.
Borderlanders: neglected, misunderstood, disdained,
at once defensive and proud of their aberrant world.

Yes, *la frontera* has them all:
those who live behind their cultural wall,
and those who wish to see it fall;
those who would keep foreigners out,
and those who want them all about;
those inclined to alienate,
and those who prefer to ameliorate;
those driven by a nationalistic bent,
and those committed to a global tent.

Suggested Readings

Anzaldúa, Gloria. *Borderlands: La Frontera*. San Francisco: Spinsters/ Aunt Lute, 1987.

Arreola, Daniel D., and James R. Curtis. *The Mexican Border Cities: Landscape Anatomy and Place Personality*. Tucson: University of Arizona Press, 1993.

Conover, Ted. *Coyotes: A Journey through the Secret World of America's Illegal Aliens*. New York: Vintage Books, 1987.

D'Antonio, William, and William H. Form. *Influentials in Two Border Cities: A Study in Community Decision-Making*. Notre Dame: University of Notre Dame Press, 1965.

Fernández, Raúl A. *The Mexican-American Border Region: Issues and Trends*. Notre Dame: University of Notre Dame Press, 1989.

———. *The United States-Mexico Border: A Politico-Economic Profile*. Notre Dame: University of Notre Dame Press, 1977.

Fernández-Kelly, María Patricia. *For We Are Sold, I and My People: Women and Industry in Mexico's Frontier*. Albany: State University of New York, 1983.

Fowler, Gene, and Bill Crawford. *Border Radio: Quacks, Yodelers, Pitchmen, Psychics, and Other Amazing Broadcasters of the American Airwaves*. Austin: Texas Monthly Press, 1987.

Gamio, Manuel. *The Mexican Immigrant: His Life Story*. Chicago: University of Chicago Press, 1931.

García, Mario T. *Desert Immigrants: The Mexicans of El Paso, 1880–1920*. New Haven: Yale University Press, 1981.

Griswold del Castillo, Richard. *The Treaty of Guadalupe Hidalgo: A Legacy of Conflict*. Norman: University of Oklahoma Press, 1990.

Hall, Linda B., and Don M. Coerver. *Revolution on the Border: The United States and Mexico, 1910–1920*. Albuquerque: University of New Mexico Press, 1988.

Hansen, Niles. *The Border Economy: Regional Development in the Southwest*. Austin: University of Texas Press, 1981.

Herzog, Lawrence A. *Where North Meets South: Cities, Space, and Politics on the U.S.-Mexico Border*. Austin: Center for Mexican-American Studies, University of Texas at Austin, 1990.

Horgan, Paul. *Great River: The Rio Grande in North American History*. 2 vols. New York: Rinehart, 1954.

Lorey, David E., ed. *United States-Mexico Border Statistics since 1900*. Los Angeles: UCLA Latin American Center Publications, 1990.

Maciel, David R. *El Norte: The U.S.-Mexican Border in Contemporary Cinema*. San Diego: Institute for Regional Studies of the Californias, San Diego State University, 1990.

Maril, Robert Lee. *Living on the Edge of America: At Home on the Texas-Mexico Border*. College Station: Texas A & M University Press, 1992.

Martínez, Oscar J. *Border Boom Town: Ciudad Juárez since 1848*. Austin: University of Texas Press, 1978.

————. *Border People: Life and Society in the U.S.-Mexico Borderlands*. Tucson: University of Arizona Press, 1994.

————. *Troublesome Border*. Tucson: University of Arizona Press, 1988.

McWilliams, Carey. *North from Mexico: The Spanish-Speaking People of the United States*. Updated by Matt S. Meier. New York: Praeger, 1990.

Meinig, D. W. *Southwest: Three Peoples in Geographical Change, 1600–1970*. New York: Oxford University Press, 1971.

Miller, Tom. *On the Border: Portraits of America's Southwestern Frontier*. New York: Harper and Row, 1981.

Moyano Pahissa, Angela. *México y Estados Unidos: Orígenes de una relación, 1819–1861*. Mexico City: Secretaría de Educación Pública, 1985.

Nathan, Debbie. *Women and Other Aliens: Essays from the U.S.-Mexico Border*. El Paso: Cinco Puntos, 1991.

Paredes, Américo. *George Washington Gómez*. Houston: Arte Público Press, 1991.

————. *"With His Pistol in His Hand": A Border Ballad and Its Hero*. Austin: University of Texas Press, 1958.

Poppa, Terrence E. *Druglord: The Life and Death of a Mexican Kingpin*. New York: Pharos Books, 1990.

Price, John A. *Tijuana: Urbanization in a Border Culture*. Notre Dame: University of Notre Dame Press, 1973.

Rippy, J. Fred. *The United States and Mexico*. New York: Knopf, 1926.

Ross, Stanley R., ed. *Views across the Border: The United States and Mexico*. Albuquerque: University of New Mexico Press, 1978.

Ruiz, Vicki L., and Susan Tiano, eds. *Women on the U.S.-Mexico Border: Responses to Change*. Boston: Allen & Unwin, 1987.

Sklair, Leslie. *Assembling for Development: The Maquila Industry in Mexico and the United States*. Boston: Unwin Hyman, 1989.

Stoddard, Ellwyn R. *Maquila: Assembly Plants in Northern Mexico*. El Paso: Texas Western Press, 1987.

Timmons, W. H. *El Paso: A Borderlands History*. El Paso: Texas Western Press, 1990.

Urrea, Luis Alberto. *Across the Wire: Life and Hard Times on the Mexican Border*. New York: Anchor Books, 1993.

Vanderwood, Paul J., and Frank N. Samporano. *Border Fury: A Picture Postcard Record of Mexico's Revolution and U.S. War Preparedness*. Albuquerque: University of New Mexico Press, 1988.

Weber, David J. *The Mexican Frontier, 1821–1846.* Albuquerque: University of New Mexico Press, 1982.

————. *The Spanish Frontier in North America.* New Haven: Yale University Press, 1992.

Weber, David J., and Jane M. Rausch, eds. *Where Cultures Meet: Frontiers in Latin American History.* Wilmington, DE: Scholarly Resources, 1994.

Weisman, Alan. *La Frontera: The United States Border with Mexico.* Photographs by Jay Dusard. Tucson: University of Arizona Press, 1991.

Suggested Films

Ballad of Gregorio Cortéz. Directed by Robert M. Young. Los Angeles: Moctezuma Esparza Productions. 1983. Based on a classic *corrido* (ballad), this is the story of a *tejano* (Hispanic Texan) who is pursued by the Texas Rangers for killing a sheriff.

Chulas Fronteras. Created by Chris Strachwitz. Directed by Les Blank. El Cerrito, CA: Brazos Films. 1976. A delightful portrait of the borderlands through the sights and sounds of Tex-Mex music.

Del Mero Corazon. Produced and directed by Chris Strachwitz. El Cerrito, CA: Brazos Films. 1980. Sequel to *Chulas Fronteras*, offering additional enjoyable music from the borderlands.

Geronimo and the Apache Resistance. By Neil Goodwin. Alexandria, VA: PBS video. 1988. The tragic story of the legendary Apache leader told from the Indian point of view; includes moving interviews with several of Geronimo's descendants.

The Global Assembly Line. By Lorraine Gray. Produced with María Patricia Fernández-Kelly and Anne Bohlen. Educational Television and Film Center. 1986. Examines global forces that sustain assembly industries in underdeveloped parts of the world, including the Mexican border area.

The Hunt for Villa. By Hector Galán and Paul Espinosa. Austin: Galán Productions. 1993. Relates General John J. Pershing's unsuccessful chase of Pancho Villa following Villa's raid on Columbus, New Mexico, in 1916.

Leaving Home (We Do the Work). Produced by Patrice O'Neil and Rhian Miller. 1992. Examines the closing of factories in the United States and the transfer of jobs to cheap-labor havens like the Mexican border communities.

The Lemon Grove Incident. Written and produced by Paul Espinosa. Directed by Frank Christopher. San Diego: KPBS. 1985. Docudrama about a school desegregation case in 1930 in the San Diego area.

The New Tijuana. Produced by Paul Espinosa. Directed by Frank Christopher. San Diego: KPBS. 1990. Describes the transition of Tijuana from a small tourist town to a thriving metropolis facing multiple challenges.

The Nine Nations of North America: Mexamerica. Written and narrated by Joel Garreau. New York: PBS. 1988. Focuses on transnational forces that are reshaping the southwestern United States and northern Mexico.

El Norte. Produced by Anna Thomas. Directed by Gregory Nava. CBS-Fox movie. 1984. This fascinating, sometimes sad, and sometimes funny movie relates the story of a Maya brother and sister who seek a better life in the United States.

One River: One Country. New York: "CBS Reports." 1983. Suggests that people on the border live in a "third country," neither mainstream United States nor mainstream Mexico, but a blend of both.

The Trail North. Produced by Paul Espinosa. Directed by Thomas Kario. San Diego: KPBS. 1983. Anthropologist Robert Alvarez and his son recreate the journey made by their ancestors from Mexico to California.